YOU AND YOUR MIND

Studies and scientific investigations in popular psychology

Edited by

Kenneth Ryan

CARILLON BOOKS   CB   ST. PAUL, MINNESOTA

YOU AND YOUR MIND

A CARILLON BOOK
Carillon Books edition published May 1977

ISBN: 0-89310-019-6

Library of Congress Catalog Card Number: 77-72770

Copyright © 1977 by Carillon Books

All Rights Reserved

Printed in the United States of America

CARILLON BOOKS is a division of
Catholic Digest
2115 Summit Avenue
St. Paul, Minnesota 55105
U.S.A.

Introduction

Popular psychology may seem to be of only casual interest until one considers that it really was the subject matter of all successful novelists, playwrights and even poets. The way the human mind works has always been a subject of fascination for persons with the intelligence and time to investigate it. Shakespeare, Dostoievsky and Browning were men who had natural insights into the human mind's workings and proved it in their masterpieces. It remained for modern science with its experimental methods to furnish an ordered study of man's reactions to his environment and the possible ways of modifying, improving or eliminating those reactions according as they were good or bad for man's well-being.

A good deal of the scientific study can be filtered down to the general public through publications of the general interest type. This present collection of studies and investigations falls readily into its chapter subjects. They are: self-analysis, personal improvement, narrative stories of psychological experiences, youth-maturity-old age, and the effect of environment on the human mind.

CONTENTS

6 CONTENTS

Chapter I

What Am I?

"Why did I do this?" and "Why didn't I do that?" are the commonest questions of people talking to themselves. Everyone engages naturally in self-analysis, and those who do it most scientifically do themselves the most good. Realizing that you do fit into recognized categories of people and are likely to act and react as others in your category do is the first step in self-knowledge. You have to know at least the general guidelines about who is and who isn't normal, the emotional boundaries between the psychotic, the neurotic and the merely moody person before you can make valid judgments on even your own thoughts. The articles in this chapter from a wide variety of magazine sources furnish a fairly good foundation of study, if you are really interested in yourself.

Who's Normal?

Nobody seems to know, the experts least of all

By Edward Edelson

"Conforming to the standard or the common type; usual; not abnormal; regular; natural." That is *normal* according to the dictionary. But what does *normal* mean? Is anybody normal?

That is no trivial question. It has fascinated psychiatrists, dominated general practitioners, intrigued philosophers, worried statisticians, confounded industrial designers, baffled lawyers, and troubled scientists.

Those who ponder the idea of psychiatric normality might think about the Midtown Manhattan Study, in which investigators went door-to-door to get in-depth interviews with 1,600 residents of a New York neighborhood. Roughly one person in five was found to be mentally healthy, with no noticeable symptoms. One in five was mentally disturbed enough to require immediate attention. The rest, 60% of those interviewed, has symptoms of mental problems ranging from mild to moderate. So if you accept the idea that *normal* means "the common type, usual," the normal person is just a trifle off center, psychiatrically speaking.

Psychiatrists usually throw up their hands when they are asked to give any definition of *normal*. "That depends on the expectations of a culture," says Dr. Marvin Stern, a psychiatrist at New York University.

Even when people come from a common cultural background, Stern says, your normal is not my normal. "Everyone knows what is normal, but no one quite agrees with the definition of other people," he says. A sneaky way out, Stern goes on, is to substitute the concept of "average" for that of "normality." He doesn't think much of that idea.

"Statistics are O.K. because you can put them into a computer and do things with them," he says. "But in terms of what life is all about, the computer just doesn't work."

Surprisingly, statisticians agree with that. Frederic Selzer, who as assistant statistician of the Metropolitan Life Insurance Co., keeps numerical track of millions of people, believes that "average" may not even exist. He says, "The average number of children in the American family may be 2.2, but we can't find such a family."

So statisticians fall back on the idea of "the normal range," the average with a wide margin for individual differences. But even that doesn't work too well, as physicians have been finding out in recent years. Once upon a time, they had neat ideas about what constituted normal physical measurements, from heart rate to red blood cell count and all on down the line of almost anything measurable. Then came automated equipment that made it possible to test large numbers of normal people, and the neatness disappeared.

For example, the Technicon Corp., which produces automated blood analyzers, lists the normal range of cholesterol in the blood as anywhere from 150 to 300 milligrams per cubic centimeter.

If a 100% variation bothers you, consider that the normal range of uric acid is from 2.5 to 8.0 milligrams, more than a threefold difference. The same range of variations has been found in almost every physical test.

And if that bothers you, there is another curve ball: all these average readings are not necessarily normal. Physicians think the average American is abnormal in many important aspects.

That is true of blood cholesterol, which has been linked to heart disease. Heart experts say the average American has an abnormally high cholesterol reading.

The same is true of weight. Metropolitan Life tries to talk not of average weight but of "desirable" weight, which is something below what most of us tip the scales at.

Even the desirable weight leaves a large margin for error. The desirable weight of a 6' man can be anywhere from 148 to 184 pounds, depending on his body frame.

And if you think actuaries have trouble fitting people into slots in the basis of statistics, consider the harried industrial designer who is trying to make machines that will be comfortable for everyone to operate. "The average man is like the unicorn," says Peter Kyropoulos, technical director of General Motors' styling department. "He is a mythical animal." Kyropoulos is fond of quoting a study done several years ago, in which two consultants took eight "average" measurements, added a 30% margin for error, and then tested 4,000 Air Force men against the average.

Only 25.9% were of average height. Only 7.4% were both of average height and had the average chest circumference, and had average sleeve length. And no one at all was average in all eight measurements. "One thing is certain," says Kyropoulos. "If we pick an average, we can be sure that we have maximized the number of unhappy users."

So designers do the only thing they can do: they deliberately decide to make some people uncomfortable. Your average car, and your average almost everything else, is designed for people whose standing height is taller than all but the shortest 5% of women and shorter than all but the tallest 5% of men.

Perhaps the final word on normality came from a recent experiment reported by D. L. Rosenhan, professor of psychology and law at Stanford University. In the experiment, eight sane volunteers sought admission to mental hospitals. All were admitted. Then the reaction of both staff and real patients to these pseudopatients was studied. The result: the real patients recognized that the pseudopatients were sane, but the staff members did not. "The fact that the patients often recognized normality when staff did not raises important questions," says Rosenhan.

What was that definition again?

Three Kinds of People

Love, power, and achievement are their basic drives

By Marilyn Mercer

Putting people into categories has its pitfalls. Not all men, all women, all blacks, all whites, all Americans, nor all Russians behave alike. Still we think we know what liberals are like, what businessmen are like, what Republicans are like. Often we trip on these generalizations.

Prof. David C. McClelland of the Harvard Department of Social Relations is a behavioral psychologist who has spent a good part of his life studying human motives. He categorizes people by their motives, not by the surface facts of their lives, or what they appear to be, or say they are, but by the inner needs that really drive them. The three primary needs are for power, achievement, and love.

Condensed from "Glamour", 420 Lexington Ave., New York City 10017. December, 1969. ₵1969 by the Conde Nast Publications, Inc., and reprinted with permission.

Power people are those whose greatest need is to have impact on others, to be recognized, to be important. Achievers basically want to get the job done, and then look around for new worlds to conquer. Love people get their greatest satisfaction from personal relationships, and will sacrifice other satisfactions to that end.

The needs are not always filled, of course, and everyone has all three needs to some degree. But in most persons just one need predominates. Most of us would say that the need for achievement is good, the need for power is bad, and the need for love should be in women only, but McClelland's categories are morally neutral.

Politicians are almost always motivated by the power need, so are actors, entertainers, and celebrities. Thus the power category very probably includes such statesmen-heroes as Franklin D. Roosevelt, Winston Churchill, as well as rock-and-roll singers and Jacqueline Onassis. The role of achievers includes Henry Ford and Thomas Alva Edison, as well as a large percentage of the Mafia. Hippies, as well as the suburban good-lifers with their mortgages, barbecue sets, and swimming pools, are basically motivated by the need for affiliation, and thus are love people.

Successful politicians are classic power types. The man running for office, not matter how eloquently he may promise achievement to come, is usually power motivated. The rigors of a political campaign and the gamble involved hold little attraction for the true achiever. Achievers, says Professor McClelland, have a built-in fear of failure and do not like to take chances. A hereditary monarch can be an empire-building achiever, but in a democracy you have to be a power person to get to the top in the first place.

John Kennedy would seem to be a pure power type. Robert Kennedy, who ran his brother's organization quite effectively, was very probably a power-achiever. And the tragedy of Edward Kennedy may be that he has inherited the role of power achiever, but is basically motivated by genuine fondness for friends and associates. Real power people and real achievers do not go to cookouts with old office mates, except for token appearances.

Whereas Richard M. Nixon, with his announced determination to apply sound management to government, with his caution (fear of failure?) and his distaste for television performances, may have been the first achievement-motivated chief executive we had in a long time.

Entertainers, actors, performers, television personalities, from Sir Laurence Olivier to Huntley-Brinkley to the Rolling Stones, are usually power motivated. The achiever in the arts is likely, after a stint as an actor, to turn director-producer, Mike Nichols for example. Performers have a tendency to incorporate themselves, like Bing Crosby and Barbra Streisand. There are power-love people in the performing arts, too, who often lead soap-opera lives. The plight of the power-love celebrity is a story dear to the hearts of the American public.

In separating out the power-love figures, we sometimes confuse form with content. Judy Garland, though she was often cast as achiever, as the show-must-go-on girl, was quite probably a power-love person. And Arlo Guthrie and others in that genre, no matter how much their material extols universal love, seem in full command of their personal situations, and are quite probably power people.

Preachers and teachers are power people, too. Billy Graham, John Kenneth Galbraith, William Buckley, and Shirley Temple, far apart though they might be in their thinking, share a common need to air that thinking in the public arena and get a little feedback, which is what the power drive is all about.

Not all power people are public personalities, however; some power people stay home. These are usually power women, and they usually have large problems. The woman who needs and wants public acclaim and attention outside of the family circle may work at running the PTA or League of Women Voters. On the other hand, she may demand them from her family. Power women are better off working.

The achievers in our society are easy to spot. They are Professor McClelland's "salesmen-entrepreneurs;" they are the men who made model airplanes, had paper routes and sold lemonade as kids, and grew up to own gas stations, build housing complexes, and mastermind conglomerates.

Woman achievers run businesses, devise and set into motion community programs, operating effectively but usually inconspicuously. If it is advantageous, the woman achiever will get someone else to front for her: a local political figure, a female celebrity. The power woman, no. If she cannot be the star of the show she produces, she generally does not want to play.

The woman achiever at home fills her needs by making a project out of home life. Sometimes she makes a project out of her children: teaching them to read; encouraging their shell collecting; broadening their range by visits to museums, concerts, and the like; supervising their homework. The achiever mother generally contributes to their growth and development. However, her project can get out of hand, and the achiever mother can be as destructive a force as the power mother or the overpossessive mother.

Professor McClelland says achievers do not like to try anything that is too easy or too hard. Putting a group of servicemen through tests to determine motivation, he discovered that the achievers, in a ring-toss game, when told they could stand any distance they chose from the pole, elected to stand midway. If they stood too close, tossing the ring over the pole was no achievement. On the other hand, if they stood too far away, they were afraid they might fail. And a negative trait of the achiever, says Dr. McClelland, is fear of failure.

Who are the love people? You know the love woman. She gets her primary satisfaction from her husband or family. She may work, but the job is something secondary. She will quit it or change it to suit the needs of her husband. While she is at it, however, she enjoys office life mightily. (She is the one who takes up all the collections for departing co-workers.) Wherever she works, she makes friends and she cares about them. However, friends or no, she will quit or change her job to suit the needs of the man in her life.

The love woman at work has other manifestations, too. She may be a teacher, nurse, social worker. If she is an executive it is usually in a noncompetitive field. You can find achieving and quite powerful love women running schools, counseling services, and community programs. The waitress who jokes with all her customers, the department-store saleswoman who sets special dresses aside for special clients, the friendly grandmother who runs a corner candy store—all are motivated basically by the personal relationships that are built into their occupations, and thus are love people.

The professional heartbreaker, the girl who usually has a flock of men following her around, seems to be a love person, but is not. Essentially, she manipulates men for ends known only to herself, which makes her a power person.

All of the three drives have their negative sides. Certain characteristics define the frustrated power person, love person, and achiever.

Drinking, seemingly, enables the frustrated power person to enjoy the illusion of power he does not get in real life. Politicians and generals for example, when they retire, tend to drink a lot. The aging actress who turns to drink and drugs as she reads her old press clippings alone in her hotel room is the cliche' figure of the frustrated power woman.

The achiever fears, above all things, failure. So the ulcer is the classic ailment of the executive with bad problems.

The negative side of the love drive has made "women's fiction" a subliterary art form. "Love," says Professor McClelland, "is polymorphous and perverse, and people get it all mixed up with sex."

So far we have been talking in terms of public figures and familiar types. Where do you fit in the picture?

One easy test is to ask yourself what you would do with a million dollars. This is one of the questions asked by recruiters for business in an attempt to smoke out true achievers.

Well, what would you do? If you have 16 schemes for investing the million, you are a true achiever. If you would invest it in a new and impressive life style—clothes, cars, a house in town and one in the country—it is the need for power that drives you. A love person would probably spend a little, then put the rest into a home or invest it for the children.

Or, say you would spend it on travel. The achiever would not be likely to, except for a purpose, such as establishing a string of boutiques in the Middle East. A love person might take friends of a trip around the world. A power woman might take the trip but not the friends. The million, she would reason, entitled her to a completely new set of friends.

And once it is established what you are, whom do you match up with? Love men and women get along marvelously with each other. So do two achievers. However, two power people are likely to clash.

An achiever woman can be the perfect backstop for the power man: the public man's perfect hostess wife is an example. She may also fill in as his secretary, business manager, accountant and generalized trouble shooter.

An achiever woman does well with a love man, too. These are the couple who have marvelously run homes, showplace gardens. A domesticated, happy love man does not object, usually, to his wife having her achiever projects on the side.

A power wife will generally overpower a love man. She works nicely, however, with an achiever husband, as a power man works nicely with an achiever woman. A love woman is usually unhappy with a power husband. She does not want to share him with the public, she wants him all to herself; and no power man born has ever been satisfied with an audience of one.

At the present moment, the achievers are most highly valued by our society. Achiever men, that is. Achiever woman are tolerated, but love women seem to be the popular social ideal.

This is so for obvious reasons. Achievers are what make the wheels turn in an expanding economy, like ours in the 19th and early 20th centuries. All the myths of the early 20th century were built around the achiever hero: the Horatio Alger boy, the empire builder, the winner of the west, Get-Rich-Quick Wallingford.

The achiever hero, however, fell into bad grace in the 1930's when the economy collapsed and left the businessman-entrepreneur with a certain amount of egg on his face. At that moment, the power hero came in.

Who was, for the moment, Franklin D. Roosevelt. The country needed an authority figure, a man on a white horse, a charismatic father, and FDR filled that need. The country wanted, as well, to be cared for and manipulated. It wanted a strong central government that would set everything that had gone wrong to rights.

Our culture heroes from then on to the 1950's were largely power people: statesmen and folk singers, political ideologues of all varieties, union leaders and generals.

In the 1950's, the togetherness era, the love person came back into style. If we had a culture hero, it was the domestic father. A popular novel of the time, Sloan Wilson's *The Man in the Gray Flannel Suit*, extolled the praises of the love man, who turned his back on the achievers and power people in his company and decided life was too short. Nine to five for him, and the rest of the time with the family.

Power, of course, came back in a big way in the 1960's. The protest movements were not only power movements, as all protest movements are, but they called themselves power movements, which was something new. Student power. Black power. Even flower power. And within the protest movements, power people—teachers, preachers, manipulators and demonstrators—were the cultural heroes.

It is possible that the achievement hero may come back. A likely bet is the scientist-hero, the super-technician of the New Technocracy, who must, if he is going to be able to build the world of tomorrow and make it function, be an achiever. Professor McClelland has worked out a method of training achievers. He has been successful with groups of Indian would-be businessmen and black owners of small businesses in the U.S., as recorded in his book, written with Dr. David G. Winter, *Motivating Economic Achievement.*

Where do the love people fit into all this? It is hard to imagine a true love-motivated person running the country. If we are heading, as we seem to be, into a cooperative rather than a competitive society, Professor McClelland may have to take on unmotivating and untraining power people and achievers, and redirecting them into love. For only love would make such a world go round.

Signs of the Psycho

*Among them: emotional immaturity, immunity to guilt,
self-centeredness*

By Ruth Doehler

Most of us have probably at one time or another been
bewildered, baffled, or hurt by psychopaths. In the U.S. their
number is greater than the number disabled by any other
psychosis except schizophrenia.

In a U.S. Veterans' hospital for mental cases, out of 857
new admissions, 102 were psychopaths. An additional 134,
first admitted as drug addicts or alcoholics, were later found
to be in a lesser degree psychopathic.

This situation is startling because psychopaths are not
technically eligible for admission to any mental hospital in
the U.S. or Canada. The reasons: 1. psychopaths refuse
medical help, and the law upholds their refusal because they
have no hallucinations or delusions: 2. the psychopath is a
manipulator who can often talk his way out of a hospital by
playing one staff member against another.

Most psychiatrists agree that there are two types of
psychopath. In the minority is the very cold, destructive mur-
derer whose actions have no reason that a sane person can
understand. More common is the milder type whose actions,
though senseless, are less serious and are mainly harmful to
himself.

The two distinct types have ten traits in common: The
psychopath does not profit by experience, lacks a sense of
responsibility; is unable to form meaningful relationships;
lacks control over impulses, lacks a moral sense; is antisocial;
does not alter his behavior after punishment; is emotionally
immature; unable to experience guilt, and self-centered.

A frightening aspect of society is the way in which young
people identify with psychopathic behavior of both types.
James Dean, the young actor who became associated with his
title role in *Rebel Without a Cause*, created a Dean cult after

Condensed from "Chatelaine", 481 University Ave., Toronto 2, Ont., Canada. July, 1966 ⸳1966
by Maclean-Hunter Publishing Co., Ltd., and reprinted with permission.

he carelessly killed himself in a sports car. The movie was based on a study done by psychiatrist Robert Lindner of the goalless, charming psychopath who is unable to align himself with any values.

Charles Schmid was of the murderous type. The 23-year-old son of respectable parents in Tucson, Ariz., had a large following among local teen-agers, though many knew he had murdered three young girls "for kicks." Instead of seeing Schmid in terms of his actions, they accepted him. Schmid was the genuine article, cool and unable to be emotionally involved. When sentenced to death, his comment was, "Well, that's the way it goes."

The psychopath is never motivated by passion, or strong feeling. If he commits a murder it is because he has no ability to resist an impulse, however faint. Psychopaths do things "just for the hell of it." Perhaps this is why some fun seekers identify with this behavior, although they don't imitate it: the psychopath dares to do what others only think of.

The two types, the potentially violent and the nonviolent, have different backgrounds. The primary or true psychopath lacks any ethical sense, demands immediate satisfaction of pleasure impulses, cannot bear suffering or loss, and has no capacity for guilt or love. It is impossible to treat him. His personality may have been damaged in the first 18 months of his life by the absence of maternal love.

Picture an infant who is left on a dirty mattress for hours on end, without a voice to comfort him crying and falling asleep to awake crying again, because his mother leaves him like that day after day. He falls into despair and grows up with no expectations of love, which he has never experienced. Other examples are babies who are beaten by their fathers.

Such a child may react all through life with destructive rages to even minor frustrations. The needs which he felt as an infant were never met, and therefore he cannot mature past this state, remaining an infant emotionally.

The nonviolent psychopaths have had some love, but not enough. Either the parent has acted inconsistently with the child, or has not always been present, during the crucial years up to age 14. It is during these years that a child can identify with a loved parent figure and pattern his behavior accordingly.

A British research study of 100 psychopathic prisoners found that only 38% of them had spent their formative years with the same two parents. The most severe cases ("cold, hostile, affectionless, capable of calculated acts against others") were found to have lacked any loving figures from infancy on. Seventeen per cent of this group were illegitimate, compared with 5% in the general population of Britain. The milder cases had had parents who gave them love one day and indifference the next; or deaths, separations, divorces, or boarding or foster homes entered into their backgrounds.

Frequently the psychopath has been a stepchild. The stepparent, father or mother, sees his new role as a moralizer, not as a loving parent. He or she may unconsciously regard the child as a representative of the earlier mate. To establish his position as parent, he may be overzealous about right and wrong, and without love. He represents his actions as an unpleasant but necessary duty.

In one such case a domineering stepfather relegated all the farm chores to the boy, and constantly nagged and preached at him. The child never expressed his resentment. Instead, one day the lad, in grade 6, failed to come home until after midnight, when he turned up with a wild story of having been kidnaped by two boys whom he described in great detail. The story set the town on its ears for two days, until an understanding policeman got to the bottom of it.

This was the beginning of a behavior pattern. The boy throughout his life would tell people that he thought they desired to hear. He never came to the attention of any authority who could help with his real problem: a moralizing, hypocritical stepfather and a sentimental, ineffectual mother.

A second case involved a mother who had been frequently hospitalized, leaving her little girl in the care of a nurse who disliked children, but made a show of conscientious duty. The mother's absence was felt by the child as a desertion. This feeling, plus her rebellion against the hypocritical nurse, contributed to her first small delinquencies, stealing, running away, lying. She convinced her father that she would be better, only to repeat her behavior. Because of sex adventures at age 14 she was sent to a girls' school.

She married well, only to desert her husband inexplicably after a few months of marriage. She later formed casual alliances, and abandoned an illegitimate child. She was frequently found in the society of criminals. She was trying to escape from the voice of the moralizing, domineering nurse which had become her own hated conscience.

Is the psychopath responsible for his own repetitive, destructive behavior? Only 1.7% of psychiatrists in a Canadian survey think that he should *never* be held legally responsible. Fewer than 32% felt that he should *always* be held responsible for his acts.

If caught early enough psychopaths can be treated. But it is so difficult to treat an adult psychopath that the answer to the general problem is prevention. There must be suitable care for the infants of mothers who must work or are seriously sick. Neighbors must immediately report suspected cases of neglected and battered children. It is the right of every child to have a good substitute in these cases, such as day care or a visiting homemaker who is skilled with children. The child must be assured that it is not his fault that the parent is away or ill. Parents who are irritable, unsure of their own values, allowing the child to believe they are right even when they are unjust, are asking for trouble.

When the Trouble is 'All in Your Head'

Laboratory tests point to good and bad ways of dealing with stress

By Flora Schreiber and Melvin Herman

Imagine yourself as a human experimental subject, hooked up to a formidable array of apparatus. The doctor leaves the room. suddenly something goes wrong. There is a shower of sparks. After a moment the doctor rushes back, "Hold still!" he warns, and fiddles with the apparatus. The sparks subside. "How do you feel?" he asks. What would you answer?

This planned accident-in-the-laboratory experiment is designed to arouse anxiety. The response a person makes shows his defenses against stress. A person who always tried to avoid trouble might reply, "I just refuse to think about it." Someone else might say, "I knew you are a doctor and wouldn't let me be hurt." Still another, with no defenses, might say, "I practically fell apart."

The investigators at the Institute for Psychosomatic and Psychiatric Research and Training of the Michael Reese hospital in Chicago think that these typical responses to stress are clues to psychosomatic disease. "If psychomatic illness is to be understood, it is not the illness itself that must be studied, but the basic processes leading to it. All of us have defenses by which we avoid being stirred up. If we let

Condensed from "Science Digest", 1775 Broadway, New York City 10019, March, 1966. ©1966 by the Hearst Corp., 959 8th Ave., New York City, and reprinted with permission.

everything bother us, we would be at the mercy of the world," says Dr. Roy R. Grinker, Sr., institute director. "Anxiety long felt becomes unendurable. What we call psychiatric disturbances are really abnormal means that some individuals use to avoid anxiety. Some persons even escape into mental illness."

The particular form that defenses take is an individual matter. It varies according to one's personality type and his physiological response to stress. In psychiatric interviews, a doctor can note the degree of anxiety, anger, or depression shown by patients subjected to stress. The physiological effect of emotion can be recorded as changes occur in heart rate, blood pressure, the secretion of hormones by the adrenal cortex, and blood and urine analyses.

In his new kind of research, Dr. Grinker finds that the type of physiological reaction to stress varies with the individual. In one person, stress will cause a faster heartbeat; in another, higher blood pressure; in a third, abnormal muscle tension. Some persons have abnormal tension in all their muscles all the time.

These responses may reflect, or even cause a particular type of psychosomatic illness. A person who consistently reacts to emotional stress with a rise in blood pressure may develop permanently high blood pressure. One who reacts by tightening his neck muscles may suffer from a chronically stiff neck.

The type of response, though probably not inborn, is established early in life. When an infant reacts to stress, such as hunger or cold, he reacts with his whole being: he gets angry, his face flushes, he cries, he breathes faster. All his muscles are in action. As the child develops, this total reaction is narrowed. The response that finally predominates is determined by the way the child has been treated. In cases of extreme anxiety in adults, as in soldiers reported on by Dr. Grinker during the 2nd World War, there is a return to the broad, undifferentiated response of infancy.

The institute research shows a distinct relationship between muscle tension and certain character traits. The degree of muscle tension was measured by an electromyograph, which records a muscle's electric activity through electrodes taped to the skin. Under induced stress, anxious persons showed muscle hypertension. When patients were criticized, their speech muscles grew tense. Praise relieved the tension.

A generalized muscular hypertension, according to Dr. Donald Oken, may not only be a reaction but also a defense that keeps painful emotions from being recognized. Dr. Oken thinks that persons with a need to oppose strong feelings with strong controls develop unconscious anxiety.

He says, "Clarifying the psychophysiology of muscle tension should lead to a better understanding of psychosomatic illness in general, and of many cases of illness mistakenly diagnosed as rheumatism, fibrositis, or lumbago, in particular."

He declares that treatment of patients complaining of anxious tension may be fruitless, and perhaps dangerous, if directed only at reducing tension." Merely reducing tension through drugs may lead the patient into an unnatural relaxation, resulting in a loss of self-control. This loss, in turn, many lead to an increase in anxiety or the development of undesirable defenses. Dr. Oken says that those patients who do benefit from medication that reduces muscular tension are those in whom psychological conflict is no longer acute. He stresses the relationship between anxiety and muscle tension, and warns that "patients cannot be treated as mere collections of tense muscles."

Many persons have competent defenses against emotional pain. Even when showing physiological changes under stress, they remain outwardly calm. Now these changes are being measured in the laboratory.

When a child who has been to the dentist plays the game of dentist over and over again with her doll until the anxiety of the real experience is gone, she is overcoming stress. By reliving and repeating a bad experience in our thoughts, we can master the anxiety originally associated with it.

Dr. Mortimer Ostow of Montefiore hospital, New York City, says, "Every mental illness brings with it a struggle to establish or to maintain affectionate relations. The struggle is always painful. After a certain period, the patient may abruptly give up the attempt and withdraw from himself. He shows detachment from other persons and extravagant self-love. He remains aloof, and cultivates solitary pleasures. This maneuver, when successful, spares the person pain. But if this goes on very long, he may never resume normal emotional attachments."

Draw a Picture of Yourself

When you finish, you have taken a personality test

By Peggy Anderson

Before you read further, get a piece of paper and a sharp pencil and draw yourself. Take your time, and don't worry if you're not an artist. Just draw the best picture of yourself that you possibly can.

Finished? You have just taken a psychological test. It's called Draw-A-Man. About 9,000 children in the Philadelphia schools take this test each school year. And, though the test was developed for use with children, adults may be asked to take it when applying for a job or being considered for a promotion.

Draw-A-Man is usually given along with other tests (a single test of any kind never gives an adequate picture of the person taking it), but it has two advantages over many other tests; it requires no verbal skills, and it can give a lot of information in a very short time.

Your drawing for example, took you perhaps five or ten minutes to do. A psychologist could look at it and tell you quite a bit about yourself. He might tell you that you are worried about being clumsy. He might tell you that you're unrealistic or a dreamer. Maybe you think your drawing couldn't possibly reveal that much about you.

Well, look at it. Where did you place yourself on the page?

Are you in the middle of the paper, or in a corner? Do you fill the page, or are you a tiny figure in a snowy wasteland? Do you have stick arms and legs? Did you give yourself eyelashes, knees, thumbs? Are you wearing a print dress or a plaid tie? Did you draw anything besides yourself: a line to stand on, a house, another person, a supermarket cart? If you ask yourself why you draw a certain feature a certain way, and give yourself an honest answer, you can probably figure out part of what your drawing says about you. But don't expect to figure it out completely.

Condensed from the Philadelphia "Inquirer", 400 N. Broad St., Philadelphia, Pa. 19101. December, 1970. ᶜ1970 by the Philadelphia Newspapers, Inc., and reprinted with permission.

Dr. Thomas Atkins, a psychologist at Children's Hospital, Philadelphia, who is administering this and other tests to 12,000 seven-year-olds for a research project, is reluctant to generalize about just what characteristics mean what, even as an automobile mechanic won't diagnose a rattle without looking pretty carefully at the car. But Atkins will say that the person who draws himself two inches high on a blank sheet of paper 8 1/2 by 11 inches long is feeling at least a little inferior. He also says that the child who draws himself as a scribble, or even several scribbles, is not ready for first grade. He also says that a parent whose child's drawings are appreciatly different from those of his classmates is justified in wondering why.

He also says that if you draw yourself as a stick, you're evading. You are not made of sticks, obviously, and it's unlikely that you think you are. You are not an artist, you say? Dr. Atkins would not accept that evaluation. Anybody who can make one line can make two, and there's no excuse for one-dimensional legs except evasion.

You are also evading if you sketched yourself very quickly and then spent ten minutes making flowers on your dress or stripes on your shirt. You're not getting down to the business at hand. Why? That's for Dr. Atkins to know and you to find out. Or perhaps vice versa.

If you are 13 or 14 years old, Draw-A-Man can estimate your intelligence. After 40 or 50 years of study, psychologists reached the conclusion that a child's drawings reflect his mental maturity. So, as a child gets older, his drawings should mature along with him. And you can expect certain features at certain ages. Scribbling is a perfectly good way of putting crayon to paper if a child is only one year old. In the next year or so, the scribbles should turn into something, at least in the child's mind. The drawing may still look like a scribble to an adult, but the child calls it "mommy's face."

By the age of three or four, the child's drawing of a human figure should roughly resemble a human figure. Since faces and eyes are what is most important to babies, the figure, according to a colleague of Dr. Atkins, will usually have a very large head. It will have eyes and arms, but no trunk. By five or six the trunk should be added, though the head may still be over-sized. By seven the child may be drawing profiles.

Until he is eight or nine a child is likely to draw a figure with legs inside the pants or even bones inside the leg. That is because the child draws what he knows, not what he sees: He knows the legs are inside the pants, so he draws them there. A year or so later he may try to draw the body in profile but will draw a frontal view of the trunk, arms, and legs, and a side view of the head, by 13, all the parts should be in their proper places. Proportion should be roughly accurate, and the child should be drawing what he sees, not what he knows.

The child who doesn't stay fairly close to this schedule may only be immature. He could also be seriously disturbed. But Dr. Atkins is quick to point out that the child who shows himself to be seriously disturbed on the Draw-A-Man test is likely to be recognized as seriously disturbed by anyone who spends 15 minutes with him.

Mrs. Julie Sadtler, a psychologist who works with Dr. Atkins, recently showed a number of drawings to a group of pediatricians at Children's Hospital. The drawings and her comments illustrate the variety of information that Draw-A-Man can give.

A boy of five, considered normal and bright, drew a vertial rectangle for his body, a circle on top of it for a head, and stuck two undetailed feet at the bottom. "The boy said he drew his body that way because he was wearing a package" came the psychologist's explanation. "I guess he wasn't feeling very good about himself that day."

A seven-year-old drew herself with a huge head and a small body, which is the way a typical four-year-old would draw herself. Part of the drawing was a scribble. The child is considered "severely retarded."

A six-year-old drew himself with no mouth. "He has immature speech." A five-year-old drew himself small, with a lot of shading. "The shading indicates anxiety." A six-year-old drew himself in an agitated state, with his hair standing on end. "This boy suffers from occasional seizures." A girl drew herself with her eyes closed. "She falls asleep in class a lot." A boy who was failing in school drew a large, classic-looking, successful salesman type and a huge smile. A boy who is big and inept drew himself in giant proportions with thick, graceless limbs. A child dashed herself off in a hurry and then drew an laborate supermarket cart with elaborate boxes of cereal and cocoa, jars of peanut butter, and jelly, cartons of milk. "Evasion." A child drew himself close to one side of the paper. "Maybe he feels the need for support."

Mental capacity develops continually until the age of about 13, then reaches a plateau. The human figure varies, but not essentially; the normal figure may be seven feet tall or three, but either way it still has two legs, two arms, two eyes, one nose, and so on. This is why the Draw-A-Man test tells less about the intelligence of an adult than it does about the intelligence of a child. Once you have reached the state where you are drawing a complete, proportionate person, what you do with your drawing from then on is a question largely of personality or interest: you can draw your hand with a cane in it, but the cane describes your taste, not your intellect.

How Quick Are You?

*A simple test will show the current state
of your reflexes*

By R. S. Tripp

4	3	10	12
6	11	8	9
1	7	2	5

See how long it takes you to touch each square in numerical order. 9 seconds? Your reflexes are about average. 7 seconds? Very good. 5 seconds? Excellent. More than nine seconds? Your reactions are too slow.

You are driving your car. A hundred feet ahead a boy on a bicycle wobbles into your path. The split seconds that elapse between the time your eyes see him and the time your foot applies the brakes is "reaction" time. It varies from person to person and in the same person under differing conditions. It consists of the time required to sense the signal, plus time required to decide what response to make, plus that required to respond.

Simple involuntary reflexes take from 0.06 to 0.1 second but in spite of all the research that has gone into reaction time (RT), it is still impossible to state what any one person's RT will be at any particular time. RT will vary within a person from moment to moment. Any statement about someone having fast or slow reactions is misleading if the conditions are not specified.

Here are a few common beliefs about reaction time and what scientific studies have revealed about them.

A warning given to you ahead of time shortens your reaction time. Logical and usually true. It is most effective if the warning is given one to eight seconds before the response signal.

As you grow older you grow slower. False. You do not slow

Condensed from "Science Digest", 1775 Broadway, New York City 10019. May, 1965. ⸳1965 by the Hearst Corp., 959 8th Ave., New York City, and reprinted with permission.

down with age until you are 60. By then experience will usually balance off any physical slowdown.

Men are faster than women. True. Men have an edge over women in most tests, particularly complex ones.

Rewarding a person will cut down his RT. True, but punishment for reacting slowly is even more effective. Bullfighters, racing drivers, and pilots, who face both positive rewards and the most severe negative reward (death), have both factors working for them.

To be a jet pilot or an astronaut your reactions have to be exceptionally fast. False. Jet pilots and astronauts are not even tested for simple RT. If a man has some neurological disturbance that upsets his RT capability, it will show up in other tests. The small individual RT variability existing between pilots is overshadowed by each pilot's ability to learn, exercise good judgment, perform under pressure, and adapt to conditions.

There is a link between a person's intelligence and his RT. False. Intelligence as measured by standard IQ tests produces results only at the extremes of the scale, particularly in complex tasks. Even this effect is still debatable.

Lack of sleep slows down your RT. Sleep deprivation produces no change in RT until the subject is near the point of collapse. Then the usual result is no response at all because the subject temporarily becomes unconscious.

Drinking coffee or taking benzedrine will cut down RT. Neither seems to have any effect on wide-awake subjects. When used after a sleep loss they can cut down RT.

Smoking slows down your RT. False. Cigarette smoking produces no measurable result.

Drinking liquor slows down your RT. The question of liquor's effect on human performance in general and RT in particular is debatable. A small amount of liquor will improve the RT of persons who are normally too emotionally inhibited to make rapid responses. Do not use this as an excuse, though. It works only with certain personalities, and after more liquor is taken there is a definite lenghtening of simple RT. The degree varies with individuals and the rapidity with which the alcohol was consumed. Each person's rate of alcohol absorption may vary considerably, but alcohol-burning rate is constant for a given body size. All the airlines and military and government agencies now have preflight abstinence rules, though the abstinence period varies from eight to 24 hours.

Outstanding athletes have superior RT. RT tests were made of athletes during and after competition. First results indicated that, for the tests given, athletes did have shorter RT's than nonathletes. A later check revealed that the shortened RT's were due to the competition itself. The raised body temperature and emotional and mental set of the contestant speeded up his reactions.

RT becomes most important for people when they are driving. Do you know how quickly you can stop your car? Oh, of course, you have read the tables on speeds and braking distances, but what does 50, 176, or 230 feet really look like to you? The best way to find out is to take your car to a large deserted parking lot, airport, or road, and try stopping as quickly as you can from various speeds. You may be shocked. You may find that one wheel locks up, or that the brakes fail. Unfortunately, for most people, they find out their reaction time only when they have to make their first emergency stop.

Some drivers are so confused and frightened in an emergency that they "freeze"—don't react at all. Anyone who holds an airplane pilot's license has spent much of his training time studying and practicing for various emergencies that might occur in the air. The only emergency test given to auto drivers is usually a quick stop from about 20 mph.

Who is Happy?

Scientists are finding that the poets were right

By Paul Brock

Once only poets and philosophers tried to find the formula for happiness. Now doctors and psychiatrists are making discoveries which concern us all.

One is that intelligence and happiness do not go together. Investigations at Ohio Wesleyan university proved that those with high IQ's were less happy than those with lower IQ's. The results suggested that intelligent persons find more to be discontented about. Clever men and women are usually sensitive; they are more keenly aware of life's disappointments.

Women have a greater capacity for happiness than men, according to Dr. David H. Fink, a psychiatrist. He says that

Condensed from "Science Digest", 1775 Broadway, New York City 10019. September, 1965. ᶜ1965 by the Hearst Corp., and reprinted with permission.

"when a women's desire for a home, family, and loving mate is satisfied, she is far happier than the man who is similarly blessed. Men tend more toward restlessness and dissatisfaction."

Hard work can make a man happy. Sociologist Judson Landis found that men of leisure are likely to suffer more from boredom. They feel frustrated. Businessmen are the happiest, followed by teachers and clerical workers.

Prof. C. E. M. Joad said, "Work brings happiness, but the pursuit of wealth does not." Yet in a recent "happiness survey" of French men and women, money was ranked above everything else as essential to happiness. Most of them were quite certain they would be happy if they had wealth. Good health came second, and peace third. Love came last. Only 1% of the men and 5% of the women considered love essential to happiness.

The same survey revealed that people who stifle their anger have less chance of happiness. Those who give vent to their feelings enjoy life more. One couple reported that they throw old plates at a wall when they are angry at each other. After the first couple of plates the anger is replaced with laughter.

When 1,000 elderly people were questioned in a research project sponsored by the University of Wisconsin, they said their happiest years had been between the ages of 25 and 45, news that must astonish the harried people living in those years. It was found that though young adults may describe themselves as "happy," many of them are really frantic with worry over the passing of time. They can sense the years sweeping by without any evidence of accomplishment. Worrying over imagined mistakes, they give parties, drink too much, and say too little. They think old age is a catastrophe.

Yet when the same people reach the age of 65, they, too, will probably conclude that the years from 25 to 45 were the happiest in their lives. In the Wisconsin survey only one person chose childhood as the happiest period. Youth came a poor second. The link existing between work and happiness was again apparent with "both men and women happiest during that period in life when they were working hardest and carrying the most responsibilities."

The survey asked a representative group of men and women to write down the things they had done in the last three weeks that had given them the most happiness. Here are some of them. 1. Visiting friends, having dates, meeting new people. 2. Achieving some wish, desire, or ambition. 3. Games, sports, and amusements. 4. Conversation. 5. Dressing up, improving personal appearance, and acquiring new articles of apparel (mainly among women).

Dr. W. Beran Wolfe, of the institute of Psychiatry in London, says that science has reached much the same conclusion as the poets: that to find real happiness we must seek for it outside ourselves. If we live only for ourselves, we are always in danger of being bored. "It matters little," says Dr. Wolfe, "whether you interest yourself in making your town cleaner, or whether you go in for boys' clubs. Choose a movement toward greater human happiness and join it. No one has learned the meaning of living until he has surrendered his ego to the service of his fellow men."

Daydreaming

Psychologists used to think that it was harmful, but recent research shows that it actually be necessary

By Eugene Raudsepp

Daydreaming once was considered a waste of time. Psychologists regarded it as evidence of maladjustment, an attempt to escape from reality. They warned that habitual daydreaming could reduce a person's effectiveness in real life and hamper his ability to cope with problems.

Even the more indulgent psychologists considered daydreaming a childish habit which caused students to get bad grades and adults to fail at their jobs.

As with anything carried to excess, daydreaming *can* be harmful. Some substitute a fantasy life for the rewards of activity in the real world. And when a person can no longer cope with reality, his mental health is impaired. But these situations are rare. Most people suffer from a lack of daydreaming.

Our attitudes toward daydreaming have been much like our attitudes toward dreaming in our sleep. Night dreaming was once thought to interfere with normal sleep, to rob us of necessary rest. But experiments have indicated that dreams

Condensed from "Success Unlimited", 6355 Broadway, Chicago, Ill. 60660. November, 1975. ᶜ1975 by Success Unlimited, Inc., and reprinted with permission.

are a normal part of sleep, and that dreaming each night is necessary for mental health.

Dr. William Dement, who is experimenting on the significance of dreaming at Mt. Sinai Hospital in New York, reports that those subjects whose dreams are interrupted regularly exhibit emotional disturbances: hypertension, anxiety, irritability, and difficulty in concentrating.

"One of the subjects," Dr. Dement reports, "quit the study in apparent panic, and two insisted on stopping, presumably because the stress was too great." As soon as the subjects were allowed to dream again, all psychological disturbances vanished.

Prolonged *daydream* deprivation also results in mounting anxiety and tension. And many daydream-deprived people find that eventually the need can no longer be suppressed: daydreaming erupts spontaneously.

During times of stress, daydreaming erects a temporary shield against reality, in much the same way that building a house protects our bodies from the elements. Both may be seen as forms of escapism, but no one wants to spend life in an unrelieved battle for survival. We are entitled to occasional strategic withdrawals to regroup our forces.

Recent research on daydreaming indicates that it is an intrinsic part of daily life. Daydreaming, it has been discovered, is an effective means of relaxation.

But the beneficial effects of daydreaming go beyond that. Experiments conducted by Dr. Joan T. Freyberg, a New York City psychotherapist, showed that daydreaming significantly helps intellectual growth, powers of concentration, attention span, and the ability to communicate with others. Dr. Freyberg also discovered that her parents who easily engaged in fantasy-making usually responded more quickly to treatment.

In one experiment with school children, she observed that daydreaming improved their concentration. "There was less running around, more happy feelings, more talking and playing with each other, and more attention to detail," Dr. Freyberg reports.

In still another experiment, psychologist Dr. Sara Similansky discovered that people who were taught how to daydream significantly improved their language skills. And Dr. Jerome L. Singer at Yale found that daydreaming improved self-control and enhanced creative thinking ability. Dr. Singer feels that daydreaming is a way to improve upon reality, that it helps a person to cope with delay, frustration, and deprivation.

An electronics executive makes it a habit to daydream a few minutes every day. He says that it has added considerably to his mental energy. He reported that after a brief respite of daydreaming he feels more vigorous and zestful, and that he is better able to handle sudden pressures and crises.

Others who daydream regularly have reported that they emerge from the "vacation" of daydreaming not only relaxed, but more optimistic, enthusiastic, and purposeful. Some even claim a feeling of "lightness" in their bodies. Senses, too, are heightened: colors seem brighter, and objects seem to take on greater depth.

Daydreaming improves a person's ability to solve everyday problems. Contrary to popular belief, conscious effort at solving a problem can be an inefficient approach. Initial effort is necessary when we face a problem but it has been discovered that an effective solution frequently occurs when conscious efforts have been suspended. Inability to "let go" and daydream often prevents a solution.

Many famous scientists and inventors have performed best in relaxed moments of daydreaming. Sir Isaac Newton solved many of his toughest problems when his attention was diverted by private musings and fantasies. Thomas Edison also knew the value of "half-waking" states and whenever confronted with a seemingly insurmountable obstacle that defied all his efforts, he would stretch out on the couch in his workshop (brought there for just this reason) and let fantasies flood his mind.

Many artists, writers, and composers have indulged in daydreaming and reverie. Debussy used to gaze at reflections of the setting sun on the river Seine. Schiller kept rotten apples in his desk drawer. Their aroma helped him to evoke a mood of reverie. Dostoievsky found that he could dream up his plots and characters best while doodling. Brahms found that ideas came to him effortlessly only when he approached a state of deep daydreaming. Cesar Franck is said to have walked around with a dream-like gaze in his eyes while he was composing, seemingly unaware of his surroundings.

Daydreaming need not be the pursuit of the impossible. For many people it is a way of making reality more meaningful. Daydreaming helps them to find out who they are, why they are doing what they are doing, and what they really want to do. They use daydreaming for considering alternatives and discovering fresh directions.

John Uelses, former pole-vaulting champion, deliberately dreamed before each meet about winning, and vividly pictured himself clearing the bar at a certain height. He visualized the stadium, the crowds present, even the smell of the grass and the earth.

Golfer Jack Nicklaus daydreams before each tournament to attain what he calls "the winning feeling." This feeling, as he puts it, "gives me a line to the cup just as clearly as if it's been tattooed on my brain. With that feeling all I have to do is swing the clubs and let nature take its course."

President Harry S Truman used daydreaming as a retreat from stress. "I have a fox hole in my mind," he used to say.

Several alcoholism clinics use daydreaming to cure alcoholics. Dr. Edward McGoldrick, whose Bridge House has a high record of recoveries, instructs his patients each day to relax, close their eyes and deliberately picture themselves as sober, responsible successful persons, enjoying life without liquor. After a few weeks of this fantasy therapy, many patients attain sobriety and a new, more positive outlook on life.

Why would a vivid projection of success help to bring success? "Your nervous system cannot tell the difference between an imagined and a real experience," says neurosurgeon Dr. Maxwell Maltz. "In either case, it reacts automatically to information which you give it from your forebrain." He says that daydreaming "builds new memories into your midbrain and central nervous system." These positive memories improve self-image, and a good self-image improves a person's behavior and accomplishments.

To get the best results, you should picture yourself as you want to be. The important thing is that you picture your desired objectives *as if you had already attained them.* Go over several times the details of these pleasant fantasy pictures. This will impress them upon your memory. And these memory traces, or "engrams," will soon start influencing your everyday behavior.

While exercising your imagination this way, you should be alone and undisturbed. It is also a good idea to close your eyes in order to help your imagination soar. Many people find they obtain better results if they imagine themselves sitting before a large, blank screen, and project onto it the desired image of themselves.

Everyone should put aside a few minutes each day for daydreams. Who knows? Today's fantasy may become tomorrow's reality.

Displaced Any Behavior Lately?

Why every living animal sometimes does stupid things

By Keith Ellison

A seagull sits atop its nest of thatched grass. The bird's long wings lie close at its sides, and its crimson legs are tucked beneath its body helping to warm three incubating eggs. Suddenly the bird hears a strange noise from a passing sailboat. She seems uncertain whether to protect the eggs or investigate the disturbing sound of children's laughter. So she does neither, but dives into the water and begins vigorous bathing.

A short-haired gorilla walks through the rain forests of western Africa, its 450 pounds resting on all four brawny limbs. About 200 yards away, a hunter drives his jeep through the undergrowth. As the gorilla sees the intruder it throws all of its weight back on its two hind legs, rises to its full 5 1/2 foot height, and pounds on its chest.

A young housewife jumps from her car after her carelessness at an intersection has caused a collision. As the other driver mutters angrily and a patrol car pulls up, the woman looks into her pocket mirror and hurriedly brushes back her hair.

What do these three incidents have in common? Quite a bit. The gull, the gorilla, and the housewife, like many other animals, are engaging in "displacement activity." Confronted with conflicting emotions, each is undecided between two logical responses. But, instead of choosing the most obvious alternative, each makes an apparently illogical response. The gull does not know whether to nest or explore; it decides to bathe. The gorilla is not certain whether to stand its ground or flee; it thumps its chest. The driver wants to escape from her predicament but she also wants to resolve the trouble; she primps.

Displacement behavior was not recognized by pshychologists until 1940. Researchers have still not investigated all of its manifestations, nor have they reached a consensus ex-

Condensed from "Science Digest", 224 W. 57th St., New York City 10019. March, 1971. ᶜ1971 by the Hearst Corp., and reprinted with permission.

planation of it. In 1947, ornithologist Edward Armstrong suggested that it is a kind of "sparking over" from one behavior pattern into a new, irrelevant pattern. According to Armstrong the gull is "energized" by a sense of danger, but, in the confusion of the moment, the energy sparks over to bathing.

An important modification of Armstrong's sparking-over concept was suggested by anthropologists J. J. Van Iersel and A.C. Bol. After extensive field observations the two researchers concluded that displacement really is a form of "disinhibitionism." They think that animals' behavior patterns are arranged in a kind of hierarchy, with those of higher importance, such as the gorilla's impulses to attack or to flee, disinhibiting patterns of lower importance, such as the gorilla's chest beating. According to Van Iersel and Bol, when two such impulses of equal importance in the hierarchy occur simultaneously, they cancel one another out and neither is performed. Instead, a behavior pattern of lower rank in the hierarchy is set loose; hence, displacement.

Whatever the true explanation—sparking over, disinhibitionism, or something entirely different—displacement behavior is obvious among animals. Some varieties of insects eat voraciously when experiencing conflicting drives. In the fish family, the stickleback often engages in seemingly irrelevant nest-building when its territory is approached by an opponent. As the danger comes closer, the nest-building becomes more animated. Many birds go into mating patterns when disturbed by a real or imagined threat. Baboons, mountain gorillas, and people all have been seen yawning in displacement situations. Anthropologists say that during important examinations some students, even if well-rested, yawn repeatedly as they consider the questions.

Many men and women resort to shoulder shrugging, head shaking, and head scratching in uncertain circumstances. Whistling can be a displacement activity of some persons when they are frightened and unsure of how to cope with their fright. Some anthropologists think that regrettable human traits like compulsive eating and alcoholism may be attributable to displacement behavior.

Displacement behavior can sometimes be seen on a large scale among a mass of people. Anthropologists cite the cheers of a crowd at a football game and ask: is that really a rational response to the events on the field or is it a form of displacement activity? Skilled demagogues like Mussolini and Hitler were ominous examples of displacement. By arousing in their followers a fervid sense of national or racial feeling, national leaders can direct the efforts of thousands into some important but unrelated activity, like the creation of a new economic system or the introduction of a radically different religious ethic.

But many anthropologists, psychiatrists, and sociologists are optimistic about the uses of displacement behavior. They feel sure that some organized displacement activity can be found to redirect marital tensions that otherwise might end in divorce. Colleges may provide the first opportunity for planned displacement; student unrest might be intentionally directed toward some peaceful end. Even international feuds may eventually be resolved by a rigorous application of a well considered displacement pattern.

Emotions on the Job

They can make or break a business enterprise

A few years ago we used to worry about the husband who brought home a briefcase full of work. Now we are concerned about the employee who brings his home troubles to work.

In an East Coast firm, employees complained about schedules, co-workers, office equipment, and things like noise, glare, heat and cold. They also had headache, backache, and abdominal pain, so they were referred to the medical office.

The company physician, who happened to be a psychiatrist, found that only one complaint could be traced to work conditions. The others were made by a stenographer who was panicky at the thought of losing her boy friend; an account executive who feared he would inherit the heart disease that killed his father, a salesman who had two girls in love with him; and a foreman who had a feeling of guilt for his wife's depression.

Dr. William C. Menninger says, "From 60% to 80% of all dismissals in industry are due to social incompetence, and only about 20% to 40% to technical incompetence. One emotionally disturbed employee can mess up his whole department, and the cost of his illness can hardly be estimated."

Condensed from "Medicine at Work", 1155 15th St., N.W. Washington, D.C. 20005. May, 1966. ©1966 by the Pharmaceutical Manufacturers association, and reprinted with permission.

In one General Motors plant of 5,800 employees, emotional problems were found in more than half of those reporting for medical care. Emotional problems cause the $12 billion loss in absenteeism, employee turnover, alcoholism, industrial accidents, and lowered productivity.

A worker's problem can often be talked out in a few visits with the company physician; therefore, many firms are hiring psychiatrists. Difficulties exist for the common laborer as well as the top executive. Some occupations are more vulnerable than others. The engineer-scientist's intense absorption in his own work makes him especially vulnerable to emotional upsets. Transition from the leisurely atmosphere of a university laboratory to hard industrial work often causes emotional difficulties.

About 40 years ago the Western Electric Co. found that better lighting increased output, but so did reduced lighting. Just by showing interest in workers, management turned drudgery into happy productivity. But there are also pressures on executives: frustrations and fear of failure, which can harm or improve the attitudes of their workers depending upon their own handling of the pressures.

In some companies the psychiatrist sits in on executive meetings. He never advises on corporate matters, but he does tactfully point out any irrelevant emotions getting in the way of objectives.

Psychiatrists are convincing management that there should be greater emphasis on capacity for human understanding in the selection of executives. Dr. Menninger puts it this way, "When I say a leader must understand men, I mean he must understand the unreasonableness in all of us and the hostilities we all have."

Advisors to both labor and management are insisting that a neurotic employee should neither be fired nor demoted. One psychiatrist says business may be defeating itself when it tries to screen out all emotionally tense employees or job seekers.

Dr. Frederick W. Bershimer, who was hired as a full-time psychiatrist for E. I. du Pont de Nemours in 1943, said, "The most valuable people are sometimes screwballs. If you do a good enough screening job you may get people who are perfectly normal. But you will have screened out people who discover things like nylon."

If we can build mental health in a complex occupational environment, a side benefit may become the greatest reward of all: the personal well-being of generations to come. When a boy hears his father constantly complain about his job, he is likely to have a similar attitude toward his own work.

Neurosis may be communicable, but emotional well-being is even more catching. Says Dr. Ralph T. Collins of Kodak, "the work that men do is an essential part of their lives, not mainly because of it they earn bread, but because a man's job gives him stature and binds him to society. The man who is satisfied at work, confident in his employers, and cooperative with his fellow workers will spread his contentment throughout the community."

Your Voice: The Most Personal Thing About You

It reveals your ups and downs, your health or lack of it

By Mary Virginia Moore and J. Buckminster Ranney

Your voice registers your ups, and your downs, your good health, your fall from it. It reflects the many aspects of your personality with cruel honesty. It is as unique as your fingerprints.

The tiny muscles which produce the shout of a baseball official or the high *C* of an operatic soprano are called vocal cords, but they have other functions than production of sound.

The vocal cords are protected by a cage of cartilages. The cords stretch across the upper portions of the windpipe to make a pair of sliding doors to the lungs. The cage is the larynx. Together, they tell some things to come and go while keeping others in or out.

Most of the time, the doorway is open, allowing air to pass freely through mouth or nose, down the throat, through the trachea to the lungs. Seconds later, carbon dioxide leaves the lungs and travels out.

The vocal cords spread apart a little during each inspiration and come a bit closer together during each expiration. The cycle is completed 15 times a minute, day and night.

The vocal cords close tightly to trap air in the lungs for the

Condensed from "Today's Health", 535 N. Dearborn St., Chicago, Ill. 60610. December, 1967.
ᶜ1967 by the American Medical association and reprinted with permission.

elimination of waste products from the body, for labor contractions during childbirth and strenuous activity.

The vocal cords also exclude unwanted guests from the
lungs. Particles of dust, grains of salt, drops of water, safety
pins, pennies, and fish bones may try to crash the gateway.
The vocal cords bar the entrance and, if need be, they will use
the mighty cough. A cough can blow out foreign material
with the force of a 100 mph gust of wind.

Birds possess a vocal organ, the syrinx, designed
specifically to make sound. Man was not endowed with this
bit of anatomy, only with the intelligence to adapt other
structures to make sound. At first the sound was a cry, a
grunt, or a sigh. By modifying the basic tone, he produced
several dozen speech sounds. Further refinements of pitch,
loudness, and quality make it a musical instrument and, when
man knew the meaning of words, he sang.

The voice became the most important means of communication and an art form of the highest order. With voice,
man is able to talk to those around him. He can release pent-
up emotion. He is able to make his own music. In sighing,
sobbing, laughing, humming, singing, screaming, and cooing,
as well as in speaking, he reveals his moods and thoughts.

Each of us has felt a lump in the throat that seems to be
located directly in the larynx. Each of us knows the "I can't
trust myself to speak now: feeling that goes with deep
emotion. We have heard the whiny voice that betrays an
unhappy woman; the weak, thin voice of a self-conscious
child; and the quivery voice that accompanies fright. We have
heard the husky, low-pitched voice of a man who is deeply
moved and the high-pitched, shrill voice of an excited birthday child. Each one of them is produced by emotions.

If two objects of equal length and size are caused to
vibrate, the more tense one will produce the higher-pitched
sound. The muscular tension that accompanies the excitement causes the vocal muscles to be tighter and thus to
produce a higher-pitched sound than they do when relaxed.

The opposite occurs during emotional depression. Bodily
activities are slowed down, muscle tone is lowered, and the
sound coming from the relaxed vocal muscles is lower in
pitch. Less energy may cause the voice also to be less loud
than usual.

Your blue moods and your gay moods are mirrored in your
voice. If you wake up with a dull, fuzzy voice but enjoy a
clear, vibrant one at dinnertime, you are an evening person
rather than a morning person.

Slight hoarseness reveals a bad cold, a little nasality indicates a sore throat, and a "thin" voice suggests anemia. Almost any vocal variation may indicate a general condition of the body.

Luckily, cancer in this region is one of the easiest of all to cure or remove. But, unluckily, there is little warning of cancer there: No pain, no bleeding, no swelling. A change in voice is one of the seven danger signals of cancer. Whenever hoarseness persists for more than two weeks or when it occurs with no known cause, consult your doctor!

But most cases of hoarseness are not caused by malignant growths. Whenever the cords are swollen, irritated, infected, scarred, or damaged in any way, there is a change in voice pitch, loudness or quality.

From the birth cry of a healthy baby to the feeble good-by of a dying man, the voice grows old along with the rest of us. The cry of a newborn baby is proof to the doctor that the child's passageway to the lungs is open and that he is breathing. During infancy and childhood the voice in boys as well as girls is often shrill and loud.

Voice becomes important to a baby as he finds satisfaction in the wonderful sound he produces and as he finds rewards in the responses of other people to his vocalization.

Children constantly abuse their voices by screeching, screaming, and imitating sounds. Yet they usually do no permanent damage to their vocal cords or their voices.

The most drastic voice changes take place during adolescence, when rapid growth and changing hormonal secretions cause the vocal cords to become thicker and longer so that lower pitches are produced.

All of us have noticed changes in the voice of an aging person. Not only does the voice often become weaker and the quality poorer, but the pitch changes. The pitch of a man's voice gradually rises as he grows old.

Occasionally a man or woman may preserve a clear speaking voice long after physical health has declined. This is more often true when he maintains an active interest in other people and a good supply of things to talk about.

From birth to old age, from mood to mood, in sickness and in health, the real you is shown in your voice. There are many you's and each has its own voice. Your voice is the most personal thing about you. It belongs to you and you alone. A single *hello* on the telephone can identify you with absolute certainty to a friend. Scientists using sound analyzing instruments find voice samples a sure method of identification.

What is probably the most variable thing about you remains also the most constant thing about you.

The Danger in Unspoken Anger

Suppressing one feeling can lead to a loss of all feeling

By Carol Hoover

I am a family therapist dealing with disturbed adolescents, and I have noticed that parents of such children seldom express their feelings toward each other directly.

In one kind of family, a good deal of hugging and kissing may go on, but at the same time, everybody seems to be mad at everybody else. Each person is busy explaining how angry somebody else is, what somebody else wants or thinks, how another person does terrible things. It may take months of therapy before a wife can say to her husband, "I am angry at you," instead of "My husband does these terrible things all the time." Tenderness toward her husband can emerge only when she admits she herself is angry instead of insisting only that her husband is doing something wrong.

In another sort of family the feelings the parents have for each other are expressed not verbally but through family-wide sequences of action. One husband, who was angry at his wife but felt unable to say so, suddenly drove to visit his mother in a distant city, taking one of the children along with him in the car, without a word to his wife. In another family, the wife habitually left the room whenever her husband began speaking to her angrily, so there was never a chance to thrash out a disagreement. In retaliation, the husband secretly supported the daughter in behavior of which the mother disapproved.

Sometimes the parents silently convey their anger in such a way that one or more of the children acts up in an unconcious effort to get the parents talking again. One teen-age boy would get himself picked up by the police whenever his parents were at odds; this always forced the parents to talk to each other. But the couple's fundamental disagreement remained because they could not express their anger at each

Condensed from "Word", 1312 Massachusetts Ave. N.W., Washington, C.D. 20005. January, 1968. ⟨1967 by the "Word" and National Council of Catholic Women, and reprinted with permission.

other in words; and another silent alienation followed. This is called an emotional divorce.

Husband and wife may fear that talking about their anger will result in physical violence. They see little difference between words and action. To them, the statement "Sometimes I get so mad at you, I feel like hitting you over the head with a baseball bat" means that the next step will be the swing of a bat at the head, and it appears dangerous to utter such thoughts.

Other persons are more afraid of emotional hurt than of physical violence. They don't realize that anger which is ignored, or turned off like a faucet, does not simply disappear but accumulates and affects everyone in the family.

Unspoken anger can kill tenderness between husband and wife, and lead them to concentrate on a son or daughter, which can greatly disturb the child. When a child is in trouble, the parents usually speak to the child. Father and mother may speak to each other about the child. But it is at least equally important that husband and wife speak to each other about their feelings.

When I am consulted by parents about an adolescent daughter, say, I am likely to remark at some point, "Forget about Sandra for a while. Let's talk about the two of you."

It is amazing how much trouble many husbands and wives have in staying on the subject of their own relationship. Try it yourself: can you and your mate talk for even five minutes just about the two of you? Some couples find this almost impossible. Hardly a minute goes by before a child's name is mentioned. Such couples are the ones who have great stores of hidden anger.

In some cases, the buried anger has been converted into a sense of hopelessness. What is the use of trying to change yourself or the other person? The pair gives up making any real attempt to clarify issues between them. One wife, who decided her husband was upset by seeing her cry, used to sit in the car and weep, rather than let him feel the force of her angry tears.

Sometimes you meet families who are so discouraged about themselves that nobody bothers to get mad. Everyone sits around looking bored, or keeps busy in a succession of small, tiresome tasks. When not at his job, the father gets away from it all at the golf course, while mother hides behind the whine of her vacuum cleaner.

Then there are the couples who with sarcastic taunts manage to avoid any direct, honest expression of anger. These partnerships are usually masochistic; both husband

and wife would find it hard to do without each other's thrusts. The taunts from someone else drown out for each of them their own self-criticism. Their mutual scorn is thus a valued state of affairs for both, although they complain bitterly to outsiders. Frequently they inform everyone that they would get a divorce if only it weren't for their religion, or the children, or any other reason but the main one: that neither can live without the other. They avoid any acknowledgement of feeling as their own; it is rare to hear either husband or wife say, "I am angry at you," "I care about you," "I am disappointed in you," "I love you."

Parents can help children learn how to express anger usefully in words, particularly but tolerating such anger when it is spoken toward them. The small boy who bursts out with "I hate you" when his mother refuses permission for a trip to the movies may make a more effective husband later in life than the boy who silently swallows his anger. And the mother who leaves him free to say it, without needing to change her ruling about the movies, is helping him toward a more fruitful existence.

If mother and father are able to speak openly of their disagreements, show anger and love and tenderness as they are felt, they will show the child that the expression of real feeling between adults can be one of the best parts of his life.

Wear Your Neighbor's Shoes

Though you may not like the fit, you will get a different outlook

By Jewel Maret Jenkins

Sometimes it's a good idea to put yourself in another's shoes. All one winter I watched a man who rode the bus to work each morning, carrying his lunch pail. One stormy day I thought to myself, "Here is a man trapped by the treadmill if ever there was one!" His eyes were deep set, his mouth stern; the planes of his face were as if carved from granite.

Condensed from "A Treasury of Success Unlimited", Edited by Og Mandino. ©1966, 1965, 1963, 1962, 1961, 1960, 1959, 1958, 1957, 1956, 1955 by Combined Registry Co., and reprinted with permission of Hawthorn Books Inc., 70 5th Ave., New York City 10011. $5.95.

"What has this man to look forward to?" I asked myself. "Obviously he is dressed for hard outdoor labor. Probably he will eat his cold lunch out in the snow. No wonder his face is so grim."

Yet in his face there was some gleam of inner contentment; in the eyes, some calm acceptance of life.

One day, during school vacation, the man got onto the bus with a glow of excitement about him. Holding tightly to his hand and looking up at him was the most beautiful child I had ever seen. She swept her long auburn curls back from her pink cheeks, and said with delight, "Today is the most wonderful day of my life, daddy, because you are taking me to work with you!"

Smiles appeared all over the bus at the little girl's words. Suddenly I saw what this man worked for, the hidden treasure that explained the contentment in his eyes. The glow on the little girl's face made the daily grind a little less tiresome for all of us that morning. We felt we had stepped for a moment into this man's shoes and found that any job may have compensation.

If you change jobs occasionally, you can put yourself into another's shoes. Try some unfamiliar occupation. Dig a few ditches, saw some logs, scrub a few floors, and get the feel of life from a new angle.

You can do a mental change of jobs, so that another's problems are brought home to you. Jane was inclined to be impatient with clerks. She never realized it until the day a customer mistook her for a clerk. The large woman, whose eyes glittered behind steel-rimmed glasses, called out, "See here, Miss! You have kept me standing here too long. Don't apologize. It's too late for that now! I'm reporting you."

Jane just gasped at the angry customer. Suddenly she had visions of tired sales clerks with aching feet and throbbing heads. Since then she has put herself in the clerk's place whenever she shopped.

One summer a friend of mine spent enough time outdoors to deepen her naturally olive skin to a dark tan. One day she slipped into a bright red sun dress and went downtown to shop at a fashionable store. She waited while customer after customer who had come in after her was served. At last she stopped a clerk, asked to see some dresses and went into the dressing room to try them on. The clerk was surly about her request to see the merchandise, and it was some time before the dresses came. When they did they were not handed to her, but were thrown rudely into the booth. All at once my friend realized that she had been mistaken for a Negro.

Her eyes filled with tears. She felt deeply hurt, and as if she had no means to fight back. She hung the dresses neatly on the hangers, put on her own red dress, and walked quietly from the store.

This woman has always been tolerant of others. She had thought she understood the problems of minority groups before that day, but the incident shocked her to real awareness of another's feelings. She told me, "My feelings for people of other races have been different since that day. I used to suppose they must have certain attitudes; not I *know* how they feel."

Wear your neighbor's shoes for a while. You may not like the fit: the pinch of poverty, the bruise of ill health, the tight lacings of color or class prejudice—but you will learn.

Your Brain: Still the Champ

It can outperform any computer

By John Pfeiffer

Suppose you sat down with paper and pencil to write out everything you remembered: names of people you know or have heard about, experiences from childhood on, plots of movies and novels, descriptions of jobs you have held, a list of your hobbies, and so on.

This game would not be worth playing, because even if you wrote 24 hours a day, you would be at it for at least several thousand years. The brain's storage capacity has been estimated at 10,000,000,000,000 (ten million million) units of information.

The main theory of a large-scale computer may contain from 1 million to 4 million storage elements, tiny washer-shaped magnetic cores each capable of holding one "bit", the basic unit of computer information.

The cores, with associated equipment, may occupy 70 cubic feet, or roughly the space of a telephone booth. This represents an enormous advance over ENIAC, the first of the electronic computers, which required a much larger space for 600 bits of 17 words.

Condensed from "Popular Mechanics", 250 W. 55th St., New York City 10019. January, 1965. Ⓒ1964 by the Hearst Corp., and reprinted with permission.

But the brain is still champion when it comes to compact design. A blob of nerve tissue about the size of a pinhead can hold more information than any computer. In a volume of about 1/20th of a cubic foot, the brain includes 10,000 million nerve-cell elements or neurons, each of which can store an average of 1,000 bits. So a human brain can store 2 1/2 million times more information than the most advanced computer.

The large-scale computer can retrieve a given item of information in half a millionth of a second. The brain may take a second or more. But the machine has far less to "thumb through." If it contained as much information as the brain, its searching processes would take much longer.

How such a tremendous amount of information is stored in the standard-size brain is only one of the great mysteries of memory. Some of your brain cells change in a very specific way every time you register a new experience. But the nature of the changes, the nature of our built-in memory traces, continues to elude investigators at medical and biological laboratories. Nevertheless, recent work has provided some interesting clues.

The first stage of learning involves a kind of short-term memory. A very young child may look at a totally new thing, say a shoe or the letter *B*, a number of times, and each time represents an entirely new experience: no persisting record has been made. The experience only begins to "take" after the child has viewed the object on and off for a total of about 15 minutes. Even then the record may fade overnight. To store something permanently in the mind, a process known as consolidation, demands 12 or more hours.

Temporary disorders of short-term memory are fairly common. Drinking too much seems to interfere with the formation of new traces, and the morning after may find the person without any record of the night before. A blow on the head may have the same effect. After his first professional fight, Mickey Walker, later welterweight and middleweight champion of the world, was showering when he called out to his second, "What round did I knock out the guy?"

"You didn't knock him out at all," the second explained. "He knocked you out. In the first round, too."

The mechanisms of short-term memory may work less efficiently among older persons. The veteran who recalls full details of battles fought 40 years ago often has trouble remembering what happened last month or the day before yesterday. The aging brain tends to make only incomplete records of recent events, though ability to retain what is recorded may not be affected.

Alcoholism, on the other hand, can produce severe trouble at a relatively early age. A 52-year-old taxi driver admitted to a Chicago hospital lives in a strange and fleeting world. He has a memory span of just about two minutes. If you tell him your name and ask him immediately to repeat it, he will have no trouble. But after two minutes are up, he will have completely forgotten it.

Such disorders involve a complex of nerve structures called the "Papez circuit." Buried in the depths of the brain are a number of centers arranged in a kind of loop and interconnected by nerve fibers, some of which are nearly as big around as a pencil. Damage in this region may interfere with our ability to form and store memory traces, records of the past. Research also indicates that these mysterious traces may be chemicals of a very special sort.

James McConnell and his associates at the University of Michigan are probing the workings of memory by studying the flatworm, a tiny "cross-eyed" creature that can be conditioned to react to a flashing bright light. Normally, it ignores the light. But if each flash is accompanied by an electrical shock, the flatworm finally learns to react to flash alone.

Cut a thoroughly conditioned worm in two, and the head end grows a new tail and the tail end grows a new head. But new worms remember most of what the original worm had learned. Under proper conditions, one worm will eat another, and the worm that has fed on an educated friend is a better learner than its brother who has eaten uneducated worms. It appears that recently acquired information has been passed from old to newborn cells. Studies at Michigan and at a number of other laboratories suggest that the information may somehow be incorporated into the structure of molecules of substances knows as ribonucleic acid (RNA).

RNA is a hereditary material found in all cells, including those of flatworms. Experiments performed at the University of Rochester, N.Y., show that a "magic-bullet" substance that breaks up RNA without affecting other chemicals also prevents the passing on of information from a flatworm to the creatures formed from its severed halves. In related research on rats, Swedish investigators report that learning increases the amount of RNA produced in brain cells. Not only that, but it also produces changes in the chemical composition of the hereditary material, as if memory left its traces in the form of subtle alterations in the structure of giant RNA molecules, alterations that endure like symbols graven in stone.

If memory consists of such "marked" molecules, one aspect of the storage problem would be solved: there is ample space for them in the brain's 100 billion nerve cells. We know very little about how and where our records are stored, however, except that they are probably not stored in any single center. Large areas of the brain may be damaged beyond healing or removed surgically without causing measurable memory loss, suggesting that memory traces may be duplicated over and over again and stored in many places. No one knows how the duplication is accomplished, but the process is something like making copies of valuable documents and then keeping them in widely scattered strong-boxes as a safeguard against fire and theft.

Sometimes it seems as if the scattering is almost too effective, and we fail to find the records. Notice that forgetting is not involved in cases like that of Mickey Walker. Strictly speaking, he had nothing to forget because he had formed no new traces. As a rule, genuine forgetting implies that we cannot get at memories that presumably exist intact somewhere. Perhaps nerve pathways are blocked, and, if we knew how, we might be able to restore the past in full simply by using the proper drug.

Another unsolved puzzle is how we recall information once it has been registered. Again, there is no special "recollecting center," although certain areas of the brain seem to play a part. Wilder Penfield, director of the Montreal neurological institute and one of the world's foremost brain surgeons, stimulated points on the sides of an exposed brain by touching them lightly with a wire electrode or electrical contact. Since the brain feels no pain, operations may be conducted with a local anesthetic only, and patients are fully conscious and capable of describing their reactions.

One of Penfield's famous cases was that of a 26-year-old secretary. The instant he stimulated a certain point on the side of her brain, she heard an orchestra playing the song *Marching Along Together*. Furthermore, it was not a "silent" memory, the kind of experience you have when you merely think of a tune. The woman felt as if she was sitting in an auditorium with all the individual instruments playing loud and clear, though at the same time she knew that she was actually in an operating room. She was vividly reliving a previously forgotten event. When the surgeon moved the electrode, breaking the contact, the music stopped as suddenly as if an "off" button has been pushed. But the most unusual thing happened when the same point on the brain was stimulated again. The woman immediately heard the same music, but it did not continue from where it had stopped. The entire song started all over again from the beginning. It was as if the memory was stored on a cerebral soundtrack, a tape that automatically rewound itself after every use in preparation for the next playback.

But recollection involves far more than retrieving information in its original form. We can rearrange and classify the information with the speed of thought, and that represents perhaps the greatest mystery of all. Indeed, some of the things we do so routinely that we take them for granted are among the most baffling mysteries of science.

For example, think of what must go on inside your head when this kind of question is put to you: "Did you ever see a movie called *Life Begins at Forty?*" Or a question like this: "Do you know Evelyn Mayo?" Think of how many movies you have seen and how many people you have met and worked with and read about. Yet your brain contains a filing system, since you can come up with an answer (usually the correct one) within a few seconds.

There is also a searching system that usually works so swiftly that we are not aware of it. But its nature may be guessed at by considering what happens when we fail to recall something immediately; for example, when we have trouble answering the question, "What was the name of the motel you stayed in last summer?" Most of us would run through the letters of the alphabet and decide that the name starts with a particular letter or combination of letters. Then we run through a list of words that meet those specifications. The odds are that something of this sort is happening when you answer a question "without thinking," only the search proceeds at a fantastic speed.

Nature continues to set standards that we try to match. A host of now unsolvable scientific problems could be solved if thinking machines remembered and recalled as efficiently as does the human brain.

Chapter II
Help Yourself

After you learn a few things about yourself and why you are as you are, you are ready for pointers on how to change yourself, and the evaluations others have of you, for the better. There are well established, fundamental ways of breaking habits, controlling fears, making friends, improving your emotional states and reactions. These points and others equally important appear in the articles in this chapter on self-improvement.

Cure Your Blues

*A new kind of psychotherapy employs
old-fashioned fatherly advice to treat
persons who think they are unworthy*

By William Krasner

In a cartoon, a pompous psychiatrist stands over a skinny, sad little man and says, "There isn't anything wrong with you. You really *are* an insignificant worm."

Psychiatrist Aaron T. Beck has been working with depressed people for 20 years. He thinks the humor is O.K., but not the technique. "That's one of the myths about depression, that maybe the patient is simply facing facts about himself, or our terrible times. But when you get down to work with a real patient, you always find that he has it twisted around worse than it is. At the heart of depression is a *false* idea about how bad he, the future, and the world are."

Dr. Beck, director of the Mood Clinic at the Hospital of the University of Pennsylvania, is white-haired, handsome, friendly, and apparently not depressed about anything. For a man who spends so many hours a day, and has spent so many years, listening to the dreariest stuff imaginable ("I'm no good, doctor. The world stinks. My family and everybody else would be better off if I'd just get it over with the pull the trigger.") he is surprisingly cheerful. And why not? He feels that his life's work is bearing fruit, and the method he uses can relieve depression in most people.

"The beauty of it all," says Beck, "is that the patient has learned a technique that can help bring him out of depression again if a new crisis develops. He can come in for refresher treatments, or even do it himself."

There is another advantage to cognitive therapy, Dr. Beck's method. "Compared to most other forms of depression therapy, it's relatively simple. It doesn't require extensive digging into the past. It doesn't require drugs. It doesn't take a lot of time or a lot of money. Maximum length of treatment

Condensed from "Philadelphia Inquirer/Today", 400 N. Broad St., Philadelphuia, Pa. 19101. Feb. 3, 1975. ‹1975 by Philadelphia Newspapers, Inc., and reprinted with permission.

is 20 weeks, one session a week. It's not like psychoanalysis, that might run on for years. It doesn't even require a specially trained psychiatrist."

To appreciate what this might mean, we must know what depression means. To psychiatrists, depression is not the gloom or sadness that might come after a bad day or a disappointment. It is not even the anxiety, immobility, and feeling of great loss that comes when you lose a loved one, a job, or a cherished goal. Though the symptoms might be the same, the cause is real, and you will come out of it. There might be something wrong with you if you didn't show temporary gloom.

Clinical depression is a sadness and feeling of isolation and unworthiness so intense that it dominates your life, your thoughts, and your functioning. It is more crippling to more people at any one time than is any other disorder except the common cold. About 15% to 20% of Americans are depressed right now.

During our lifetimes, most of us will need treatment for depression, even if we don't realize it, or get it. The exact number can't be known because most depressed persons don't come in for treatment, or even know they are depressed. Depression is "the great pretender," masked as stomach trouble, vague aches, laziness or weakness; loss of appetite and sex drive; alcoholism or drug addiction; or even as just the normal condition of things in a naughty world. This is especially true of men, who are supposed to be stoic and so go to physicians with physical complaints instead.

But many will not even see a physician. Some cannot get up the courage. Some think their misery is a richly deserved punishment for persons as lowly as they are.

Says Dr. Beck, "The majority of infanticides are committed during depression. Usually they are followed by suicide attempts." Though depression debilitates, it does not kill directly, like cancer. Suicide, and sometimes the murder of loved ones, provide the mortality rate.

Symptoms of depression vary with the condition and the person. Some victims merely drag along, day after day. Others go along about their business rapidly enough, but get no meaning or joy from life. Good-time Charlie in the bar, or the sociopath who acts on selfish impulse, may be depressed persons who are trying to fill up the empty spaces within.

To the deeply depressed, nothing is worse; they would prefer pain. "It's like looking into the mouth of hell." The comparison with hell comes up often. Some theologians believe that depression is the primary tool of Satan, to bring man to despair of the goodness of God and his creations, and surrender to darkness.

The deeply depressed *know* that they are worthless. The world is desolate and terrible, a surrealist landscape. They can only wait for the sword to fall. They may be agitated and anxious, often can't sleep or sit still, and yet they have trouble performing the simplest tasks.

Some of the best descriptions of how depression feels come from famous writers, who were either unusually gloomy, or maybe just able to say it better. It's very hard to do creative work while deeply depressed, but they were there, or they wouldn't know the country so well. "Hence, loathed Melancholy," ordered Milton. "Of Cerberus and blackest Midnight born. . . ." "In the real dark night of the soul," said Scott Fitzgerald, "it is always three o'clock in the morning."

One of the most famous victims of depression was Abraham Lincoln, who dreamed of his own funeral. Friends were afraid he might commit suicide. Some of the traits that most endeared him to us, the soul searching and sadness in his speeches, the image of a suffering friend and father, probably reflected his depression.

Against this archenemy of mankind, what do Dr. Beck and his colleagues put into the field? They are practicing cognitive therapy, one of the newer schools of psychotherapy. In the Mood Clinic offices, decorated and furnished in the style that could be called standard hospital depressive, nothing dramatic seems to be happening.

The patient, sometimes with a spouse or family member, discusses things with the therapist and sometimes performs little exercises or answers questions. He weeps or sighs; listens or talks; sometimes he argues.

"We try not to play God here," says Dr. Beck. "We want the patient to be an independent person." To make sure that the patient really is depressed, in an early visit he is given the Beck Depression Inventory, a questionnaire with 21 sections describing his feelings. Then the therapist tries to find out, or to help the patient find out, what distorted beliefs he has that are responsible for the depression, to bring them into the light, and then to change them.

The patient is given simple instructions: try hard to remember the thoughts you have each time you feel depressed; keep a list of them. Therapy is tailored to the individual patient and his needs. Compared to the more familiar ways of treating standard mental and emotional problems—such as Freudian psychotherapy or psychoanalysis, drugs, electric shock, behavior modification—all this seems a little too simple. It even appears rather old-fashioned and unscientific, with overtones of the fatherly talk and positive thinking.

But though the theory is straight-forward, the practice is often subtle and sophisticated. We see and understand the world through the windows of our perceptions, colored by our biases and pre-set ideas. If that window is cloudy or the glass distorted, it will twist what we think reality is, and how we react to it.

"People will find that some event will continually bring on a feeling of depression, and won't know why," Beck explains.

"For instance, a woman reported that she saw an old boy friend and felt sad. Why? She doesn't know. With the help of therapy, though, she comes to remember that between the meeting and the feeling she had a cognition: "I'm not as young or attractive as I was. He'll notice. He'll turn away." That was what made her sad, not the meeting, which was pleasant enough. In fact, she is still attractive. It was up to the therapist to help her recognize that cognition, show her that it was exaggerated or wrong, and break up that cause-and-effect relationship."

How can such a simple cause explain a disorder that brings so much crippling and death? Wouldn't a deep depression have to have a long history of bad experience behind it? Or a chemical imbalance in the brain? Shouldn't it take stronger medicine?

"We have to work in the present, not the past, because the crippling feelings are in the present, and may be getting worse," Beck explains. "True, some forms of depression have physiological causes. We know that manic-depressive psychosis, in which there are wild swings between elation and hyper-activity on one hand and deep depression on the other, responds very well to lithium. But manic-depression makes up only about 5% of all depression. Most of the rest can be reached by cognitive therapy.

"The great damage in depression is done by the vicious cycle that the distorted perception sets off, that then get deeper and deeper. The depression affected the perception, exaggerated it, so that she interpreted the way he acted toward her as scorn and rejection. This made her more depressed, and so on. Eventually she could have became completely withdrawn. The job of therapy is to stop that vicious cycle and reverse it."

The person who is in depression did not become depressed through one chance, bad idea. Throughout his development he picked up and had reinforced negative ideas about himself, the world, and his future. These attitudes became persistent patterns of seeing and intepreting whatever happened to him.

They might not dominate his life for a long time. And even if he did have a depressive episode he would probably come out of it, at least until the next crisis threw him back. But he would remain especially sensitive to being rejected, thwarted, or deprived.

These are not accidental events, or "part of the game"—not to him. They would reinforce his own feelings about his basic unworthiness, and the untrustworthiness of the world.

Most depressed persons feel that they have suffered some deep personal loss, Beck says, even if they can't always define what it is. They have lost the love of someone close or a goal they had tried to reach. "Characteristically, there is a 'crisis of expectations.' They had expected to achieve something great, were sure they should have, and now realized, or felt, that they weren't going to, and never would."

Next, what Beck calls the "primary triad" of idea patterns takes over and determines the final symptoms.

First, the depressed person interprets all his experiences in a downbeat way. Nothing good ever happens to him. That's the kind of world he lives in, and the way he, and it, affect one another. As in some giant, frustrating Charlie Chaplin comedy, everything conspires to defeat, humiliate, or reject him.

Second, he sees himself in a negative way. He probably deserves everything that happens to him because he is such a shabby, inept, unworthy specimen. "Oh, what a rogue and peasant slave am I!" cried Hamlet, "I'm just no good," is more typical of the average person.

Finally, the future is terrible as well. His troubles won't let up. Things will get worse, never better. Nothing will work out. Hamlet again: "Oh God! Oh God! How weary, stale, flat, and unprofitable seem to me all the uses of this world."

All experience is filtered through these viewpoints and is colored by them. The conclusion is inevitable: everything is hopeless. The emotional response has to be sadness and depression. The depression makes the idea of hopelessness more intense.

Take another, common example: a student believes that he is hopeless, beyond his depth. He must have failed. In class, the professor does not call on him—seems to ignore him. This means that he already has failed, that the professor no longer considers him part of the class. The next time he takes a test he may be so depressed that he *will* fail—or he may not take it.

A man sat across from the therapist. Sometimes he clutched his girl friend's hand; sometimes he wept. He was well-dressed. Though he had lost weight and his face was lined, he still looked young and prosperous. He had an important job with a large corporation; he had risen rapidly, but he was sure he was a failure and his life was practically over. He would be fired soon, he said.

For over two years he had been depressed—sometimes worse than at other times, but never without symptoms and feelings of despair. He had been hospitalized four times, had been given electric shock, and had taken anti-depressant drugs. For a while after each treatment, he felt a little better; but it had not lasted long.

He was tired all the time, had little appetite, no longer enjoyed the things he used to. He spent much of his time brooding about his troubles or thinking of suicide. He had trouble concentrating; he cried often.

He did seem to feel a little better when he was doing something, and felt that activity was better than sitting around, so the therapist asked him to keep a daily record of what he did for the next three months, noting if he felt any sense of pleasure or mastery at any time, and how much.

Nothing was taken for granted. When he came in and said, "Boy, what a miserable week," he and the therapist went over the list together, and the doctor could show him that he had really accomplished a lot. Yet he still had not known any pleasure or feeling of mastery.

For instance, the day after he had attended a party for a friend—the first time out in weeks—he became depressed. Why? What had he been thinking? They looked at the record. Well, he had drunk too much. He was an alcoholic. Not only that, he was a hypocrite, a sham. He had actually felt good and laughed during the party—and that feeling was a fake, because he was depressed and unworthy.

As he talked, his fiancee stared at him in astonishment. According to her list they had both had a good time, he had seemed to be sincerely enjoying himself, and his drinking was no more than that of the other guests.

In time he began to see the problem in the way he looked at things: the twisted glass. He took 14 treatment sessions over five months. By the end of that time his most important symptoms of depression were down within normal range, and he went off treatment. A year later he was checked again. He was doing well at work, and was due for a promotion. He had married the girl friend.

"The real tragedy of depression," Dr. Beck explains, "is

not that it is hopeless, but that it isn't. Not at all. So little of all the suffering is necessary. The great majority of patients, if they don't commit suicide, will come out of it, at least until the next crisis.

"You'll get complete recovery from an episode 70% to 95% of the time. Among kids, 95%. Yet think of those high school and college kids committing suicide!

"And apart from that, therapy can help. Drugs can reduce symptoms. And we are finding that cognitive therapy is getting results.

"The test of a system of therapy in whether the percentage who show improvement is greater than the percentage who would get better anyway, if nothing was done to help them. Our new studies are showing that our method has a better percentage that spontaneous recovery. We can't be certain until we can do follow-ups on our cases for a few years longer, but so far we are getting results. About 80% are improving."

How to Live With Fear

It is natural to be afraid, but there are
ways to prevent dread from overshadowing
everything you do

By Lucille DeView

Fear can sneak up on anyone. Fear of the latest illness. Fear of losing a job. Fear of loneliness. Fear of crime in the streets. Fear of old age. The list is endless. Small wonder this is called the Age of Anxiety.

Some people allow fears virtually to paralyze them. They fear going out at night to the theater or a symphony. They refuse a promotion in another town because they fear a new environment.

Others, however, find common-sense ways to handle their fears so they can live full, satisfying lives. The experts say:

Condensed from "Detroit Sunday News", 615 Lafayette Blvd., Detroit, Mich. 48231. Nov. 17, 1974. ᶜ1974 by the Detroit News, and reprinted with permission.

Don't worry. Everyone has fears. The trick is not to be so obsessed that we hear noises when there are none.

"If you live in fear, you're going to have to live in seclusion," says Msgr. Clifford F. Sawher, chairman of the Detroit-Wayne County Community Mental Health Board. "So have a little confidence, trust and faith. Do the things you are accustomed to do, and probably nothing will happen. If you build up fear in your mind, it spoils your life even if nothing happens.

"People with strong faith take things in stride. They do not fear death because they know they can't live forever, and they believe there is a reward awaiting them. One man in our parish is 95 years old and comes to Mass every day. Others are uplifted by his example of courage and faith."

Doctors, psychiatrists, philosophers, social critics, and anthropologists offer these ways to deal with fear:

Realize that the things you probably fear most are not likely to happen. People panic at the thought of being mugged, yet 40 times more people are seriously hurt in home accidents. People fear murder, but 11 times as many people die in auto accidents as in homicides. Our fear of crime is really fear of the unexpected, the unknown. We like to be in control of the situation. At home or in a car, we think we are. Taking common-sense precautions (locking doors, parking cars in lighted areas) will lessen the chances of your being victimized by a crime. And getting involved in community efforts to combat crime, where you can examine how much of your fear is really justified, should lessen your anxiety.

"Use your fantasy life to deal with your fears," suggests Dr. Cereta Perry, psychologist at Merrill-Palmer Institute. "For example, when a fourth-grade child is afraid to go to school because of a conflict with the teacher, I ask him to tell me a story about what might happen." When the child imagines a specific fearful situation, then he can deal with it. Vague, unnamed fears are much more difficult to control.

Learn to look and feel self-confident. This begins in childhood and may be as simple as doing your job well or having faith that what tomorrow brings will be good.

Take care of your health. Fears prey on us when we are weakest. Balance work with play. Get enough sleep, balanced nutrition, and physical exercise. Avoid self-medication: have regular checkups.

Talk out your troubles. Learn to accept what you can't change and realize that nobody (including yourself) is faultless.

Develop a healthy sense of humor. Laughter is good

protection against harm or fear of harm.

Don't try to escape or submerge your fears. Alcohol and drugs make things worse instead of better. So does ignoring warning symptoms of illness.

Do something about the things you can do something about. If you're really afraid of financial problems in your old age, maybe you should try to get a job with a better retirement plan.

Analyze your associates and your activities. Are your friends always glum? Maybe you need new friends with a more cheerful, positive outlook.

Don't use fears as an excuse to shut yourself off from others. If you're too lazy to visit someone in the city, admit it. Don't say: I'm afraid to drive at night.

Have goals and dreams. Expect the most from life. People with low expectations cower alone in their rooms when they could be having a good time.

Contribute to life. Vote. Be a community activist. The problems won't seem so fearfully big and beyond solution. As anthropoligist Margaret Mead writes, we are not sheep. We can be vigilant in our own behalf.

Get involved with people. We fear strangers. Even husbands and wives can hide their feelings from each other and become alienated. When we know each other we lose our fear.

Remember fear itself can be as great a killer as bullets or disease. Soldiers, hospital patients, shipwreck survivors, have been known to die, not from illness, lack of food, water or the hope of rescue, but from fear.

Evolve a religious attitude towards life. Faith gives you guidelines to keep unfounded fears away.

The Science of Kicking a Habit

Compulsive behavior is easy come, not-so-easy go

By George A. W. Boehm

There are probably as many recipes for breaking habits as for stopping hiccups. And the chances of success are about the same: not very good.

Treating habits is generally so unrewarding that many psychiatrists will have little to do with them. Some years ago a survey showed that almost half the members of the Southern California Psychiatric association had a policy of turning away alcoholics. Almost half of those who did treat them set up a strict quota. The reason generally given: alcoholics demand too much time and respond poorly to psychiatry.

Nevertheless, some people have been conspicuously successful in breaking habits. They get their methods from what psychologists have learned about making habits. The strategy is like running a film backwards. That is to say, when you find out what psychological, physical, and social factors support a habit, you try to counter these with contrary conditioning.

Thousands of scientific papers detail theories of conditioning. Actually, however, there are only three basic types: classical conditioning, operant conditioning, and modeling.

Classical Conditioning. This theory stems from the experiments of the Russian Ivan Pavlov in the late 1800's. He started by letting a dog see and smell food, whereupon the animal drooled. Then every time he presented food he rang a bell. After several such experiences, the dog drooled even when Pavlov rang the bell without bringing food. It had been conditioned to associate bell with food and to respond alike to both.

Most habits are partly sustained by classical conditioning. Though the smoker has a craving for the biochemical effects of nicotine, he also associates the act of puffing with those effects. Thus each of his 100,000 puffs a year adds a bit of muscle to his habit.

Condensed from "Think", Armonk, N.Y. 10504. November-December, 1969. ©1969 by International Business Machines Corp., and reprinted with permission.

Classical deconditioning can sometimes accomplish wonders in breaking habits. More than 15 years ago Robert Efron performed a notable *tour de force* with epilepsy, which some medical men consider a symptom, like a sneeze, rather than a disease. His strategem came right out of Pavlov.

Efron's patient was a woman who had been having frequent and severe seizures. At the onset of each attack, she was aware of a nasty, pungent odor. Efron started by giving her a vial of a liquid with an odor entirely different from the one she associated with her attacks. By sniffing at the vial whenever she felt a seizure coming on, she was able to break the familiar chain of events and thus abort attacks.

Later Efron went much further. He gave the woman a bracelet and told her to concentrate on it when she sniffed the vial. Like Pavlov's dogs, she eventually came to associate bracelet with vial so intimately that she was able to avoid seizures by looking hard at the bracelet. At the end, when the woman began to feel the strange aura that precedes an epileptic attack, she was able to nip it in the bud simply by *thinking* about the bracelet.

Operant Conditioning. Most habits are fueled by this kind of conditioning. It consists of an immedite reward for right behavior or an immediate punishment for wrong behavior.

The reward or punishment need not be great. In fact, some years ago psychologist William Verplanck discovered that by simply expressing mild approval, nodding and smiling, he could condition friends and students to many sorts of bizarre habits. For instance, if a person to whom he was talking happened to scratch his nose, Verplanck would beam and murmur soothingly. The person would soon scratch again; Verplanck would again make comforting noises and gestures. After several such subliminal reinforcements a typical victim would be clawing compulsively at his nose.

Nor need rewards be given consistently. Indeed, many tests with people as well as pigeons show that once a habit is established it is most strongly maintained if reinforcement is applied erratically and only occasionally.

This strange fact, says psychologist David Pearl of the National Institute of Mental Health, may help explain the persistence of superstitions, which he regards as habits of sort. Say that a baseball player happens to take a drink of water before coming to bat and then hits a home run. If he is inclined to be superstitious, he will then make a habit of going to the drinking fountain before stepping to the plate. Even though he may only hit five home runs a season, every one will reinforce his belief.

Punishments are usually not nearly so effective as rewards. This is particularly true with children. Verplanck observes that harsh parents often reinforce the very habit they are trying to eliminate. The reason seems to be that the child craves attention. Even a slap is more gratifying than no attention at all. A better plan, therefore, is to shower the child with kindness when he is not behaving according to habit.

Modeling. This third form of conditioning has received much study in recent years. Really this is little different from putting the picture of a famous football player on a package of breakfast food in the hope that youngsters will choose the cereal their hero endorses. But modeling techniques have been greatly refined.

Albert Bandura of Stanford, for instance, has cured small children of an unreasonable fear of dogs by showing them pictures of children with dogs. He may start with a picture of one child with a small dog, then work up gradually to groups of children romping with big dogs that look savage. He gets good results by showing one child with a succession of different dogs. But he does even better when he uses several different children.

Evidently, although most people like to copy a hero, they find it even more reassuring to follow a crowd. This is behavior that advertisers often take into account when they show ordinary people using a product.

There is much more to many habits than psychology can explain. For one thing, the body easily becomes so accustomed to some strange chemicals that it can hardly survive without them. This can be demonstrated with animal cells grown in a glass dish. The tissue culture remains healthy if a little morphine is added to its nutrients. But if, after a few days the morphine is removed, the cells sicken and die, a typical drug addiction in a test tube. It seems that in accommodating to morphine, the cells substitute it for some essential part of their nutrition so that it becomes, in effect, a vitamin or hormone.

Many addicts suffer terribly and may even die when abruptly deprived of drugs. Agonizing withdrawal symptoms are usual with opiates and barbiturates. Most authorities agree also that the "cold-turkey" treatment for heavy tobacco smokers has pronounced biochemical effects, although people who suddenly stop taking marijuana or LSD do not suffer similar physical pangs.

Nonetheless, too much has been made of purely physical withdrawal symptoms. "Would you believe that we know how to cure the strictly physical craving for heroin in just two

weeks?" says Robert C. Petersen, chief of the National Institute of Mental Health Center for Studies of Narcotic and
Drug Abuse.

Psychological craving will take much, much longer to
squelch. The Narcotics Addiction Rehabilitation Act of 1966
prescribes three full years of aftercare to keep former addicts
from backsliding. And Dr. R. Gordon Bell, head of the Donwood foundation in Toronto, which has had striking success
with various addictions, insists that his patients (mainly
alcoholics) commit themselves to 11 months of outpatient
treatment after about a month in his clinic.

There is probably much truth in the dictum preached by
Alcoholics Anonymous that a reformed alcoholic can never
again in his life take a drink. But the danger may lie in his
outlook on alcohol rather than in any permanent alteration to
his body chemistry.

Beyond the simple craving for a drug—nicotine is a
drug—the addict is fixed in a complex behavior pattern. The
ritual of reaching for a cigarette, lighting up, and watching
the first puff of smoke curl up toward the ceiling may be more
pleasurable than any immediate effects of nicotine in the
blood stream. Similarly, the ceremony of mixing the day's
first martini may be intensely gratifying in itself. This
association of familiar routines with purely chemical effects
makes addictions especially tenacious.

All but a few heroin addicts go back to their habit after the
usual cooling-off period in an institution. The records are little better for alcoholics who "dry out" at a health camp or a
municipal hospital; even Donwood with its year-long treatment has a success rate of no better than 70%. Addictions
(or, as some people call them, chemical dependencies) are in-
scrutable. Heroin addicts, for example, often seem to get as
much satisfaction from an injection of milk sugar as from the
real drug. "I am convinced they are addicted primarily to the
needle," says Peterson.

Scientists still do not understand all the subtleties of addiction. One man who may have a better grasp of the total
problem than anyone else is Jerome Lettvin, a former
psychiatrist who has become a noted neurophysiologist at
MIT. In 1967 Lettvin took most of the year off to visit drug
users around Boston.

He arrived at many unconventional ideas during this
research. He learned, for instance, that psychedelics, such as
LSD, are probably not nearly so innocuous as phar-
macologists believe. Some of his friends who experimented
with a "trip" were able to function normally in their social

life a day or two later, when no traces of the chemical could be detected in their blood. But their professional work was subpar for another two or three weeks. He observed that sleeping pills also depressed the intellect considerably longer than might be expected from blood analysis.

It was about the social aspect of habits that Lettvin made his most profound observations. Often when talking with a young Roxbury black hooked on heroin, he would ask, "Wouldn't you like to get off the stuff?" Usually the boy would reply, "I sure would, man. That would be the best thing that ever happened to me."

Then why was he lukewarm about submitting to treatment? Lettvin explains, "Sure, he wanted to get away from heroin. But that wasn't all he wanted, by any means. He also wanted to stop being black and living in a ghetto. What he really wanted was to be someone else, and at some other time in history. And who can blame him?"

The social pressure that makes and sustains habits is enormous. In some circles, for example, young people must smoke or drink heavily or take marijuana to demonstrate that they belong. Conversely, social pressure, consciously applied, can also help to break habits. Such organizations as Alcoholics Anonymous, Synanon, and the Weight Watchers rely mainly on the buddy system in which former addicts help neophytes with advice and moral support. When a Weight Watcher steps on the scales during one of the chapter meetings, her fellow members cheer or boo according to whether she has lost or gained.

Rational man would like to undo his own habits simply by saying to himself, "This is harmful to me. I will therefore stop it forthwith." Will power, unfortunately, is seldom strong enough to make this approach effective. Nevertheless, people can often extinguish their own habits by carefully planned strategems.

The tactic of swearing off "for today and for today only" is undeniably sound. It has worked wonders for members of Alcoholics Anonymous.

Usually, though, the would-be habit breaker needs a crutch, some gadget or chemical or even another habit, that will interrupt the compulsive behavior. Many are available. Nail biters can apply a colorless fluid to their fingertips; its bitter taste serves partly as punishment, partly as reminder.

An electric device is now available commercially for a person with a habit to carry in pocket or purse. When the impulse comes to light a cigarette or duck into a bar for a drink he or she grabs the box and gets a nasty electric-shock in the fingertips, a simple negative reinforcement.

Many people follow elaborate programs for cutting down a habit rather than cutting it out. Dr. Bell is convinced that they are all on dangerous ground. Say that a smoker resolves to postpone his first cigarette until noon. The chances are that he will be so obsessed with this schedule that he will waste half the morning watching the clock and thinking about lighting up that first smoke.

Some habits cannot be eliminated entirely. One is overeating. Bell says that some of his most difficult cases are grossly fat men and women who come to Donwood to change their eating habits. Under strict medical supervision they take off weight rapidly enough. But a year or two later they are likely to come back as fat as ever and ridden by guilt. The reason is that the patterns of normal eating and overeating are so similar that it is virtually impossible to break one without breaking the other. In fact, the Canadian psychologist D. O. Hebb explained years ago that hunger itself is as much as addiction as is the craving for morphine.

Another way to break habits is to mimic them with conscious, purposeful behavior. Some years ago Knight Dunlap, a Johns Hopkins psychologist, had great success with stammerers who could read aloud smoothly but had trouble conversing. He made them deliberately stammer while reading passages from a book. Many of them gained enough insight into their habit so that they were able to break it gradually by regularly practicing stammering. Along similar lines, David Shapiro and Bernard Tursky of Harvard Medical school recently have been curing smokers by forcing them to smoke when they do not particularly crave a cigarette.

The most sensational habit cure reported in the last few years is a one-shot treatment by New York psychiatrist Herbert Spiegel. He first hypnotizes the patient, then teaches him to recite: "Smoking is injurious to my body. I need my body to live. I owe it to my body to give it all the protection it deserves." Then Spiegel shows the patient how to put himself into a mild state of hypnosis and repeat the words whenever he feels the urge to smoke.

Why should hypnosis be more effective than simply having a heart-to-heart talk with yourself? Spiegel explains that hypnosis is not magic. It is just a way of focusing attention on a single thought. While in a trance the patient brings to bear extraordinary concentration about his problem, enough to overwhelm all the subconscious ideas that underlie smoking. In other words, if you want to break a habit you have to try with all your might.

How to Say No

Some pointers in the gentle art of tact

By Robert Wacker

The passport to freedom is a two-letter word: *No!* It offers escape from boring parties, kittens in need of a home, office collections for people you do not know, and similar plagues. But how do you turn someone down without being called a slacker? Most of us take the coward's way out: We give away our lunch money and our leisure time.

This quiz may put some iron in your soul. You are to reject the proposals made, in one of the ways suggested. Watching over your shoulder will be Mrs. Connie Prendergast of Houston, Texas, who, besides being a wife and the mother of a teen-age girl, is International Secretary of the Year, representing the 25,000-member National Secretaries association. Most members are secretaries to corporation officials who are deluged with appeals for time, money, and the use of their name. Their secretaries are experts in the gentle negative.

Decide how you would handle each situation. Then see how a pro like Mrs. Prendergast rates your answers for tact. Her analysis may show you how to do what you really want to do without hurting either your principles or your reputation.

1. "We have never met, but your daughter Jean and my Marilyn are good friends. Marilyn is having a 'sweet-16 party' Friday night, and she would like Jean to come. Some neighborhood boys will be in, and there will be dancing and soda pop. It may be a bit late, but there is no school the next day, so that doesn't matter, does it." "No, we're not planning to chaperone the party. We think it's important to let the kids know we trust them."

(a) "I'm sorry, but we have told Jean she may not go to unchaperoned parties until she is 18."

(b) "Oh, isn't that too bad! Jean has already promised to visit her aunt and uncle this weekend. They're having a party, too."

(c) "We really don't approve of unchaperoned parties for 16-year-olds."

2. "I'm selling these Easter cards for $3.50 a box. If I can sell just 25 boxes, the company will give me a bicycle. Will you buy two boxes?"

(a) "That's a lot of money for Easter cards, but if you come back when you have sold the other 24, we will buy your last box."

(b) "We've been getting our cards from an organization that gives the profits to charity."

(c) "I wouldn't pay $3.50 for a box of those cards. They aren't worth it."

3. "Old pal, do me a small favor. I'm a little short of cash, so I went to the Sweetheart Finance Co. they told me they would let me have a couple of hundred on my signature, as long as somebody who knew me signed the note, too. You don't have to worry, I'll never miss a payment!"

(a) "I'd lend you the cash if I had it, but I won't co-sign a note for anybody."

(b) "Sorry, I already owe those people myself. My signature is no good there right now."

(c) "Oh, I trust you, but what if something happened? Do you know how many people were killed just crossing the street last year?"

4. "I hope you don't mind my barging in while you're still unpacking and all, but I just must be the first to welcome you to our friendly little town.

"You are going to love it here! And I do hope you'll join our Wednesday Afternoon club. All the people who really count belong to it, and we have such a stimulating program."

(a) "Thank you so much, but I'm afraid we'll be too busy for any organized social activities for a month or two at least."

(b) "We aren't joiners. I'm sorry."

(c) "Thank you. I'd like to discuss it with you and perhaps meet some of the other members after we've been here awhile. Won't you sit down and have a cup of tea?"

5. "Do you think this miniskirt looks good on me, dear?"

(a) "Darling, you do have beautiful legs, but let's keep them in the family."

(b) "I think these mod styles are too harsh for someone as warm and feminine as you."

(c) "Really, dear, you're not a teenager anymore."

6. "That roast we had at your place last Sunday was so marvelous, I thought we ought to get together again! I've put a tray of popovers in the oven . . . do you have steak in your

freezer? We'll drop over.

(a) "No, we don't. Why don't you pick one up on the way?"

(b) "We were going to have salmon loaf tonight."

(c) "That's a lovely idea, but the steak wouldn't thaw in time."

7. "Dear Cousins: How are all of you? Arlene was saying last week it's a shame our families don't see more of each other! We're taking the kids to the Interstate Exposition next month, and we thought we might stop by and spend a few days."

(a) Telegram: "Company transferring me Fairbanks, Alaska, next week. Great disappointment. Must get together when return."

(b) "Dear Cousin George: We'd like to see you all and hope it can be arranged, but our house isn't very large, and the kids are sleeping two to a bedroom now."

(c) "Dear Cousin George: Great idea, and I'll make the motel reservations. There's a very nice place about a quarter of a mile from here with a fine restaurant.

8. "I think it's idiotic the way Americans make such a fetish of being young. I'm willing to tell anyone my age. I'm 38. How old are you?"

(a) "It's silly, but our company's personnel office doesn't agree, so I've never put my age on record anywhere."

(b) "I admire your frankness. I don't know if I'll be that brave when I'm 38."

(c) "My, you certainly don't look 38! Oh, by the way, I've been meaning to ask for the recipe for that creamed liver we had at your house last week."

9. "Everybody does it at this plant. All you have to do is take any timecard out of the rack with yours and punch us both in. The timekeeper never watches. I'll cover for you sometime."

(a) "No dice. With my luck, I'd be caught for sure."

(b) "How could I do that and then go home and tell my kids it's wrong to steal?"

(c) "No, and if I ever find out you've pulled a stunt like this, I'll report you to the foreman!"

10. "It's going to be the biggest cocktail party of the year. Simply everyone is coming."

(a) "We've sworn off parties where there are more than five couples. It's so frustrating—just as you get interested in what someone is saying, he is interrupted by someone else."

(b) "That's the trouble. Everybody is going, and all the sitters are spoken for. We can't get a babysitter."

(c) "Oh, dear! We have tickets for a show!"

ANSWERS

1. (a) Tell your party-throwing neighbor that you have high standards for your daughter's conduct, if that's how you feel, but do not add the slap of saying you "really don't approve" (c) of the way she's raising her Marilyn. If you say your girl is leaving town for the weekend (b), you will have to hide her.

2. (b) This is the only possible answer, and if you don't buy your cards from a charitable organization, it may be a good idea. Why teach a child to cheat? If you say you'll buy his last box of cards (a), he will probably come back and say he has sold the others, whether or not he really has. Saying (c) the cards are not worth the money is being frank, and possibly insulting.

3. (a) Turn down your insolvent pal with a flat "I won't cosign for anybody." If you say you owe the same company (b), he might point out that in your state that's no reason for not being a cosigner, and what could you say then? The other excuse (c) hasn't held water since debtor insurance.

4. (a) Your overfriendly new neighbor and her club could be the town bores, but they could also be people you would enjoy knowing. Hold her off until you have had a chance to investigate. Answer (b), and you simply offend her, and if you offer her tea (c), you'll get the whole sales pitch.

5. (b) Be flattering but negative. You may think miniskirts are too mini (a), but your wife doesn't or she wouldn't have brought one home. Any married man should know better than to tell his wife she's too old for anything (c).

6. (a) Tell your freeloading neighbor to buy her own steak. Suppose she likes salmon loaf, too (b)? Or she might delay on the popovers (c) until your $8 porterhouse has thawed.

7. (b) Telling Cousin George that your house is really too small for a clan reunion should be enough. Forget the telegram (a), and no matter how brash George may be, he surely deserves kinder treatment than (c), unless you're at war with his family.

8 (b) Commending her bravery should embarrass the snoop enough to deter further cross-examination. Anyone with enough nerve to demand your age won't be turned aside by a change of subject (c) or a reference to company personnel policies (a).

9. (b) People who ask you to do something dishonest don't deserve a polite reply. Saying you fear getting caught (a) puts you in the same class. On the other hand, it's not your responsibility to tattle (c) and could make you very unpopular with fellow employees.

10. (c) You had better have tickets for a show. Don't an-

nounce you've sworn off "any kind" of party (a). There may be some reason why you would like to be invited next time, and don't say you can't get a babysitter (b). If others can, so can you.

How did you do?
If you got more than six answers right, your instincts are fairly trustworthy, and you probably aren't cornered by too many pests. Fewer than five suggest that you often put your foot in your mouth.

More important than numerical scores, however, is what you got wrong. Did you pick answers 1 (c), 2 (c), 4 (b) or 7 (c)? If you did, you may be needlessly curt, even cruel. Try to put yourself in the other person's place and avoid blunt answers. You'll have more friends.

On the other hand, if you picked 1 (b), 2 (a), 2 (b) or (c), 4 (c), 9 (a), or 10 (b), your excuses seem more likely to get you into deeper trouble than off the hook. Suppose you were doing the asking and you were answered in that way. You can see how easy it would be to talk a person out of that objection and have your way.

Be firm. Be tactful. Be truthful. Whatever you do, don't say Yes! That is, unless you want to.

Learn From Your Mistakes

The boo-boo is often the mother of invention

By Douglas Lurton

You make mistakes, as we all do, but there are intelligent as well as stupid ways of confronting them. You are smart if you recognize that it is not so much your mistakes as what you do about them that really counts.

1. You profit by facing mistakes squarely. Man tends to alibi failure and rationalize what he does. That way he loses. He profits, however, if he accepts the responsibility for his mistakes.

Condensed from "A Treasury of Success Unlimited", Edited by Og Mandino. ᶜ1966, 1965, 1964, 1963, 1962, 1961, 1960, 1959, 1957, 1956, 1955, by Combined Registry Co. and reprinted by permission of Hawthorn Books, Inc., 70 5th Ave., New York City. 250 pp. $5.95.

He who alibis and runs away may live to alibi another day, but he is not likely to be a winner. You can rationalize yourself into a rut of mediocrity or even into an asylum. You can alibi yourself out of a job or a promotion. In a study of why thousands were fired from corporations, it was found that more were discharged for carelessness, or failure to cooperate, than for lack of a specific skill on the job.

2. You profit if you don't let mistakes get you down. Strong men and women bounce back after making mistakes. They have the courage to try to avoid repeating errors and to improve.

Babe Ruth hit many home runs, but he also fanned 1,330 times. Thomas Edison made countless mistakes. Abraham Lincoln failed in many ventures. But they had one thing in common: they did not let their mistakes get them down.

3. You profit if you learn how to take criticism. The first, instinctive reaction to criticism is resentment. Your feelings are hurt. Your ego seems under attack, and an assault on your ego is like a small attack on your life. Many of us resent even our own self-critical thoughts and dismiss them quickly. Many resent criticism coming from others and set up face-saving defenses. But the fully mature man or woman determines to profit from criticism and learns how to take it intelligently.

Adverse criticism may reflect outright hostility or it may come from a sincere desire to help. Anyone interested in self-advancement should listen to criticism either unworthily or honestly offered. The more true the criticism is, the more it will hurt. Unjust criticism can be easily brushed aside, but if it really stings the intelligent approach is to seek out the element of truth in it and do something about it.

4. You can profit by learning both from your own mistakes and those of others. We do not necessarily learn much by experience. A doctor with 50 years' experience is not necessarily better than one with ten years' experience. It all depends on how selective a person is in piling up his experience.

Experienced bricklayers laid bricks for thousands of years in the same old way. From generation to generation master bricklayers repeated the methods they had been taught as apprentices. Their instruction included experience in repeating the mistakes as well as the skills of their craft. They learned to lay brick through experience, but they didn't learn from mistakes how to eliminate lost motion. It was not until Dr. Frank Gilbreth studied the old methods and applied scientific methods that experienced bricklayers were taught how to lay many more bricks in much less time and with much less effort.

Step 1. Determine carefully just what it is you are trying to accomplish and why. What is the job of the moment? What is its purpose?

Step 2. What are the pertinent facts involved? Can you get additional facts bearing on your problem from reading, or friends, associates, or others in a postion to know?

Step 3. After considering all of the facts available you should be able to determine possible courses of action. Study each one.

Step 4. Narrow down the possible courses of action to the one that comes closest to accomplishing your purpose.

Step 5. If you have carefully followed the first four steps and not jumped to any conclusions, you may be sure that your analysis has given you the one best course of action for you. The important step is to do something about it right away.

You learn by taking courage from the fact that others make mistakes. Mistakes in full or in part were responsible for certain wallboards, vulcanized rubber, X-rays, aniline colors, photography, dynamite, fiber glass, and many other inventions.

How to Get More Out of Your Reading

Private reading takes as much technique as public speaking

By Norman L. Cahners with John Kord Lageman

How can busy people read with greater speed, comprehension, and enjoyment?

As a publisher I have had a special interest in how the reading experts answer this question. I learned that reading is discovery. That is the basis of all effective reading techniques.

The good reader isn't primarily a reader. He is detective,

Condensed from "Think", 590 Madison Ave., New York City 10022. September-October, 1964.
©1964 by International Business Machines Corp., and reprinted with permission.

explorer, scientist, critic, and editor. All these are active, seeking roles. You can't use words simply by looking at them any more than you can use swords locked up in a glass case.

When I was growing up in Bangor, Me., our family taught me a basic lesson about reading. At the table, one of us would introduce a topic and we had to be prepared to discuss it.

From those dinner-table forums I learned: "Use it and you won't lose it."

Reading is surrounded with entirely too much ritual. There's no point in telling a busy man to seek a relaxed posture or to insist on quiet or freedom from interruption.

Reading requires active participation. It is you who must supply the imagery, interpretation, application, and relevance.

Most of our reading mistakes are forms of patient plodding. The main ones are these. 1. Reading all material at the same speed. 2. Word-by-word reading instead of phrase or idea reading. 3. Going back again and again over the text to be sure that something is understood. 4. Not starting with the right line on the return sweep. 5. Daydreaming while the eyes continue to follow the lines automatically.

The most helpful advice I got from reading experts was to make a habit of previewing material before you actually read it. Who wrote it? When? What are his qualifications? What is he trying to get at? How has he organized his material? Take a few minutes to answer these questions in advance and you will save yourself hours of unrewarding effort.

At Harvard, William G. Perry, Jr., tells how the Bureau of Study Counsel devised a reading test for Harvard and Radcliffe freshmen. "We gave students a 30-page chapter from a history book. They were to suppose that an examination would be given in about a week. Twenty minutes later we stopped them and asked them what they had been doing."

Some of them had read as many as 20 pages and were able to answer all questions about detail. But when they were asked what the chapter was all about, only 15 out of the 1,500 students could do so. One out of 100 had what Perry calls the "moral courage" to look at the end of the chapter. A half-minute study of this summary paragraph enabled them to make sense of the details.

Pick a dozen business letters at random. Most of them are constructed like a day-coach sandwich: a thin slice of meat between two thick layers of conventional prose. Make a habit of opening the sandwich and getting at the meat.

In the board meeting or seminar, the person who shines is

the one who can instantly marshal relevant facts and bring them to bear on the issue at hand. How often have you heard, "But I knew it all along. I just couldn't think of it." Slow recall, absent-mindedness, inability to recapture the relevant are the bugaboos of every student, businessman, and scientist.

How can you retain what you read or recall it as needed? The important aspect of memory is not storage but retrieval of the unifying idea or dominant theme around which facts cluster. Unless detail is placed into a structured pattern, it is rapidly forgotten.

Experiments have also demonstrated that rereading isn't nearly as effective as recalling what you have read.

When you finish a session of reading, ask yourself, "What have I read?" Close your eyes and try to recall it. You will find that you will learn a lot more this way than by rereading the material.

Forgetting is rapid at first, then slower. A recalling shortly after learning reduces the amount forgotten.

Your feelings, too, have a tremendous influence on what you retain and what you forget or distort. You more easily remember facts and arguments which support your side than the material for the other side.

Our second President, John Adams, read perhaps 50 books during his four years at Harvard. Today, a single course may require that many books; the average Harvard undergraduate has to spend at least 1,000 hours a year with books. This is fairly light compared with the reading load in a first-rate graduate school. The student who thinks that graduating into the business and professional world will relieve him of pressure to read is mistaken.

Over half of all the technical information printed in the U.S. since the Revolution has been published in the last ten years. The world's research centers are producing 60 million pages of technical papers a year. A fast-reading scientist would have to read eight hours a day until the year 3363 to finish this year's outpouring of facts.

Another survey, by the American Management association, found that the average top executive spends four hours a day reading: two and three-quarter hours on essential reports, correspondence, newsletters and magazines; and a hour and a quarter to improve his general competence.

Prof. Paul Witty of Northwestern university estimates that the average college-educated person uses only about 20% of his capacity for reading. Merely by trying harder most of us can double our reading speeds without any loss of comprehension. Paradoxically, the better you read, the more effortless it becomes.

Finding time rather than saving time is the greatest problem of all. A simple way to clear the boards for concentrated reading is to make a definite time for it, ten minutes or an hour, however long you decide. Put it on your agenda every day.

How to Make Small Talk

*It is a fine balance of listening and
telling, governed by kindness*

By Amy Gross

Three people, a couple and a friend, are in the couple's apartment. Another couple, strangers to the friend, enters. Drink orders are taken and filled, and the host is re-embedded in his chair. Then comes that moment, when five people are looking at their drinks, the pictures on the wall, the cat—thank God for cats—that moment, in short, of blank-minded, excruciating silence.

The hosts turns to the new couple and smiles, "Busy day?" So simple. Embarrassingly simple. But the guest does not sneer in disgust. In fact she looks relieved, and begins an amusing-enough description of her day. The conversation takes care of itself the rest of the evening.

I started studying small talk a few years ago, when I noticed that some people were totally at ease in situations that made me clammy. Some people were perfectly comfortable when meeting strangers. Not me. I would become a stranger to myself.

Some people always had a pleasantry for the butcher. But I could never manage anything more friendly than "Two pounds ground round please no that's all thank you," and hope that my sincere smile conveyed my neighborly feelings. Some people, I could hear them, enjoyed seeing a friend off at an airport. Why was it that I had used up everything to say on the drive out to the airport? No matter how beloved the friend, nor how I regretted the separation, I'd be waiting for

Condensed from ''Mademoiselle'', 350 Madison Ave., New York City 10017. May, 1974. ʿ1974 by the Conde Nast Publications, Inc., and reprinted with permission.

the boarding announcement, and thinking, "Go, already."

Small talk is, when you think about it, a greatly underrated sport. The prejudice against it is only sour grapes. People say, "We were just making small tallk." But if it was *just* small talk, it was bad small talk. There's good small talk. People say, "I'm not good about it." But this disclaimer is usually a boast, implying that the speaker's mind functions at a level too lofty for small talk. Did Madame Curie discuss hairdos with the girls?

The fact is that almost all the talk we talk is small. If we were to limit ourselves to big talk, social life would need to be entirely restructured. Small talk is the language of hospitality and courtesy. It is a relaxant, a warm-up before getting down to business.

Small talk serves as an audition for friendship. You and a stranger build a rapport from the initial game of "I like blue/Me, too!" And when the small talk snaps you together (Me, too!), there is an excitement that is absolutely invigorating. It seems then that the world is rife with possible people, and that you can connect, you are valuable . . . and all because you like blue, too. A man I met six years ago at a dinner party asked what kind of books I read. I named a few writers, he picked up on Jane Austen, and we've been friends ever since.

Silence is the enemy of small talk. In the conventions of small talk, silence is completely outlawed with strangers, and permitted with friends only after approximately an hour and 45 minutes of constant verbiage. I don't know what would happen if two people, meeting each other, said only hello and wordlessly studied each other. But whatever would happen must be calamitous, or else why would small talk ever have developed? Maybe small talk is the human equivalent of the sniffing ritual of animals, or the grooming custom of champanzees. At any rate, it serves to say, "I am still here, the link between us holds."

The ideal small talker achieves a fair balance of listening and talking, but such a person is rare. Most people fall into one of two lopsided roles. One is a question-asker and audience. The other is an anecdote-teller and star. The first smiles, grimaces, or grunts at appropriate moments, reinforcing—applauding—the flow of words from the second.

In most cases, the questioner is of lower status/power than the talker. But occasionally a talker will suddenly perceive the existence of the conversational partner, and ask a question. Stunned, impaled by the unfamiliar spotlight, flushed with gratitude and embarrassment, the other will rush through her answer as quickly as possible so as not to overstay her visit in the talker's ear. Panting to the finish, the questioner will berate him/herself for not being able to tell a story well.

How should one tell a story? I have no idea, but I know a way to kill one.

Specificity, the telling detail, makes for good talk. Bad small talkers never fix their scenes precisely. But there is also the risk of over-detailing your story. And the surest way to kill a story is to interrupt yourself to check on the correctness of a point. "You see, they were in Paris, at the Hotel de Croissant . . . Croissant? No, I think is was the Palais de Collette . . . Oh, no, I know, they were at the LaLa in Lyons. . . . Anyway they were in France, in early spring, I guess . . . George? Where Etta Rose and Ted in Europe in the spring or was in late March? . . ."

Footnotes are another good story-killer. For some reason, perhaps a traumatic experience with a college term paper, some people are afraid to repeat an anecdote without giving proper credit. You can hear them apologetically prefacing their remarks: "That reminds me of a funny incident Lysbeth told me about. She heard it from Olive, who said she overheard it at the horse show. . . .

People are also embarrassed to repeat their own witticisms. They have gotten off a good one-liner, too good to use just once. But just in case anyone present today might have heard the same line yesterday, the wit must protect herself. With a small, self-deprecating chuckle, she will say, "Well, I was with Ashley yesterday and we talking about the same sort of thing, and I said, 'Well, Ashley, life isn't a fountain, it's a leaky faucet.' " And then she will wait, modestly, for the roar of appreciation from her audience.

I think it is also a mistake to preface a story with something like "Hey listen to this, it is fantastic. Bette-Jane, you will love this, it is just your kind of humor." If I am Bette-Jane, the call to reassure the speaker that yes indeed, he or she does have any humor pegged, is a strain. Imagine what would happen if Bette-Jane did not laugh. If she did not even smile.

Responding well is a very serious business. The world needs some more good responders. If you frequently wish, in the middle of a story, that you had never opened your mouth, don't be disheartened. There is a place for you in the world of small talk.

A friend of mine, the Gracious Man, will spin out one after another pleasant, funny story after day's outing. I have no stories. But listening to him reporting on our day I realize what an entertaining time we had. And I admire his energy. It is hard work, constructing a plot line, worrying about character development, choosing the perfect details, and timing—timing is really a challenge. It is too hard. Being the listener, you may run a greater risk of being bored. But if you are a good listener, you have the satisfaction of a job well done.

The principle of good responding is: never leave your talker's side. Fill every pause with the appropriate response: intelligent interest, sympathy, musing, wonder, etc. Punctuate with uh-huh's, mmmmm's, I see's, yeah-I-know's, right's, etc. Nods are nice. Most talkers will cue you to the reaction they want. What you are doing is called giving "feedback." To withhold feedback is to strand the talker, a great cruelty. Even the most self-confident raconteur needs to know how she or he is doing, and your role is to be there nodding, "just fine." A caution: don't let that responding distract you from hearing the story. One important convention of listening is eye contact. One is supposed to look straight into the speaker's eyes. This is reassuring to the speaker, but again, mildly distracting to the listener. For myself, I cannot look and listen at the same time. My best listening is done when my eyes are unfocused, when "I" am in my ears, letting the words go through me and weighing them, waiting for my response.

A skillful small talker also must be unflaggingly pleasant. No matter what tricks life has played on you that day, a stranger or an acquaintance must be received with smiles and *politesse.*

What if you are bored? Simply wait for the bore to pause for a breath and then excuse yourself; or lasso a passing friend whom you must speak to "for just a second." Neither of these ploys fools even the most self-involved bore. But both are effective, and should be used unhesitatingly and without guilt. They release you from the conversation and allow the other person to save face. If they seem too hypocritical, consider the alternative. A cartoon in the *New Yorker*: two couples are sitting in a living room; one man, half-rising from the couch, says, "We really must go. We're bored to death."

Driving more than ten minutes in a car is a high-pressure situation, small talkwise. There is always someone who reads aloud every sign passed, and wants a laugh for his trouble. Another fun-loving spirit is bound to suggest a word game. Then there is usually a Commentator. "Oh, look at the mountain," he will say in an enraptured tone of voice. "Oh, look at the sunset." Oh, shut up.

A big inhibitor of small talk is the fear of saying something obvious. For instance, we all know that "What do you do?" is a cliche', so we forbid ourselves that question. But those who are good at small talk leap into the obvious interpidly.

A woman who is the world's best small talker, one of the few to admit her own talent in this area, reveals her strategy: "The general principle is to ask a short general question that elicits a long answer. How-does-it-work questions are the best. If I know someone who knows a lot about cars, or wine, I will ask for advice about buying a car, or I will ask him to recommend a wine for a specific main course. Or I will ask someone about their vacation, school, food, health—people love to talk about health—even weather." Obvious. But backed by a kindly desire to make a situation more comfortable, it always works.

Finally, much of the agony associated with small talk comes from the false premise that one person has total responsibility for the direction and quality of the talk. Once, working very hard at a conversation, I suddenly decided to give up, let go. I sat back and threw the whole burden of talk to the other person. Amazingly, he introduced a subject all by himself without my help.

When the chemistry is right, small talk can be a silken experience. No one has a point to prove, every word is new, and there is a sense open-ended exploration. It is friendship, if only for that moment.

Are You Listening?

It involves a lot more than just paying attention

By Caren Rubio

Robert Benchley once ambled from group to group at a cocktail party cheerfully announcing, "Tonight it may snow if the whistle stops." Nobody asked him what he was talking about, because no one listened to him. Indeed, most people do not know how to listen. What they really do is wait until they can begin to speak.

Condensed from New York News Magazine, 220 E. 42nd St., New York City 10017. July 21, 1974. ᶜ1974 by the Chicago Tribune-New York News Syndicate, Inc., and reprinted with permission.

Some do not even wait. A Manhattan research director has a chronic case of "interruptitis." One day a co-worker, presenting her a handsome box of notepaper, wrote on the top sheet, "Nancy, what can I say? You never listen to me!"

Jeff Freeman is manager of product development at Xerox Learning Systems, which has trained 1.5 million people in over 1,000 companies to become effective listeners. He says, "The average person forgets 43% of what he has just heard. After one hour, he has forgotten 56% and after eight hours, 64%."

If we can hear, why can't we listen?

Part of it is that we have been trained, since the invention of the printing press, to see printed words rather than to hear spoken ones. Added to that are the anxieties and fears of modern life, the myriad distracting sounds we have learned to tune out, and the fact that we think four or five times as fast as others speak. What's more, we have a psychological need to be heard rather than to hear.

Fortunately, listening can be learned. But it involves concentration, comprehension, analysis, and assimilation of new material.

Daniel J. Friedman is a busy Manhattan trial lawyer. Listening is just part of his profession.

"A day in court is comparatively short," he says, "averaging about five hours. Yet it knocks me out completely, more than a couple hours on the tennis court. It takes considerable concentration, which goes beyond the ideas and impressions that witnesses try to convey. I also try to take the new information and correlate it with data I already have, so that I can formulate further questions, and see where it's all going to lead."

Another trained listener is Hermione Gingold, star of the Broadway hit, *A Little Night Music.* She has to give eight fresh and lively performances a week, even though she knows exactly what she is going to hear. "I have to listen to what my fellow actors are saying on stage," Ms. Gingold says, "or my responses would be false and I would be cheating my audience. So I focus my attention on the speaker as if my life and my career were dependent on every thought he utters."

How do the rest of us listen?

Dr. Ralph G. Nichols, author of over 20 books on communication problems, says, "We listen with our experience. There is nothing else with which we can listen."

Unfortunately, this does not mean that we listen better as we grow older and broaden our experience. "If we define the good listener as the one giving full attention to the speaker,"

Nichols says, "1st-grade children are the best listeners of all."

In their book, *Are You Listening?*, Nichols and Leonard A. Stevens describe an experiment conducted with the cooperation of Minneapolis teachers from 1st grade through high school. Each teacher was instructed to interrupt herself suddenly and ask her pupils, "What were you thinking about?" and "What was I talking about?"

The results were discouraging but informative. The answers of 1st and 2nd graders showed that over 90% were listening. The percentages "tapered off as the results from the higher grades came in," write the authors. "In junior high only 43.7% were listening. In high school, the average dropped to 28%."

Regardless of age or maturity, poor listening habits compound other problems, playing havoc with personal relationships. Attorney Friedman says people often hear exactly the same thing in entirely different ways. "They are listening with a preconceived notion of what they are going to hear."

That's why Dr. Isabel Collins, a Manhattan marriage counselor, uses a listening technique developed by psychologist Carl Rogers. "During our group sessions," she says, "each participant may speak only after he has repeated a previous person's statement, to that person's satisfaction. We do this because listening is an essential step toward understanding."

Another creative method for overcoming poor listening habits, recommended by most authorities on listening, was formulated by Dr. Nichols. Because people think so much faster than they speak, minds wander if not disciplined. In addition, our attention spans no more than several continuous seconds at best. Nichols' procedure involves four steps that use the "spare time" between thinking speed and the slower rate of speech, while helping compensate for the "mental-lapse" pattern:

1. Think ahead of the speaker. Guess what he is leading up to.

2. Weigh, don't judge, what the speaker says to support the points he wishes to make.

3. Periodically review what the speaker has said thus far.

4. Listen "between the lines" for non-verbal clues, such as facial expressions, body movements, and gestures.

Dr. Nichols recommends yet another exercise to improve listening ability. "For one minute of every hour give your fullest attention to a person talking, even a 4-year-old," he says, "If there is no one available, select a sound—an airplane overhead, a bird, a church bell, the hum of a machine.

Put everything else out of your mind.

"Such concentration may be difficult at first," he says, "but it will greatly improve your listening proficiency."

Of course, some situations demand that we not listen. We need quiet to sleep, to think, to study, to read, to function. Persons who live or work in noisy surroundings have trained themselves to concentrate only on the task at hand. Sometimes, however, we tune out noises so successfully that we unintentionally endanger our lives.

One young New Yorker was brought up a few doors away from a busy firehouse in midtown Manhattan. She learned while still a child to screen out all shrill sounds until the day, she says, "that a stranger saved me from casually strolling into a speeding ambulance, with a screaming siren I didn't hear."

Fear, too, can preempt good sense, impede listening, and create terror. A striking example occured Oct. 31, 1938. This was the night, Halloween, that Orson Welles and the Mercury Theater of the Air dramatized H. G. Well's fantasy, *The War of the Worlds.* The prewar conditions in Europe, coupled with the severe Depression, may have affected the mental balance of the nation. The radio audience successfully disregarded four commercial interruptions to panic at the fictional invasion from Mars.

Loaded words, arousing deeply ingrained emotions, also distort listening. Judge Howard Goldfluss of the Criminal Court of the City of New York witnessed this fact some 15 years ago during a murder trial. The district attorney opened the case to the jury. Then the defense attorney rose and began: "Ladies and gentlemen of the jury, I want you to remember that the statement just made by the district attorney is not evidence and should not be construed as evidence. The judge will so charge you. As far as I'm concerned, this man, this district attorney, is just another *homo sapiens.*"

"Simultaneously," says Goldfluss, "the jury and the spectators gasped. The judge pounded his gavel, and the district attorney, an otherwise competent, intuitive, and intelligent man, became so flustered that he jumped up, objected to the defense attorney's 'accusation,' and demanded an apology."

Live Alone Without Being Lonely

Let the married couples be the outsiders

By Harriet La Barre

You can live alone without being lonely. I know, I am a widow who has been doing just that since my husband died.

Many widows, separated people, and other live-aloners are miserable. They brood out of windows on sunny Sundays, feeling helplessly alone.

That struck me as a waste, what with all the possibilities of enjoyable living, I wanted to become part of the river again, instead of watching from the banks.

I stopped waiting to be asked to dinner occasionally by married friends who viewed me as a third wheel, an outsider. I formed my own group of friends. They were single friends, men and women, to share a meal, go to movies with, walk with, share interests with. Let the married couples be the outsiders!

I knew a few single people, but only casually. Meeting people was not difficult. I met plenty where I worked. I discovered that if you take a course in something that interests you, whether poetry, Chinese cooking, or politics, you cannot help but meet people.

Making friends was harder. I found I had to take the initiative. Most people would rather die than admit they do not have bushels of friends. I did not want to admit it either. But I did that the first step. I entertained people.

The very word *entertaining* was a chiller until I realized that giving new acquaintances a cup of tea was "entertaining" them. If you added a tunafish sandwich and it was Saturday noon, you had given them a lunch.

I finally worked up to inviting a crowd of ten to my 3 1/2 room apartment. They were all people I honestly liked. Why ask anybody else? The hardest thing was to stop worrying that people might turn down my invitations. I discovered that they were delighted to come. I also found they were happy

Condensed from "Family Weekly", 641 Lexington Ave., New York City 10022. July 29, 1973. ©1973 by Family Weekly, and reprinted with permission.

with spaghetti and inexpensive wine. Or chili, crusty bread, and beer. It is the companionship, not the food, that people come for. And they, in turn, invited me back.

Holidays were a problem. I established a rule. If nobody invites me anywhere by three weeks before the holiday, I invite eight or ten single people for a holiday buffet.

Empty weekends have been another menace. But the secret of happy weekends, I learned was simple. Plan activities ahead.

I also schedule daily activities. So many hours are for work, so many for a personal study program. I even schedule hours for lazy, luxurious grooming. With a structured day like that, it is almost impossible to be lonely.

But I also prize loneliness. This is the privacy to reflect, to listen to music, to grow, to become, to have the single joy of reading a book. I think it is a mistake to believe that aloneness must necessarily be loneliness and that you should do something to "take you out of yourself." Why not, instead, occasionally go deeper into yourself? Sophisticated aloneness is what I am talking about. It is even good to have a project like learning a language or to appreciate different kinds of architecture. In my case, my interest this season is Greek mythology.

I also insist that it is hard to be lonely living in a home or apartment that has charm and comfort. Having such an apartment does not have to ruin your budget, either. You can create plenty of charm with paint, inexpensive fabric, and contact wallpaper.

One of my best anti-loneliness investments was deciding that only the most attractive living was good enough for me. This meant having a luscious pink cushion, even if I had to make it myself; that thick bedroom rug, even if it took a billion (it seemed) green stamps to get it. It also is harder to be lonely when you are curled up cozily in a soft chair drinking tea out of a Wedgewood cup ($2.50 second-hand) and reading an absorbing book from the library, than if you are standing in the kitchen gloomily sipping out of a chipped mug with only yesterday's newspaper at hand. Eating well in comfort and warmth, I also find, does a lot to dissolve loneliness.

We all need love. Having an interesting, aesthetically satisfying full life makes you more likely to attract warm friendship.

Can You Read Body Language?

A quiz tests your comprehension of
mankind's most popular form of communication

By John E. Gibson

1. If you are trying to determine whether a person talking to you is attempting to hide something, there is one gesture that can often tip you off. True of false?

2. Individuals who often touch other people, putting their hands on their arms or shoulders, patting them on the back, usually lack self-esteem. True or false?

3. People who "talk with their hands" do so because they lack verbal fluency. True or false?

4. It is easy to tell how much someone likes you simply by observing his gestures. True of false?

5. People whose hands are seldom still when they talk are likely to be neurotic and emotionally unstable. True or false?

6. Women are more inclined than men to overlook the significance of telltale gestures when talking with another · person. True of false?

ANSWERS

1. True. The gesture is the "hand shrug," the spreading of the hands with the palms upturned in the you-see-I-have-nothing-to-hide gesture. In psychological tests at the University of California, it was found that the hand shrug increased to a marked extent in interviews in which subjects were trying to withhold information from investigators.

2. False. A study of 80 male and female college students showed that "the higher the subject's self-esteem the more intimate the subject was in communicating through touch, especially when communicating with a female." And similar studies conducted by Harvard psychologists showed that "touch privilege is a correlate of status."

3. False. There are exceptions to the rule, of course, but university studies have shown that, as a group, people who "talk with their hands," who have a high rate of hand

Condensed from "Family Weekly", 641 Lexington Ave., New York City 10022. Sept. 29, 1974.
‹1974 by Family Weekly, and reprinted with permission.

gestures, are actually, more fluent in their speech than others. Another interesting finding: when the subjects' hands were restrained, it took the people longer to describe a scene or picture.

4. True. Dr. Albert Mehrabian, associate professor of psychology at the University of California, has this to say: "Greater liking is conveyed by standing close to another person instead of far; by leaning forward instead of back when seated in a chair or at a desk; by touching; by extending bodily contact, as during a handshake; and by prolonged good-byes. . . ."

5. False. Psychological studies at the University of Paris show that people whose speech is accompanied by gestures tend to be outgoing and people-oriented, with well-balanced personalities. The investigators found that "communicative gestures in general are strongly tied to emotional stability, that is, the absence of neuroticism."

6. False. University studies show that women are much more attentive to, and affective by, gestures and other non-verbal signals than men are. A woman's greater sensitivity to this form of communication often causes her to accord it more significance than the words the person is actually speaking.

Making Friends: The First Four Minutes

They can be the last four minutes of loneliness, says a psychiatrist

By Leslie Bennett

The greatest problem in the world today is not inflation, the energy crisis, war, or famine, says a Los Angeles psychiatrist. Dr. Leonard Zunin thinks mankind's biggest problem is simply one of loneliness.

"Suicide is one of the ten leading causes of death in the U.S., and the only totally preventable one," he points out. "There is a suicide every 20 seconds in this country, and

Condensed from the Philadelphia Sunday "Bulletin", 30th and Market Sts., Philadelphia, Pa. 19101. June 3, 1973. ©1973 by the Philadelphia Bulletin, and reprinted with permission.

throughout the world 10,000 people attempt to end their own lives every 24 hours. Most people who try to commit suicide do so because of the lack of fulfilling relationships with others."

Dr. Zunin believes that the desire to be involved with other people is a basic biological need, like thirst and hunger. "A number of research studies have demonstrated that almost every civilization in the world considers prolonged solitary confinement to be the single most inhumane type of punishment that exists; far more cruel than corporal punishment. When people are isolated they go crazy.

"According to some studies of situations in underdeveloped countries, babies can actually die if they are not picked up and touched. The sad thing is that although we now have more people on earth than ever before, and more superficial contact, there is more loneliness than ever.

"In one year the average American today probably meets as many people as the average person did in a lifetime 100 years ago. And yet contemporary man is far more lonely. There is a big difference between being lonely and being alone, and the mere presence of other people does not necessarily help at all.

"For one thing, people are afraid to take risks. If you never talk to or care about anyone, you will never be rejected. But your emotional needs will never be satisfied either."

Having presented this depressing picture, though, Dr. Zunin does not merely abandon mankind to its misery. In his book, *Contact: The First Four Minutes,* Dr. Zunin suggests that what happens in a specific four-minute time period is the answer to enriching the quality of human contact in your life, whether with someone you met an instant ago or someone to whom you have been married for 20 years.

By way of example, he says that "Four minutes is the average time, demonstrated by careful observation, during which strangers in a social situation interact before they decide to part or to continue the encounter."

The same principle of crucial time interval applies in continuing relationships as well. "How does a couple behave during the first four minutes of each day?" Dr. Zunin wants to know. "And how do they handle the first four minutes when they are reunited at the end of the day? If somebody can tell me what those eight minutes are like day-to-day, I can tell then what the whole marriage is like."

Dr. Zunin offers several concrete ideas on how to improve matters. "Despite our current cultural insistence on total honesty, there is a distinct value in what, for lack of a better term, I call positive prudence," he says. "There is a time and place for everything, and during the first few minutes you are reunited with someone you care about, it is important to be considerate, and not complain.

"Here, as well as in encounters with strangers, the first four minutes is simply not the time to flood them with criticism, advice, one-upmanship, and so on. It doesn't really matter what you do talk about: the emotional tone is what counts."

Dr. Zunin contends that if you meet someone at a party who keeps looking anxiously over your shoulder, as if to find a more attractive person to move on to, you are probably not going to like him very much.

"Every time you meet someone, give him your undivided attention for four minutes. A lot of people's lives would change if they did just that. Talk to more people. Begin to break down the cultural taboos against contact. Most people respond to friendliness. And be sympathetic. Don't forget the other person has his own needs, fears, and hopes. You are not the only one."

Dr. Zunin also suggests that you try to communicate a degree of self-confidence, even if you have to force it. Train yourself not to be self-demeaning or overly apologetic or overly aggressive, either. People like people who like themselves. And don't think changing your behavior patterns is artificial, or say, "Hey, that is not me!" and just give up.

"It is like getting used to a new car: it may be unfamiliar at first, but it sure does work better than the old one," he says. "Become aware of your own nonverbal communication signals. Most people have no idea what they are projecting to others through their body language, eye contact, and so on."

This lack of awareness Dr. Zunin sees as one of the principal problems in our society. "The very fact that books on interpersonal communication have recently become so popular is terrible," he says. "It is a reflection of the extent of the problem. These books are not innovative; they are way behind the times. We have all the information we need on human contact, we just have not begun to use it.

"Interpersonal communications should be a required course in every school, along with reading, writing, and arithmetic. It would probably have much more ultimate effect on a person's success in life. Whether or not we make it in life depends at least as much on how we get along with other people as on how much we know," Dr. Zunin says.

"As it is, we are simply not taught, and most of us never learn, one of the most important tools for living a successful life, whether in professional or emotional terms. But we are all in need, and people are beginning to realize that how we find meaning in relationships with others is a lot closer to the answer than earning another $5,000 a year or possessing 20 more things."

Learn While You Sleep?

No matter what the Russians say, you cannot

By Peter Desbarats

Some 1,000 residents of the Russian atomic-research center near Moscow were subjected to a short, intensive course in English during night sleep. The volunteers, aged 18 to 50, included some of the leading intellectuals and scientists of the Soviet Union.

The experimenters predicted that sleep learning might raise the intellectual level of the entire USSR and put the Western world behind.

Students were to be sitting up in bed with their radios switched on at 10:30 P.M. Light music, intended to make them drowsy, was broadcast for 15 minutes. Then a five-minute lesson of 25 to 30 English words and phrases and some fundamentals of grammar was played three times. The students could follow the lesson in their texts and repeat the words and phrases aloud.

At 11 P.M. the lights were turned out. The students then put their books aside and stretched out to sleep. The lessons continued, played in softer tones until midnight. At 6:15 the next morning the lessons were continued for 40 minutes. At 7 A.M. the students were awakened, and half an hour later they were given another lesson to fix the new instruction in their minds.

This went on five times a week for seven weeks. At the end of the course Soviet scientists reported success. They asserted that some students learned the language faster, and some learned it better than they would have under normal conditions. They said that the lessons were particularly effective with students who had not studied languages previously, and

Condensed from "Pageant", 205 E. 42nd St., New York City 10017. August, 1955. ʿ1966 by Macfadden-Bartell Corp., and reprinted with permission.

that students came across best in the 15 minutes or so before they actually fell asleep and the 30 minutes or so immediately after they fell asleep.

However, it was admitted that many of those tested seemed to lose interest after the first ten or 15 lessons, that the learning pace fell off as the course went on.

Back in 1916 the U.S. Navy gave a course in Morse code to 16 sleeping sailors and reported that the men finished the course three weeks ahead of schedule.

Early in 1940, 20 boy campers aged eight to 14 were subjected to the recorded phrase, "My fingernails taste terribly bitter." The message was played 300 times a night for 54 nights in an effort to break the boys of their nail-biting practice. At the end of the experiment 40% of the youngsters had kicked the habit.

Through the 1940's and 50's various groups, usually male college students, were taught short words or nonsense syllables during their sleep periods, which resulted in some speeding up of the learning process.

Over the years courses of instruction in the form of books, records, tapes, and elaborate machines designed to teach everything from languages to mathematic tables, to discourage excessive drinking and cigarette smoking, and to overcome inferiority complexes and nervous disorders while we sleep have been advertised and sold.

Unfortunately, some of the most extensive research into sleep learning has led Dr. Charles Simon of the Systems Development Corp. of Santa Monica, Calif., one of the leading authorities on the subject, to doubt the validity of the theory. While employed at the Hughes Research Laboratories in Malibu, Dr. Simon and Dr. William Emmons spent more than two years going over previous studies and conducting new experiments.

They found basic flaws in most of the earlier work. In many cases they found that sleeping conditions were too far from natural to be valid, that students sleeping in test situations were not enjoying natural rest, that the experimenters relied on observation rather than scientific instruments to gauge their subjects' sleep, that control groups were inadequate for proper comparisons, and that evaluation of the results was faulty. Nor did Dr. Simon find any positive evidence that sleep learning is effective.

"My original feeling was that where there was so much smoke there had to be some fire," Dr. Simon says. "I started out with the assumption that you can learn while you sleep. But in the end we were forced to conclude that you cannot do so. In fact," he adds, "no one has established at what point a person can be said to be fully asleep."

Dr. Simon says that his tests did not indicate that a person can absorb material while he is at least partly awake. The Russian experiments emphasized training and success with instruction given in the time period immediately before and after the subject dozed off and immediately before they awakened again.

"But this is not learning while you sleep," Dr. Simon says flatly. "This is learning while you are partly awake. However, this period seems better suited to review of material already absorbed than the learning of new material. We do require incentive to study well, and we are more strongly motivated toward learning when we are awake than when we are falling asleep."

It is now supposed that some of the deep sleep can serve as an eraser, and that the sooner and deeper a person falls asleep after a learning period the less he absorbs. All this weighs heavily against the value of any instruction during the presleep and sleeping times. So students have been kidding themselves about the value of late-night cram sessions.

In some studies students were permitted to sleep after being taught. When they were awakened 15 seconds after the electroencephalogram indicated they had begun to doze off, most of the group retained new knowledge, but 30 seconds later only half the group had retention, and three minutes later none could recall the new material.

When a person dreams, he is not in deep sleep. Presumably, the depth of his sleep after his dream controls how well he is able to recall it later.

It would be far more valuable if one spent five minutes awake on a learning project than if he spent an entire night's sleep on the same program.

Reaching Troubled Minds Through Reading

*Bibliotherapy is sometimes the
first step on the road back*

By Charles Carner

"This is a book about an Indian woman," the librarian said,
extending a copy of *Maria: The Potter of San Ildefonso.* The
tall, darkeyed woman smiled in recognition. It was the first
response in months from Annette, a 28-year-old American-
Indian patient. The librarian was delighted at the woman's
smile. Once again a book might be a bridge for a patient to
return to the real world.

The scene was missed by the several patients and hospital
staff members browsing and reading in the library of the U.S.
Veterans Administration hospital in Topeka, Kan., but both
the patient and chief librarian Lorna Swofford recognized its
significance. Many other patients suffering from mental
illness have returned to reasonably normal and useful lives
through the use of reading as healing (bibliotherapy).
Psychologists, psychiatrists, and librarians have been experimenting for decades. Pierre Janet, a French psychiatrist,
was interested in therapeutic reading 50 years ago. Janet
believed that patients could be stimulated into making a better life adjustment through reading.

The severely ill psychotic is unreachable through reading,
and what works with one patient maybe no good for the next,
but librarians and psychologists have been able to establish
some guidelines.

Annette, the Indian woman, was referred to bibliotherapy
group sessions by her psychiatrist. The selection of the book
and its introduction to Annette were planned carefully. After Annette had accepted the book, Miss Swofford reported
to the bibliotherapy group, adding that Annette would "tell
us about the book at a later meeting."

Condensed from "Today's Health", 535 N. Dearborn St., Chicago, Ill. 60610. December, 1966.
ᶜ1966 by the American Medical Association, and reprinted with permission.

"Oh, it's good!" Annette had said spontaneously, and those were the first words anyone had heard from her in a long time! Miss Swofford explains, "Mostly she just paced the floor. But the book was full of Indian background, and it described things painful to Annette. She told us about how she was adopted, and she hadn't been able to talk about that before."

Annette is well today. She is out of the hospital, has recovered sufficiently to get along, and she has not needed to return for treatment.

Dr. Julius Griffin, one of the originators of the bibliotherapy groups at the Topeka Veterans hospital, says, "The reader learns that it is not merely their having problems that is important, but rather what the person does with them. Literature also offers a person an opportunity for identification with a good hero who has dealt with reality effectively."

Debby, a six-year-old, at an inpatient center for emotionally disturbed children, was aided by books. She was extremely withdrawn and poorly adjusted socially. She seldom spoke. At first she was thought to be retarded, although as her treatment progressed she was found to be above average mentally.

The first positive contact with Debby was made through a brightly illustrated counting rhyme book, *Over in the Meadow.* Soon Debby was able to talk to the librarian, read with her, and enjoy many books. As the time for Debby's discharge approached she seemed apprehensive about returning to her home and parents. One of the books which helped prepare her for this adjustment was *Lisette* by Adelaide Holl, the story of a pampered white poodle who was lost and miserable among strangers in a big city until she found a friend in a German shepherd dog.

Dr. Othilda Krug says "Stories of other children and how they deal with problems can be helpful. We try to include bibliotherapy in their treatment, and we try to get stories to fit their problems or their readiness to deal with situations. We start with a child's interest, so we can involve him in some kind of story that will include his problem. He deals indirectly with his problem for a while, more directly in real life later."

Psychiatrist Karl Menninger, chief of staff at the Menninger Clinic, Topeka, Kan., says that the big question is how to select the right book for the patient.

The use of books as therapeutic devices dates back to man's early history. In ancient Greece, over the entrance to a library in Thebes was the inscription: "Healing place of the Soul."

Fritz Redl, professor of behavioral science, Wayne State university, found that disturbed children had a definite reaction to the library. The eight to 11-year-old boys selected for his program were described as "angry," "wolf children," "furious."

Dr. Redl found that the library had a beneficial effect on the "furious children." For them the library represented a high-status location in its own right. It had a purpose and value system of its own which was well maintained. As it would for any proud customer, it offered the children a chance to "visualize themselves as people sane enough to go to a real library with class to it, not just 'one of those things the therapist make up for us to destroy.' "

Dr. Redl carefully controlled the library experience for the youngsters, since many librarians and psychiatrists hold that it is the total bibliotherapy experience that benefits the patient, not simply the reading.

When the original project was set up at the Topeka Veterans hospital, meetings of patients were held in the evening, like social events. Patients wore get-acquainted name tags, and refreshments were served.

Later, after the first few sessions had been held, patients were invited to become involved, though they were not forced to talk. The group soon began to develop certain social standards within itself. Many men wore ties and the women dressed up. Men moved furniture, women served the refreshments.

A program looking ahead two or three weeks to give patients time to prepare in advance was outlined at the end of each session, and the leaders always had something prepared so they could give a presentation without notice, in case no patients were able to talk that evening.

Some patients were reluctant to participate actively in group reading or in presenting reports. The leaders arranged for the shy or frightened patients to tape their presentations. This recording was done in private and could be edited by the patient. Then, at the meeting the patients would sit beside the recorder while their speech was being played.

After the patient gave this talk by tape, we would carry on as if he had given it in person. One person made four tape recordings before she was able to give one in person, but eventually she was able to give a live presentation that was a triumph for her and the start of her road back to emotional health.

A Lifetime Guide for Mental Health

How to live with yourself

By Dana L. Farnsworth, M.D., As told to Lester David

Mental health means more than the absence of mental illness. It means being able to live happily with ourselves and others; to find satisfaction in the things we do; to deal capably with stresses; to tolerate anxieties; to endure frustrations; to exhibit sincerity, compassion, and humanity toward others. Here are some suggestions that can help you and your children achieve that mental health.

Children. Your goal as a parent is to help your child grow up with the good inner feeling that he is a worthwhile human being, able to stand on his own feet.

Give your child emotional support when he needs it most, right at the start of his life. A baby comes into the world utterly dependent upon other human beings. If help is prompt and consistent, accompanied by love, he learns that he can rely on people.

If parents are not warmly responsive, an infant is likely to develop mistrust of people. He may later withdraw from them to protect himself from hurt. Such a person cannot become a warm, loving wife or husband.

Start children early on the road to independence. Once I watched a small child trying to button his coat. His mother said, "Here, let mommy fix it." And she did. But she also did nothing to help her son feel capable.

Most parents do not realize that even very young boys and girls strive to be independent. Shortly after a child passes his first birthday, he begins to show that he has a mind and a will of his own and insists on trying to do things himself. If the child masters the tasks of this period successfully, he develops self-control and self-esteem. If he does not, he may have a lasting sense of doubt and shame about both himself and others.

Condensed from "This Week", 485 Lexington Ave., New York City 10017. June 5, 12, 19, 1966. ‹1966 by the United Newspapers Magazine Corp., and reprinted with permission.

You can help your child achieve this balance by permitting him to try his own wings. Have you seen the smile of triumph that lights up a toddler's face when all by himself he had fixed a toy, carried a package, or even just stood up? He glows inside, too, with a wonderful feeling of "I can."

As he grows, the child gains confidence by trying and succeeding. So let your son try to climb that fence, build a tree house, manage his affairs. Let your daughter arrange her own social activities, even plan her own party.

Give children time to digest new experiences. Periods of stimulation should be followed by relaxation. Play should not be tightly organized. Social changes come rapidly in a child's life; he should be given time to assimilate them.

Teach children to make up their minds. A 12-year-old-boy came home from school one day and told his mother he wanted to run for class president, but was not quite sure. That evening at dinner, while the boy sat quietly, his parents debated whether he ought to make the race, finally deciding that he should not because the extra burden would make his schedule for the next year too heavy.

Don't solve problems for your children. Every human being must make decisions all through life, and those who never learn how are handicapped.

You can teach your child to make decisions by allowing him to make them. Let him profit by his mistakes, and let him understand you have faith in his ability to unravel problems. Discuss the facts with him, suggest approaches, but avoid making his decision for him.

Keep the lines of understanding open. Parents constantly complain, "Our children never tell us anything." When communication lines break down, children may develop antagonism toward their parents that can later trigger all sorts of things, such as a rush into too early marriage to escape unhappiness at home. Youngsters may come to regard all persons in authority with fear or mistrust.

In every case of broken communications, parents themselves had begun snipping the wires when the children were young. You can keep the lines between generations intact in the following ways.

Treat each of your children as an individual, with his own abilities, personalities, and needs. Do not expect one to match anothers's accomplishments, but help him be proud of what he does well.

Curb your temper. Frequent displays of anger can so terrify a child that he withdraws from you. Justified irritation at something he does wrong is acceptable, and even beneficial, but uncontrolled rage is something else.

Don't make sex a taboo subject in the house. You cannot expect an adolescent suddenly to talk freely to you about sex if nobody has mentioned it in 16 years. Frank discussion can help instill a healthy attitude in children.

Present logical arguments for your decisions. "Because I say so" is no good. Giving sensible reasons makes you a fair and reasonable person in his eyes. He may not acquiesce gracefully, but inwardly, in most cases, he will probably see your point.

Discipline him when necessary. There is no better way to show a child he is truly loved than by firm discipline.

Commend children for what they do well instead of condemning them for what they don't. It is natural for parents to want their children to succeed, but do not be only negat've. A college co-ed under treatment for a severe neurosis told her therapist, "If I came home from kindergarten with two stars, mother wanted to know how come I didn't get three. If I got four marks over 90, she wondered how come the fifth was only 80."

Many persons with personality problems have but rarely received praise. They say, "I grew up feeling I couldn't do anything right."

A child's confidence in himself is built up layer by layer as he grows. Pounding away at weaknesses creates feelings of inadequacy, but stressing his good qualities builds up his inner strength.

Adolescents. Starting about age 12 and extending into early adulthood a boy or girl must acquire a sense of identity. The adolescent must discover what kind of person he is, what is important to him, what his goals are. He must, moreover, feel that he belongs somewhere in the world, that he is accepted there, that what he does and plans to do is important to others.

The youngster with no clear idea of where he fits into society is likely to develop a contempt for the values of other people. He will find a kind of comfort in gang fights, stealing, vandalism, drugs, and uninhibited sexual activity.

How can you help your son or daughter in this quest for identity? In these ways:

Listen to your child. The young people I have talked with in the 30 years feel that the failure to listen to their point of view is just about the most exasperating of all parental traits.

Trust your child. These are difficult times for parents. You are troubled by changing moral codes, youthful experimentation with drugs, teen-age drinking, auto accidents. Exercise proper supervision, of course, but at the same time trust them and let them know you do. They will become responsible persons sooner than if they are constantly suspected of some mischief. Extremely revealing was one student's explanation of why nobody cheats in a certain professor's class. "He doesn't expect us to," the boy said.

Remember your own feelings in adolescence. Try to recall those years when you were seeking to find your way in a confusing world. Most of us can hardly remember the feelings we had in adolescence, especially the painful ones and those we were ashamed of. Dredging up some of them will help you in your job of parenthood. By being able to feel what your child is going through, you will become more understanding.

Be tolerant of their apparently strange ways. As they search for identity, youngsters will express their scorn for the customs older persons consider proper. They will dress outlandishly, wear their hair in absurd styles, voice contempt for ideas their parents hold dear, and act in all sorts of rebellious ways.

Adolescents often take their cue for this kind of behavior from the gang. Oddly enough, this allegiance to the group is a bridge toward independence. The crowd helps the individual break away from his parents, gives him a feeling that he can do things, a feeling of belonging. And this is a grouping toward identity.

Unfortunately the group also encourages bravado, shamelessness, and even a contempt for the old. The kids feel guilty about this, but the guilt is absorbed by the group as a whole. Parents find this attitude difficult to tolerate. Defiance is bad enough, but contempt is even worse. Nonetheless, such behavior on our youngster's part must be understood as a temporary defense to help him break away.

When your child implies that you're square, a fossil, and you just don't understand kids, he is saying in effect, "Look, mom and dad, the more decent you are to me, the sooner I can come back to you." Listen not to the words, but to the unspoken thoughts. It takes stability, of course, but try to accept these attacks without lashing back or becoming upset. If you can remember your own stormy adolescence and wait awhile, it will pay off.

Recognize signs of impending emotional trouble. Only an expert can tell for certain if an adolescent's conflicts in his search for identity are becoming too much for him. Some indications to seek professional advice include: an unexplained and prolonged decline in school achievement; extreme fears that persist; imaginary companions; frequent violent outbursts of temper; withdrawal from usual activity; and outright antisocial behavior.

Young Adults. Thus far I have talked to parents. Now I talk to the young adult. It is harder for him to maintain emotional equilibrium than it was in years gone by. That is because the world is no longer as simple as it once was.

For one thing, you face an uncertain future. For the first time in history, man can destroy himself. If you are to achieve security, it must come from inside yourself, because there is no security outside.

Life has become complex. Opportunities, good or bad, are almost limitless. There are so many facets in the world up ahead for you, so many specialities within specialties, that you find it hard to find a place in it for yourself. An old Dutch proverb says it best "he who has a choice has a problem."

Furthermore, you realize that to make your way successfully you must keep learning for the rest of your life. Much of what you learn now will become obsolete in a few years.

In a few more years, a small number of skilled people will produce most of the material goods we need. Most of the others, and that may include you, will have to find new ways to occupy their time.

How do you cope with these pressures? There is no simple prescription a doctor can hand out. We can, however, offer some guidelines that can help you.

Don't pick your lifework too soon. Remember that college is the place to test new ideas. Never again will you have such freedom to try new modes of thinking and behavior, to discard what is unsatisfactory, and to adopt a way of life which promises to be rewarding.

Don't be bamboozled by all the nonsense flung at you about sex. In recent years, sex has been emphasized to a degree that has become alarming, distasteful, and boring. As a psychiatrist, I can tell you that the development of a mature outlook on sex is vital to good mental health. I consider it immature to allow oneself to be propelled along without thinking out one's course of action.

Be well informed on the physiological and emotional aspects of sex. Talk about it with older persons you respect. Realize that, despite the pressure of today's freedoms, some kind of sexual morality is necessary even in the most primitive societies.

Have a few discussions with your parents. They may have learned a great deal since you last had a serious talk.

Girls, if you are planning to marry and raise a family, give careful thought now to what you will do between the ages of 40 and 70. Far too many women find themselves out of a job after their children are grown. With fewer responsibilities and nothing to do outside, they are prey to emotional ills. Prepare yourself for some kind of productive activity when your children no longer need you. Take some kind of training now, when you have time, that can be used later.

Become interested in the people with whom you live and work. When you have an investment in the human race, you help keep yourself on a level emotional keel. Directing your emotions outward toward others will prevent them from being channeled inward. Self-centeredness causes misery.

Learn to recognize all the disguises that hostility can adopt. A key to good mental health is the ability to handle feelings of anger. Hostility can take many forms, excessive griping against the boss or the job, nagging or ridiculing your mate, using money as a weapon, being to busy outside to be a loving wife or husband, excessive gossiping, criticizing, or jealously. When you recognize similar behavior, make an effort to correct it. Do not let it continue because then it will grow worse.

Ride that hobby horse you started then you were younger. If you have not acquired a hobby, it still is not too late to get started. Pick one as different as possible from your work. If you work outdoors, select an indoor one. If you are sedentary, choose an active one.

Learn to laugh at yourself. Practice if you must, but learn. President Kennedy once said he took his job very seriously, but not himself.

Rewrite your life script every so often. "How are things going?" a woman once asked a friend. "Dull," the friend sighed; "life is so daily."

I have yet to hear a more apt description. Routine followed endlessly begets boredom, which in turn causes fatigue, and then emotional problems.

Once a mother was surprised to see her seven-year-old son coming home from school from the opposite direction. "I got tired walking the same blocks and seeing the same things," he explained, "so I walked different."

Naturally, routine is essential, but try to "walk different" occasionally. Take a completely different kind of vacation than you did last year, plan surprise Sunday trips for the family, scramble your workday once in a while. Take a wild adult education course at your high school, like weaving or gourmet cooking.

Accept the fact that you will never be worry free as long as you live. Constant happiness and the absence of stress and anxiety are not reasonable goals for anybody. Conflict is inescapable.

Many persons create problems for themselves by worrying about worry. Studies show that stress may not be the dread killer everyone fears. For example, a new survey by Dr. Lawrence E. Hinkle of Cornell discloses that the hard-driving executive is no more likely to suffer heart disease than clerks, machinists, or night watchmen.

Avoid excess tension and seek help if it is prolonged, but do not grimly seek relaxation by alcohol or tranquilizers. Some worry is good for you, and you will never escape it in this life.

Wives and husbands, take a daily talk break. Rosaline Russell once told an interviewer that she and her husband have a kind of parents' hour every afternoon before dinner. They chat quietly about the day's events, each listening to the other, renewing their friendship and planning the next day. When children are young, parents' hour may be held after they have gone to sleep; when they are older, they can be told that mom and dad are not be interrupted. It is a wonderful way to prevent the sad but all too frequent drifting apart of married couples.

Husbands, include the world in your goals. Many men seek only the accumulation of money, the attainment of power, or the achievement of security. All of these objectives are self-limiting and, in the end, self-defeating. Once they are attained, there is nothing else but more of the same. And if money, power, and security should be lost, so may be the man himself.

Rather, include the human race in your personal goal. Seek money, if you wish, not for its own sake but ultimately to invest in something that can benefit mankind. Feel that you want to become the best lawyer, accountant, machinist, or whatever, not for what you can take from these occupations, but for what you contribute to them in terms of helping people. The feeling that you are part of the world gives meaning to your life.

Wives, avoid the martyr trap in those first hectic years of marriage. When the children are young, you work an endless day. You are harried, frazzled, and tired, and come evening, you are expected to be a bright, cheerful, attractive mate. It is easy to feel sorry for yourself. Don't. A wife who feels exploited does not need escape from her burden so much as an overhaul of her attitudes. It is hard lot, but complaining does no good and is bound to increase as time goes on. By middle years, such a wife is likely to be a whining, griping, unhappy person who gives little joy to anyone else and none to herself.

Accept the situation and do the best you can. Do not try the impossible. If some things do not get done, it will not be a tragedy. Experiment with different schedules of work. Rearrange your kitchen so things are easier to reach. Take an occasional rest. Enlist your husband's help. And make it your business to go out, anywhere regularly. Bear in mind that the rough period will be over soon.

Later Years. This time of life can be uniquely enjoyable. The distinguished psychiatrist Dr. Earl D. Bond has said in assessing his life, "The period from 70 to 80 was the most enjoyable of all." Dr. Bond is now in his 80's.

Dr. Bond's own recipe for happy later years is instructive. "I was relieved of organizational responsibilities and a heavy practice," he explains. "However, I kept busy seeing a few patients. I had plenty of companionship, plenty of interests in all sorts of affairs and the freedom to indulge in them, and I had good health."

Maintain your interest in people. You may have lost old friends, but it is a great fallacy to think you cannot make new ones or that they need all be older persons. You may have much to offer to younger persons.

Keep busy at constructive work that pleases you. If your job bores you, you are well rid of it in retirement. Now you can enjoy doing what has meaning for *you*. But do it. Share your experience with school boards, hospitals, churches, Red Cross, social-welfare groups.

If you haven't become involved in a hobby earlier, don't be disappointed if your efforts now meet with failure. However, this does not mean you cannot learn something new. "You can't teach an old dog new tricks" doesn't apply to people; there are many tricks that only the old dogs can do. Older persons have learned everything from golf to typewriting. By all means, keep up the interests you have had all along, whether in politics, community affairs, books, plays, gardening, or whatever.

To Get What You Want

· . . know what you want, then will it,
and use the proper means to achieve it

By David P. Campbell

Psychologists now say that if women follow certain basic principles they have established they will have a better chance of getting what they want.

First, you have to decide what it is you want. Go through the following list and mark all of the things that are important to you.

True   False

_____ _____ To be rich.

_____ _____ To be famous.

_____ _____ Lots of leisure to do as I please.

_____ _____ A husband who loves me.

_____ _____ A happy, close-knit family with at least two or three children.

_____ _____ To be talented.

_____ _____ To be married to a famous man.

_____ _____ To be popular.

_____ _____ To be a successful career woman.

_____ _____ To fall in love often.

_____ _____ To be married to a husband who will spend much of his time with me.

_____ _____ Enough authority and influence to have others working for me.

_____ _____ To be alone

_____ _____ No one ever to be angry with me.

_____ _____ To be free to come and go as I please.

_____ _____ To work in a field where I will have to compete with men to succeed.

_____ _____ To dedicate myself to others and better the world.

This check list should make it clear that there are various ways to succeed and that you can't have them all. For example, if you want to be famous, then you can't be free to come

Condensed from "Glamour", 420 Lexington Ave., New York City 10017. June, 1969. ‹1969 by Conde Nast Publications, Inc., and reprinted with permission of publisher and David P. Campbell.

and go as you please, for your public will recognize and, no doubt, annoy you.

Whatever the direction you decide to go, you must try to guide your own destiny. For example, you have to use your time wisely. Go through the following list to see how you fare.

Yes   No

_____   _____ Do you spend more than 20 minutes each day on coffee breaks?

_____   _____ Stop working each day about 3:30, telling yourself you can't really accomplish anything in an hour?

_____   _____ Play cards or games three or four hours every week?

_____   _____ Go shopping almost daily?

_____   _____ Go out with friends three or four nights each week?

_____   _____ Often spend more than ten minutes on a social telephone talk?

_____   _____ Play almost all of every week-end?

_____   _____ Having finished one task 15 minutes before lunch, do you usually defer starting another?

If you said Yes to more than three or four of these, you do not appreciate the value of your time. Fifteen minutes is important: it is long enough to write a note to your mother, call the library about a book your boss is looking for, dust off your living-room bookshelves, or file the morning's correspondence.

Ask yourself these questions about improving the way you use your time.

Yes   No

_____   _____ Have you ever kept a detailed account for a few days of just how you spend your time?

_____   _____ Ever set up a planned-time schedule for completing a large task, like a term paper, and stuck to it?

_____   _____ Taken a single routine task, like making your bed, and tried to find ways to do it faster?

_____   _____ Do you have at least a rough plan for using some time each week for self-development?

_____   _____ Can you name, quickly without much thought, someone you have noticed who does use his time efficiently?

_____   _____ Do you care if you waste time?

If you answered No to most of these you are not conscious of time and probably not very efficient. Time can spend itself. C. Northcote Parkinson, in one of his famous laws, stated,

"Work expands to fill the time available."

Use your habits to save time. You normally will not run your life like a crack drill team. Instead, you should, in an almost casual manner, try to mold your daily habits to work more efficiently.

A delightful book about using time wisely is *Cheaper by the Dozen* by Frank B. Gilbreth, Jr., and Ernestine Gilbreth Carey. Their parents were industrial-efficiency experts, who applied their working principles in rearing their 12 children.

Efficient use of time does not mean being always on edge. Someone once asked the father, Frank Gilbreth, Sr., why he wanted to save time. He replied, "For work, if you love that best, for education, for beauty, for art, for pleasure. For mumblety-peg, if that's where your heart lies."

The next step is to ask yourself what you have thus far learned to do well. Go down the following list. Be honest; do not check something unless you have already done it successfully.

_____ Can you play the piano or any musical instrument fairly well?

_____ Type?

_____ Run a 16mm sound movie projector?

_____ Cook an authentic Chinese, French, or other foreign meal?

_____ Write a newspaper or magazine article?

_____ Sketch clothes designs well enough to have them published in a school paper?

_____ Weld or solder?

_____ Play bridge?

_____ Play tennis, golf, handball, or badminton well enough to beat almost all your friends?

_____ Write poetry?

_____ Work simple problems in algebra? For example, can you factor $a^2 - b^2$?

_____ Drive a car?

_____ Tell stories to children, making them up as you go and keeping the children enthralled?

_____ Raise flowers?

_____ Fix a leaky faucet, change a tire, glue up a loose bathroom tile, retrieve a ring from a sink trap, replace a fuse, or repair a broken window?

_____ Organize a conference of 100 people, handling their travel, lodging, and meals?

_____ Skip rope for three minutes without missing?

_____ Run any kind of machine more complicated than an electric toaster?

———— Operate a camera that has adjustments for lens aperture, shutter speed and distance?

———— Identify more than ten different types of trees?

———— Plan, organize, and carry out a dinner party for eight, including all the cooking?

———— Bandage a severe cut without becoming panicky?

———— Waltz, polka, schottische, or do any folk dance?

———— Estimate distances, like a ceiling height, within 10%?

———— Do simple arithmetic in your head, e.g., which is the better buy, 15 pencils for 29c or 20 for 45c?

———— Write a friendly letter in French, German, Spanish, or any other foreign language?

———— Do a flip on a trampoline or off a diving board?

———— Handle a small sailboat by yourself or paddle a canoe in a straight line for half a mile?

———— Use a slide rule?

———— Cut out and sew up a simple dress from a pattern?

———— Operate a keypunch?

———— Make an omelet?

———— Take someone's pulse?

———— Identify more than ten different kinds of birds?

———— Reupholster an easy chair?

———— Send and receive simple messages in Morse code?

———— Maintain an average of 150 in a bowling league?

———— Swim 100 yards?

I can't tell you exactly what your score means, because some of the foregoing talents are more valuable than others. If you can play the piano well enough to appear in a public concert, that skill will take you further than any 20 of the others. No matter what you are, student, employee, wife, at liberty, there is tremendous value in being able to do things well. First, there is the benefit of the skill itself. Thus, if you can type 60 words a minute the advantages are obvious.

The second advantage of skill is the lift that it gives to your self-confidence. There is considerable inner pride in knowing that you are more competent than others, even if it is only in flower arranging. Do not worry about being best, just try to be good.

A third advantage in being talented is a flat, out-and-out social one. If you can do something well, many more doors will be opened to you.

To guide your own life in directions that are important to you, you must learn another skill: adapting to ever-changing conditions. Success is never static; we never find the end of the rainbow. Now, which of these statements describe you?

Yes   No

_____   _____   "If I could only get out of school and away from home, I could solve my problems quickly."

_____   _____   "If only I had a job and my own money, I could have what I want."

_____   _____   "If I could get married and run my own home, I would never complain again."

_____   _____   "If I just had a college degree, everybody would respect me and I'd have lots of friends."

_____   _____   "If only I could get pregnant and have my own baby, I'd never want another thing in life."

_____   _____   "If my baby would stop spitting up, sleep all night, and let me rest, life would be continually beautiful."

_____   _____   "If only our income were $100 a month higher, we'd have all the money we'd need."

If you answered Yes to even one of these, you are kidding yourself. It will not happen.

Life never stops; there are no ends; no final buzzers. But there are times of delicious success, and the trick is to enjoy them.

Chapter III

Tell Me a Story

Teachers since time began have used stories, whether in fable or truth, instead of abstract terms and diagrams to get their message across. The best illustrations of popular psychology and its workings are found in narrative rather than in firstly, secondly, etc., form. Courage, love, and good humor have their appeal when we see them in persons we know and read about rather than in arid descriptions of emotional states. The psychological reactions and states of mind related in this chapter are found in the life-actions of real people.

Bishop Sheen and the Lonely Stranger

*It began with one friend in the
dark night of loneliness*

By Paul Scott

It was Halloween night. The weather was raw and blustery
and the rain stung my face as I walked the deserted New York
streets. I always walked at night so I would not be seen. For I
had been disfigured by leprosy.

Not long before, I had been released from the government
hospital at Carville, La. After six nightmare years I was
cured. But I was only a shadow of the happy, active New
York high-school boy who loved girls and dancing and
played halfback on the school football team. Now my face
was scarred by surgery and I had lost most of the sight in one
eye. I had loved the thrill of weaving through a broken field
in football, or spiraling a pass downfield. Now, despite 16
operations, my fingers were still twisted and awkward, and I
walked with a limp.

My hopes of returning to a normal life with my family and
friends were quickly shattered by people's reaction to my appearance. When I went out in public, people stared and
whispered. I was unable to get a job. My old friends gradually
drifted away. The change in my appearance was too much
even for my parents. They moved to another city while I
remained in New York, alone and friendless.

Finally a kindly man gave me a job as a clerk in a small office and I took a room at the YMCA. I avoided the public. I
would wander along deserted beaches on weekends, or
through the empty streets of New York late at night when few
people were about. I was aimlessly walking the streets on a
rainly Halloween night when I encountered a group of
children playing "tricks or treats." They were wearing masks
and Halloween costumes. "Look at him," one of them explained, "He doesn't need a mask."

Condensed from the "Catholic Courier Journal", 36 Scio St., Rochester, N.Y. 14604. ₍1966 by
Catholic Courier Journal, reprinted with permission.

Those few childish words finally broke my spirit. I walked away in the darkness, numb with despair. Walking blindly I found myself passing St. Patrick's cathedral. Although not a Catholic, I went in, seeking to compose myself.

Kneeling despairingly in the dimly lighted interior, I suddenly thought of Bishop Fulton Sheen. While at Carville I had learned of his work with leprosy sufferers. Perhaps, I thought, if I could talk to him he could help me. Seeing a priest, I approached and asked if I could see Bishop Sheen. The priest explained that Bishop Sheen was not connected with the cathedral. "If you'll leave your name I'll try to get it to him," he said. Disheartened, I mumbled my name and phone number and walked back out into the night. It was just one more rebuff, I felt.

Not long afterwards I received a phone call from Bishop Sheen's office. The bishop had heard I was trying to reach him, the secretary said, and would like me to come to his office. As I entered his office, in a New York business building, he came quickly from behind his desk to greet me. He wore a long black cassock with a wooden cross dangling from a silver chain. Atop his gray hair was a red zuchetto.

I watched his striking, deep-set eyes for the telltale signs of shock I had come to expect on meeting strangers, but he smiled warmly and motioned me to a chair. Haltingly I told the story of my illness and disfigurement, of my abandonment by my friends and even my family. I said I had come to him, a stranger, because I had no one else to whom to turn.

"Well, you have at least one friend," he said. "Would you have dinner with me tomorrow night?"

The following night, over dinner at his residence, I told Bishop Sheen the details of my illness and the loneliness it had caused me. When I had talked myself out, he began to speak. Patiently and with gentle kindness he told me that my only salvation was to endure my misfortune with courage. "All of us suffer sometime in life," he said, "and those who bear their suffering with fortitude are strengthened by it."

Although he did urge me to face my problem with courage, Bishop Sheen did not minimize the difficulty of my situation. "You will never have many friends," he said at that first dinner.

"I've found that out," I said.

"But those you do have," he added, "will be true friends."

The first of those true friends was Bishop Sheen. Although there were a thousand demands on his time, he was never too busy to see me. About once a week I would go to his residence for dinner. Because it was difficult for me to use my hands, he would cut my meat for me. He helped me to find a small apartment and then furnished it for me. He bought clothes for me, and whenever he appeared on television he invited me to sit in the audience and introduced me to his personal guests. Afterwards he would have me driven home.

Once he asked what I planned to have for dinner the next day. I told him that I hadn't been paid yet and did not have any food in the house.

"Come with me," he said impulsively. "We're going shopping." We walked to a nearby delicatessen. There he shopped like a child turned loose in a toy store. "We'll take those," he said, indicating two plump chickens turning on a spit. "And some of these, and these," he exclaimed, scooping up cans and packages with both hands. He seemed even happier than I was as we staggered out, our arms filled with enough food to stock my larder for a week.

Bishop Sheen's kindness and good nature began to lift my despondency. All the slights and hurts I had suffered over many years faded in the face of this one man's goodness and patient counsel. Above all, he urged me to rid myself of bitterness against anyone who had humiliated me by thoughtless words or actions. "You have told me of people who have hurt you, perhaps unintentionally," he once said. "Is there no one who has been kind to you?"

Then I remembered the selfless care and devotion of the doctors and nuns at Carville. I recalled particularly the patient work of Dr. Daniel Riordan, a great surgeon who had performed the 16 operations to make it possible for me to use my hands again. Through the words of Bishop Sheen I was made to see that no matter how much I had suffered there was still much to be grateful for; that there were thousands of dedicated people working to alleviate suffering in the world.

As I got to know the bishop, I was constantly amazed at the farflung extent of his work and charity, particularly in the fight against Hansen's disease. As director of the national office of the Society for the Propagation of the Faith, he supervised 400 leprosaria around the world. Once Jackie Gleason, who sometimes is Joe the Bartender on television, gave the bishop a large check and told him to give it to "the poorest of the poor." The bishop told him the poorest of the poor were in a leper colony in the Pacific. The check was so large that Bishop Sheen took it to the leper colony himself. With it they were able to build a clinic, get additional doctors and more medicine.

When he was about to leave, an old woman, badly crippled by leprosy, came up to him. "Please tell me who did all this," she asked him. He thought for a moment and remembered his promise not to reveal Jackie Gleason's identity. Bending over, he whispered to the crippled old lady, "The man who did all this was Joe the Bartender."

Gradually, with Bishop Sheen's encouragement, I became better able to face my situation. I conquered my bitterness over slights I had suffered. Yet at times, when I was alone, I lapsed into spells of acute loneliness. Once I became so desperately lonely that I called him as he had told me to do whenever I felt I had to talk to someone. His secretary told me he was ill at home. I apologized and resumed pacing my little apartment, desperate for someone, anyone, to talk with. A few moments later the phone rang. I recognized the voice as Bishop Sheen's, although he sounded hoarse and tired.

"Paul, I want to see you," he said. I told him I was terribly lonely but that I didn't want to trouble him if he was sick. "I'm just a bit under the weather," he said. "You come right over now. It will do me good."

Guiltily I hastened to his residence. The housekeeper opened the front door. Inside, in a bathrobe and slippers, the bishop sat hunched on the stairs leading to the 2nd floor. He looked pale and weak, but he summoned up a smile and greeted me as warmly as ever. Ill as he was, he sat and talked with me far into the night. I said the hardest thing to bear was the loneliness, the absence of any friends except him.

"Friendship is a precious thing," he said; "but sometimes one finds kindness even among strangers."

Not long afterwards, his words of encouragement came true. A woman in the office where I worked, a complete stranger, became interested in my problem. She told me she thought my appearance could be greatly improved by plastic surgery. "But plastic surgery is expensive," I said. "I could never afford it."

"Don't worry about that," she said. "I have a doctor I want you to see." She sent me to Dr. Theodore Capeci, one of New York's finest plastic surgeons. He arranged for me to have plastic surgery performed by Dr. Carl Barlow, another top surgeon. Dr. Barlow performed four operations, over a two-year period, that made a marked improvement in my appearance. All of the operations and hospitalization were provided free by the two doctors, who were complete strangers. And the woman who had sent me to them was just a casual acquaintance. Later, as I thought of this, there came back to me the haunting words of Blanche Dubois in Tennessee William's *Streetcar Named Desire*: "I have always been dependent upon the kindness of strangers."

Strengthened by the kindness of such good strangers, I have finally found a purpose in life. I am now proud that the pioneering work which Dr. Riordan did in the 16 operations on my hands helped him perfect the revolutionary surgical techniques which have enabled him and other doctors to restore the usefulness of the crippled hands of thousands of victims of Hansen's disease (the correct medical term for leprosy). I also take satisfaction in working to make the public aware that today the disease is curable, that with early diagnosis and modern drugs it need not be crippling.

Above all, I am grateful for the friendship of Bishop Sheen. Once I tried to express this gratitude in words. "You have given me your friendship, your time, everything I have," I said. "And I have nothing to give you."

"That's not so, Paul," the bishop said. "You give *me* strength."

When I was with Bishop Sheen he never preached to me of religion or of Catholicism. Rather he spoke of love of God and man, and, edified by his example, I came to realize that in his kindness to me he was the living embodiment of the parable of the Good Samaritan, the man who succored the stranger in distress. His unfailing compassion and holiness inevitably kindled a spark of faith within me. It was with a deep feeling of humility and gratitude that I was received into the Church and baptized by Bishop Sheen at St. Patrick's cathedral.

We Used to Be Poor

But got rich just by unstashing things

By Ralph Reppert

My wife Harriet decided last week that we aren't ever going to be rich. She didn't blurt out, "Ralphie boy, I can see now that you're just never going to make it." No, it was more of a gradual thing that sort of took root by itself, grew, and bloomed.

It began with the Madeira table linens which somebody gave us for a wedding present and which Harriet has since

Condensed from the Baltimore "Sunday Sun Magazine", Calvert and Centre Sts., Baltimore, Md. Sept. 8, 1963. ⸀1963 by the A. S. Abell Co., and reprinted with permission.

kept stashed away in the attic.

I don't know why people squirrel away pretty things like that. Unconsciously, I think, we were saving them for the day when we could buy just the right kind of dining room furniture, china, silver, and so on. Then, in the event that we had a duchess or a movie star or perhaps a U.S. senator to dinner, we could break out the Madeira linen and show it off in the setting it deserved.

Harriet ran across the linen while looking for something else, and decided on the spur of the moment there wasn't any point saving it any longer. She also brought down a pair of silver candlesticks—another wedding present—to set off the linen.

Dinner that night had a touch of magic. The fine old pattern of the tablecloth caught in the candlelight in a way that dressed up the whole dining room, so that even the hamburger looked aristocratic.

A day or two later Harriet trotted out the good china, because the Madeira linen deserved the best we had. Then came the good silver because, as Harriet put it, "it's the *least* we can do for the china."

I broke out the bottle of brandy Harriet bought me three Christmases ago. (I had been saving the occasion for some deserving guest.)

After two glasses of brandy apiece, Harriet and I came to some conclusions.

1. Undoubtedly we will never be able to buy furniture for what we would consider a perfect dining room—or perfect living room.

2. So let's use the few nice things we have with the furniture we now have and make the most of it. In short, let's reach out right now and take a big bite out of life, while we can still bite with our own teeth.

3. Speaking of deserving guests, who is more deserving (pass the brandy, dear) than we are?

Never has a set of ideas taken over a house so completely.

I am now wearing the only pair of real silk pajamas I own, as if there were no tomorrow. I also slouch around in my good robe, which I've kept in reserve all these years in case I had to go to the hospital.

We decided to take the slip covers off the furniture in the living room. It did so much for the room that I went out and took the cold plastic covers off the car seats. It's a luxurious feeling, sitting on plush.

Harriet took our "company" percolator off the shelf and made an everyday percolator out of it. She has also pressed into everyday service a stainless-steel carving set that had never tasted meat.

I now shake up a cocktail before dinner in my good silver shaker, and I pour into the best crystal we own. I will never drink another martini out of the little jar the cheese spread came in. I hadn't realize it before, but having a cocktail out of the right kind of glass is really half the enjoyment of a drink.

I went through my golf bag, threw out all the dirty, cut-up balls, and broke open a carton of new balls I got two birthdays ago. I also bought a big bag of new tees. I now use one tee per hole, and don't even look for it after driving.

All these years I have been getting a week's mileage out of every razor blade. Toward the end of the week, I'd have to hook my toes under the bathroom water pipes and pull the razor with both hands. Now, for pennies, I use a new blade once each day, then throw it away.

Realizing that you're never going to be rich is a grand discovery. It puts a spring into your step and a gleam in your eye. It gives you a peace of mind and freedom of movement you wouldn't have believed possible. It's wonderful. It's like being rich.

Our Unspoken Language

It tells the truth that words often hide

By Barbara Frum

Psychiatrists lately are trading their couches for movie cameras and are going into homes to film the family. How the members look and move and sit tells them more than what is said.

A father with his chin on his chest doesn't have to say he is beaten down. A son may say compliant words with a mouth twisted in hate. A parent may tell his children, "Speak up and talk to the doctor," but the psychiatrist can see the real message: "Lie low or you'll get it later."

All of us use body language all the time. Our gesture messages are constantly running parallel to our spoken messages. They may clarify, amplify, or contradict what we

Condensed from "Chatelaine", 481 University Ave., Toronto 2, Ont., Canada. August, 1966. ©1966 by Maclean-Hunter Publishing Co., Ltd., and reprinted with permission.

say in words. Some suspect that families may use words to mask what they really mean.

A research group at Temple university, Philadelphia, has been inquiring into how families communicate. Dr. Birdwhistell, an anthropologist, and Dr. Scheflen, a psychiatrist, direct some film makers, clinical psychologists, and psychiatrists who have recorded families in action on film. They then study them dozens, even hundreds, of times to learn the vocabularly and grammar of family body language. Once they have mastered it, they will know what families are really saying to each other. As one psychiatrist puts it, "They will tell us by their actions what they don't know in words."

Birdwhistell wants to teach other psychiatrists to understand body language so that they can stop worrying about words and study the family's total system of communicating. When that happens, psychiatry will become more of a science and less of an art.

Dr. Ross Speck, one of the team, described a typical filming of a father, mother, and two sons. The session had been started and disrupted 20 times in one hour. When the films were analyzed it was discovered that the father had been responsible for every interruption. Each time the psychiatrist had started to ask the father what was wrong with the marriage, the father had leaned back in his chair, away from the mother, and toward one of his sons. Instantly the son would get up from his chair and either hit his brother or crash into the microphone to break up the meeting.

The session was repeatedly brought back to order by the bewildered psychiatrist. Each time, the father's leaning away from the mother and toward the son would bring another explosion, so that discussion of the marriage was impossible.

The cue discovered on the films was that leaning gesture. It was made unconsciously by the father was unconsciously received by the son. Yet the message was clear: "Break up the session."

Such cues are never consciously taught or consciously learned. Dr. Scheflen thinks they are picked up by the child at the same time he learns spoken language, probably by imitating adults.

"It's like a dialect," says Dr. Birdwhistell, "you can't teach it, yet every person learns it." But families need not have identical patterns of body language. Ask any daughter-in-law.

Every marriage unites people of different family patterns and with different body languages. Perhaps in the girl's family physical contact was used to convey affection. If she marries into a family where physical contacts are shunned, she may feel that her husband is cold, unaware that he has simply learned a different pattern of behavior.

A Jewish son may know that a torrent of words from his mother is a signal to disregard the meaning of those words. A Gentile daughter-in-law, ignorant of the family's signals, might take the words at face value.

Dr. Birdwhistell describes the We're-All-Buddies family, in which no one is allowed to be dependent, to seek comfort or emotional support from the others. This family is without strong leadership because the parents are busy being the children's pals. If the children do seek emotional support they will be rebuffed, because that would interfere with the family myth that they are all just buddies.

Another pattern Birdwhistell describes as the Muzak family. The piped-in music is never too loud, never too soft; the Muzak family, too, is always on an even keel. No highs or lows in mood are allowed. Any member who is unhappy is ignored. According to Speck, "The sickest Muzak family is the one which brags it has never had a quarrel. That family is dead for sure. They're so busy acting out their 'happy-family' charade that they haven't developed the trust in each other that would allow them to live through a real argument."

Then there is the family which has a silent member. He may be a child who never speaks, or dad who hides behind his newspaper. The rest of the family may complain that they can never communicate with dad, but they are in constant communication with him. His silence itself is a message, a running comment on the others. The wife who is trying to talk to a silent spouse becomes increasingly angry, not realizing that her anger is a response to the messages his silence is communicating.

Families have different ways of using illness. In the Sick-Mother family, no one can complain but Mother. In the Stalwart-Mother family, everyone can be sick but Mother. Some families have an understanding that no two will be sick at once so they take turns having illnesses. A variation on this pattern is the family that competes to see who is ill each morning. Dad nicks himself with his razor, Mother spills boiling water on her hand, a child throws up, a teen-ager cries.

A skilled observer picks up many clues about a family. By meeting them at home, he sees who is really the ruler. Power may reside with one of the children, the mother, or even a long-dead grandmother, according to Dr. Speck. "I visited a home in which three grown sons had to share one bedroom because the family would not disturb the room where grandma died. After ten years her clothes were still in the closet, her jewelry still in the drawers."

Dr. Speck also watches to see who sits in the power position. In the North American family the most comfortable living-room chair is usually Dad's. "It's the throne, and whoever sits in it is really running that family," says Speck.

Havoc results when two partners from mutually abrasive patterns marry. But confusions don't occur only when married people find their family patterns don't mesh. Dr. Birdwhistell thinks that even *within* families, garbled messages can be sent, so that what is said in words is completely contradicted by the body message. The trembling mother who tells her child in the doctor's office, "Don't cry, the needle won't hurt you," is saying with her facial expressions, "It is going to hurt something awful!"

The "pipe light" is a preening gesture. A woman, aware that an attractive man is present, may push her hair into place, touch up her make-up, or shift into a more beguiling stance. Men may straighten their ties, pull up their socks, or adjust their cuff links in the presence of a woman.

A mother leaving the kitchen, slumping into a chair, and wearily drawing a heavy arm across her forehead is wasting motion unless her family understands her message: Mother is tired, and wants some appreciation shown immediately.

A baby is a mass of wrigglings and squirmings. From the tens of thousands of positions and gestures that he is capable of, he will, by the age of six, have abandoned all but the few that have meaning in his particular society. The American child, while learning to speak English, also learns to move in American English.

Northern children know that a smile means friendliness. But a Southern belle learns to use a smile to mask her anger. Used by a Japanese the same smile can mean embarrassment. A smile can also be a message about a message. Accompanying a derogatory remark it can mean, "Don't take what I said seriously," just as a wink does.

An Isreali child knows that an elder stroking his beard is registering careful thought. An Arab boy knows that the same gesture signals the presence of an attractive woman.

But we cannot describe correct gestures. We only notice those that are wrong.

Our body gestures reveal the nature of our relationship to others. Family factions are revealed by posture. Members in cahoots will sit in indentical postures when talking in a group, their heads cocked at the same angle, their legs crossed in the same direction. Psychiatrists usually find that the family is, in fact, split into these subgroups or secret alignments.

How you sit at a party can reveal what side of an argument you are on. Agreeing members are often sitting in identical position. Very old friends may shift into identical postures when disagreeing, as though to indicate the discussion has nothing to do with their continuing friendship.

Happy lovers sit with their legs and arms crossed toward each other, each partner's posture mirroring the other's so that together their bodies form a closed circuit that says to all others: keep out. Quarreling lovers may pout and refuse to speak to each other, but their carbon-copy sitting positions are a signal that the quarrel is temporary.

Within the family we learn our notions of territoriality. Our territory is the space we feel we must maintain between ourselves and others. Violating a person's sense of territory can produce hilarious results. Watch two men squeezed together in the center of a crowded sofa. The closer they come the more they squirm and twist away from each other so that actual physical contact is avoided. They usually end up angled away from each other, earnestly engaged in conversation with people at the far ends of the room.

Our choice of comfortable distance from others is not a personal decision but a cultural tradition. Not everyone feels a North American's anxiety about close physical contact. A Latin American, for example, is only comfortable in conversation if his head is no more than 12 inches away from his listener's. North Americans are comfortable only at arm's length.

Often a misinterpretation of other people's motives comes from a mistranslation of their body behavior. All of our social behavior is based on the patterns learned within the family. If a person learns patterns at home that are very different from those accepted in the outside community he will be considered a misfit. The person who deviates too much from his society's patterns, whether in dress or behavior, shows ignorance, extreme rebellion, or mental illness. The community will tolerate only so much deviance. Persons whose patterns go beyond acceptable limits get special treatment or are put in mental hospitals.

Dr. Birdwhistell affirms that family patterns produce either sick or healthy members. The final test of whether a family has communicated healthy patterns is not that the child has become an adult, but that he can be a successful parent and produce mentally healthy children of his own.

A New Life for Joe

The sound of a clarinet marked the
beginning of a basic change

By Noreen Hooper

Our son Joe suffered brain damage at birth. He will never be completely normal. The fact that he has come as far as he has is nothing we can take credit for. That belongs to Joe himself.

He is now 16. He is finishing his second year of high school and his fourth year as a paper boy. He is also the proud possessor of three radios, a fine stereo hi-fi, more than 100 good LP records, and a secondhand bike, all bought from his own earnings.

Only six years ago doctors told us Joe might never be able to finish school or hold a job. That was hard to accept because, until he started 3rd grade, Joe had seemed normal.

He was, I remember, a clumsy toddler and his fingers seemed to be all thumbs. But we did not worry, because he had learned to talk earlier than most babies and he walked only slightly later. When he was 11 months old, an ophthalmologist noticed that he had double vision. Other problems arose during those early years, but our pediatrician said there was nothing to worry about: "Time would take care of everything."

But Joe's problems kept getting worse. When he reached 1st grade, and it was time for him to learn to write, it seemed to be impossible for him to make his fingers follow his brain. But later he was transferred to an excellent teacher, a woman as skilled as he was patient. By the end of his second year with her, Joe could write, very slowly and with very large letters, but he could write. He could also read as well as most other children in his class.

Then came 3rd grade and a run-of-the-mill teacher who had more pupils than patience and was certain that only carelessness could produce such badly formed letters. Joe was

Condensed from "Good Housekeeping", 959 8th Ave., New York City 10019. February, 1967.
ⓒ1967 by the Hearst Corp., and reprinted with permission.

miserable, and began to slip backwards. Both his reading and writing deteriorated and he simply gave up on learning to spell. It was the same outside of school. When he found he could not throw or catch a ball, nor even run without tripping over his own feet, he lost what little self-confidence he had, and withdrew from life, spending hours alone in his room.

Then, one day, he surprised us by saying he wanted a bike. Of course, we bought him one. Although we had no idea whether he would be able to learn to ride, we were overjoyed that he was willing to try. If he succeeded, perhaps it would give him the confidence he needed.

But he couldn't do it. After weeks of agonizing effort he still couldn't ride more than a few wobbly feet. Finally, after a particularly bad session, he wheeled the bike into the garage and turned his back on it. For the next few days he didn't utter a word, just sat and stared. It was at that point that we made an appointment with a neurologist.

After a series of tests, the doctor told us that Joe's brain had been damaged at birth. The injury was slight; only a borderline handicap, he explained. The damaged parts of the brain were the ones that controlled fusion of vision and coordination of arms and legs. That is why the injury had scarcely been noticeable at first. But when he reached school age and the demands on him were more complicated, Joe's handicap became obvious.

He said that Joe's problem might get worse as he grew older, because he had such a burning desire to do things well. He had already begun to despise himself because of his failures. If he were not helped, and quickly, he might retreat completely from a world he could not face. On the doctor's recommendation, we took Joe out of school, hired a tutor, and began the struggle to help him start living again.

For a long time it seemed hopeless. Joe did whatever he was told. He visited the places we thought he should visit, did the things we thought he should do, but he simply was not with it. He seldom talked, and when he did it was in monosyllables. Nothing could make him smile.

Then one day Joe discovered the sound of Mr. Clarinet's music. From that day on, his story sounds like a fairy tale. He had a cold and was lying in bed, listening to the radio, when I heard him call. I hurried upstairs. "Hey! Listen to that!" he said, pointing to the radio. I sat down and listened.

After a minute, he turned to me, "What do you think, mother?"

"I think it's very nice," I did, too, even though I don't know a thing about music. It was some kind of horn playing the *Beale Street Blues,* I thought, and I liked it. Of course, I would have liked anything, at that point, because I was so thrilled that Joe was taking an interest.

"That's a clarinet. Isn't it great?" I nodded, and together we listened to the rest of the number. Joe didn't say anymore, but when I went downstairs, there was joy in my heart.

On Joe's 12th birthday we bought him a portable phonograph and a Mr. Clarinet record. That afternoon he hauled his old bike out of the garage. Terrified that again he would fail, I watched from the front door. When he rested for a minute, I called, "Joe, why bother with that old bike? It's getting too small for you anyhow."

"No, it's not." He paused to get his breath. "I'm going to be a paper boy so I can afford to buy records."

That was the last sentence Joe spoke for a week. He hid the record player in his closet and ignored the radio. But twice a day he was out teaching himself to ride his bike and twice a day he came in silent, white-faced, and perspiring. Tension mounted in the house. Then one afternoon Joe's sister came running into the kitchen. "Mother!" she shouted. "Come out and watch Joe! He's going to make it! He's nearly riding!"

I couldn't make myself look. I told her to watch for me. In ten minutes she burst in again yelling. "He did it! He did it! He's off around the block!" We gave each other a hug and wept a few tears.

From them on, Joe spent every spare minute on his bike. He would come home exhausted and silent, but for the first time he was beginning to look happy. Then one day he tore an ad for paper carriers out of the newspaper and asked me to fill out an application blank for him.

Now, ever since Joe had mentioned getting a paper route, I had been hoping he would change his mind. He had never been able to make friends his own age or even speak to a stranger. I thought he would never be able to get along with the other carriers. And how could he possibly go from house to house collecting? What would it do to him if an angry customer bawled him out?

"Are you sure about this, Joe? If you can't write small enough to fill in this application, how will you sign receipts? Paper boys have to write, you know."

"No, they don't," said Joe. "I'll get a rubber stamp."

When he went out into the yard, I phoned my husband. He, too, was afraid of the whole idea. What if Joe found he could not handle the paper route? Would he not then crawl back into his shell, this time perhaps for good? That evening we called the doctor. "Let Joe go ahead," he said. If we didn't, our lack of trust might hurt him more than failing as a paper boy.

We sent in the application. As days passed and there was no word from the newspaper, I swung from hoping he wouldn't get a route to hoping he would. Joe took his bike out every day, but except for that he seemed to be slipping back into his old ways. We bought him a new Mr. Clarinet record, but he hid it in the closet without even breaking the seal. But he did watch the mail and listen for the telephone. Other times, he would sit staring into space.

Finally, the *Herald's* circulation manager agreed to give Joe a trial, when his father promised to help him over the rough spots. And in the beginning, Joe did have plenty of trouble.

The *Herald* does not give new boys route lists, but expects each to follow the old carrier for a few mornings and make up his own list. Joe found writing so difficult that each day he would get only six or eight addresses out of a total of 80. But as soon as he came home his father would drive him back over the route and make a note of the houses which Joe pointed out. He had a list by the time he started.

His first collections days were bad. Every time he had to ring a doorbell and say, "Collecting," Joe came close to panic. He was even more shaken over customer's complaints. Twice he almost quit.

But when his first payday came, all the agonies were forgotten. After paying for his papers, his carrier bag, and his collection book, he had $10 left. After stopping at a record store, he pedaled home furiously and dashed up to his room. There he took his player out of the closet, listened to the new album twice, and came downstairs to us with a huge smile. Until that moment I had had no idea what nice teeth he had! It was the first real smile I have ever seen on him.

"Now I'll play that other record you bought," he announced. Did we like the clarinet? You bet we did!

Once Joe had settled into his paper route he decided to save for a hi-fi set. He wanted to open a bank account, but he was afraid the tellers would laugh at his shaky handwriting. Every night he practiced his signature until he was sure he could do no better. Then he asked us to take him downtown. After Joe filled out the application, the bank manager took a look at the almost illegible signature, and hesitated. Then he smiled. "You know, Joe," he said, "there are only two classes of men with handwriting as bad as yours: doctors and bank managers." He countersigned the application with a huge scrawl.

From that day one, Joe has saved $20 a month and has also

been able to buy himself a full-sized, secondhand bike and scores of records. He now owns every Mr. Clarinet recording on the market and has begun to collect other instrumentalists. But his proudest possession is the fine stereo outfit. It is a dream come true for Joe and a symbol of what determination (Joe's) and kindness (other people's) can accomplish.

Joe has also made progress educationally, physically, and emotionally. He no longer needs a private tutor. He now goes to a vocational high school and has managed to keep up with his studies. He has learned to enjoy the company of other boys.

Physically, too, he has improved. His leg muscles, thanks to bike riding, are now stronger and under better control. So are his arms, thanks to swimming. It took a private coach two years to get him afloat, but Joe stuck it out and he is now a good swimmer.

He has made up his mind that he is going to learn to play a musical instrument, probably a bass fiddle. He has managed to train his legs and arms to work better, and now he will train his fingers. He tells us that he will buy his own instrument and pay for the lessons. His father and I are delighted, even though we know he may never make it, and that while he is working at it he may stop talking to us, stop smiling, and hide away in his room. If that happens we will do just what we did before: watch and hope and pray and keep our mouths tight shut. Eventually, we feel sure he will achieve the full life he has pursued with such determination.

High-IQ Club

You need a rating of 148 or better,
plus humility, to get into Mensa

By Wm. M. Hall

What has been called the world's most exclusive club is also the most democratic. Who you are, what you believe, where you live, how you look, act, or feel, or whether you are a Nobel Prize winner or a clerk in a mattress factory has nothing whatsoever to do with the club's membership requirements.

Condensed from "Grit", 208 W. 3rd St., Williamsport, Pa. 17704. Jan. 8, 1967. ᶜ1967 by Grit Publishing Co., and reprinted with permission.

There is only one requirement: you must be smarter than 98 out of every 100 people and able to prove it. If you can qualify as being in the 2% of the world's population whose IQ rating is 148 or above on the Cattell Scale, you are wanted in this club.

This society is called Mensa. *Mensa* means "table" in Latin and signifies a round table meeting of equals. Most *M's* (as they call themselves) live in the U.S. and Canada. International headquarters are in London, where the society was organized in 1945. The first U.S. chapter was formed in New York City in 1960 and is still the largest in this country.

Mensa has no official position on politics, religion, economics or social welfare. Members range from a Negro mailman in the Bronx, New York City, to a white citizens' council leader in the South. In age *M's* range from an eight-year-old schoolboy with an IQ of 200 to an 80-year-old civil engineer. They include teachers, students, housewives, doctors, engineers, accountants, lawyers, writers, artists, actors, psychologists, and a score of other occupations.

Incomes range from a $70,000-a-year industrialist down to unemployed members with no income.

Mensa's primary purpose is research in psychology and social science. In addition, it affords a meeting place for intelligent persons. It permits an exchange of ideas through lectures, discussions, correspondence, and the publication of articles in the *Mensa Journal*.

The idea for Mensa originated with Sir Cyril Burt, professor of psychology at London university. Professor Burt suggested in a radio talk that a panel of highly intelligent people might prove useful to statesmen and other decision-making people. Professor Burt is now president of Mensa.

There are 100 local chapters of Mensa here and in Canada. They meet each month. In addition, many of them have informal discussions in homes, restaurants, or other places. Whether the subject is poetry, art, bridge, investments or Japanese chess, the discussions are always lively and in good humor, even though there is likely to be considerable disagreement.

"When I joined Mensa," said jovial, red-bearded Victor Serebriakoff, international secretary, "I thought, 'Now I am joining a bunch of bright people; therefore, everyone will agree with me.' Alas, this turned out not to be so. Then I married a member and began to discover the full extent of human disagreement."

A sawmill manager by trade and Shakespearean actor by hobby, Serebriakoff is the son of a British mother and

Russian-born father. He scored a 161 on the Cattell intelligence scale.

In England, the U.S., and Canada, Mensa groups hold annual gatherings. An International Annual Gathering (IAG), is held every two years.

Membership presents some hazards, as revealed by one *M*. "My boss got wind of the fact I'm a member, and he's not too happy. I have a suspicion he took the test and flunked it." At least one couple's divorce can be traced to Mensa. The wife sought membership and made it; the husband failed.

Though Mensa is made up of the most intelligent people in the world, it is not a society of snobs. They do not parade their superiority. Their only identifying mark is a small yellow-headed map pin which they wear when attending Mensa meetings. You are not likely to spot such a badge on the street.

Mensa President Burt thinks that mental differences are largely innate, thereby making a man's abilities mostly a matter of luck in the genetic lottery. Another *M* said, "It makes me humble to think of the millions of things I don't know." Still another said, "A high IQ is no cause for feeling superior. No one should be rewarded for his abilities, but only for the use he makes of them."

Mensa is concerned with research in human behavior and its effects on society. It is concerned with the nature of intelligence as it relates to creativity, education, and leadership. Mensa branches into many subjects: The development of more accurate methods of measuring intelligence; where, and in what way, does the opinion of the highly intelligent person fit? Can it have a formative influence on public opinion, anticipate, or change it?

In 1964, Mensa volunteers participated in 13 research projects, like sensory-deprivation study, a study on social attitudes, and the theory that people born at certain times of the year are more intelligent than others.

M's also offer their services as subjects for scientific investigations. Some Mensa groups have set up their own research projects, probing such problems as the gifted child and the mystery of creation. They are also polled by various research surveys, the idea being that the opinions of the superintelligent are valuable in determining trends.

According to Serebriakoff, "More than 7 million persons throughout the world, 4 million in the U.S. and another million in Britain, could qualify for membership in Mensa. We want to get as many of them as we can."

Approximately 75,000 persons inquire about Mensa every

year. More than 20,000 tests are given annually, and about 3,000 pass preliminary tests. Out of the 3,000 who pass, some 350 are accepted as members.

To Say I Love You

We all need to say it, and someone must take the plunge

By Maria Kavanagh

How long has it been since you said, "I love you?" Not only to that special person in your life, but to the other people you love—parents, brothers, sisters.

Little children find it easy to say, "I love you," especially if they have heard it said to them, and when they do we think it is sweet and charming. But somewhere along the years, it becomes more difficult, even painful, to say, until it is often dropped altogether.

Usually, this begins quite naturally. Along about six or seven, brothers and sisters begin to think they hate each other, and sometimes their parents, too. Any show of affection becomes completely taboo.

As the teen-ager attempts to break away from parental control, it becomes terribly important not to show his true feelings, particulary toward members of his own family, and especially when anyone else is around. Often he is not sure just what he is feeling. Parents who understand this wisely wait for their almost-adult child to begin to show affection again.

But, all too often, family members, or friends, drift toward life without ever telling one another that they love each other. One warm and loving person can shatter self-consciousness and self-involvement and open the door to love for many people. Love expressed has a way of spilling over, not only on the whole family but on everyone with whom the family comes in contact.

Often a family's customs can help its members express their love. One large family developed a way of saying good night that would have baffled any coding expert.

After the children had said good night to their parents, they

Condensed from "The Liguorian", Liguori, Mo. 63057. September, 1973. ʿ1973 by the Redemptorist Fathers, and reprinted with permission.

would go to their rooms to begin the evening's resistance to sleep. Giggles, talking, and jumping around would soon bring the expected voice from downstairs. After what they knew was the last ultimatum, one of the older children would be heard saying, "D-F-T-S-Y-P-A-G-N-F-T-L-T-A-D-I-S." And the answer would come, "S-T-Y." Translated this meant, "Don't forget to say your prayers and good night for the last time and do it soon." The answer was, "Same to you." As the younger children of the family became aware of the nightly sign-off, they wanted to get into the action, but were unable to cope with the long list of letters. So they developed their own response, "A-T-Y-T (And to you, too)."

They are far apart now. Some of them have children of their own. But when they do spend a night together, they still laughingly say good night in the same way.

Perhaps our troubles over expressing love for members of our families and for our friends stem from associating the words with romantic love. In some languages there are different words for different kinds of love, but in English, the moment we use other words, we move into different concepts.

Even in our translation of the Bible, we find the word *love* with many meanings. For example, the love in the Song of Songs is romantic love. Other parts of the Old Testament refer to the love between God and man. In the New Testament, there is a new tenderness in the love between God and man, and the concept of brotherly love becomes all-inclusive.

But there is one element common to all kinds of love. Love means caring. Love means everything a person is or does and everything that happens to him matters. Rollo May, the well-known psychologist, distinguishes care from sentimentality. He cites Tolstoy's example of the Russian ladies who cry at the theatre, but are oblivious to their own coachmen waiting outside in the freezing cold. He says, "Sentimentality glories in the fact that I have this emotion; it begins in my mind and ends there. Care is always caring about something. . . . In other words, we are involved, we feel we must act."

The atmosphere of our whole neighborhood changed a few years ago, when a new family moved into our block. While the neighbors had always been courteous and friendly, they were hardly close. The newcomers had been there only a few weeks when they happened to discover that Charlie (the oldest resident of the block, who lived all alone) was 84 that day. They quickly called everyone. Within a few hours the whole block appeared with cake, champagne, and little gifts to celebrate Charlie's birthday.

Charlie was overwhelmed. It had been years since he had had a birthday party. Not long after that, he became ill. Four months later he was dead. But he had lived a full and graceful life. He had died quickly and with dignity. Those of us who knew him had the satisfaction of knowing that for once we had not been too late in saying, "We love you."

We all like to be told we are loved. We need to be told. And we need to tell. We cannot simply say, "Of course they know I love them." As George Eliot wrote, "The realm of silence is large enough beyond the grave."

Someone must take the plunge. It may be the teen-ager who has brushed his mother and father aside so often they are hoping only that they will not be rebuffed again. Or it may be the parent who risks the rebuff.

If there has been a long silence of true feelings between you and your family, it may be easier to begin by writing a note when you are away from home. But you do not have to go away. Just lay the note on a pillow, or someplace where the family will be sure to find it.

An unexpected phone call when loved ones are ill or alone, or a voluntary helping hand says, "I care about you," in a language everyone understands.

Our culture has made it almost impossible for young boys to verbally express their love for their fathers, but there are ways of letting Dad know that he is a great guy. Words of admiration for something he has done, or shoveling that walk without being asked, are eloquent ways a boy can show that he cares.

The barriers that self-consciousness and embarrassment have built will not come down in a day, or even a week. But suddenly, after a continued effort, you may be surprised at what a difference saying, "I love you" is making in your whole life.

Who Killed Romance

A statement, not a question

By George Christy

Have you lately uttered the phrase "Isn't this romantic?"
Probably not. We are more likely to shout, "Isn't this super!"

Definitions of romance range from "any fictitious or wonderful tale" to "a dreamy, imaginative habit of mind tending
to dwell on the picturesquely unusual; as, "a girl full of
romance."

The experts who observe the nation's psychological moods
concur in the opinion that we have been living with a set of
romantic myths since this country was founded. Now the
myths are being challenged.

Dr. Standford Green, clinical psychologist, points out, "A
romantic myth that is changing is that of masculine man and
feminine woman. There is too much pressure from women
today to be thought of not as feminine but as fully competent
as man. I fully accept the idea that women are as good as
men, but I do not think they have to be the same." A good
point.

Dr. Green makes another point. Can a man be romantic if a
woman is right there alongside him proving her manhood?
Strange things are happening. In California not long ago a
woman won an equal-rights lawsuit to ride on the outside
ledge of San Francisco's cable cars (which, until then, ladies
were not permitted to do). Even newspaper want ads have
been altered in the light of male-female equal rights. No
longer is a job advertised directly to men or to women: "Help
wanted—Men." The old language has changed because of the
new laws to "Jobs of Interest—Men." In other words, men
might be more interested than women in these particular jobs,
but women are certainly free to apply. Do our American
women secretly yearn to be lumberjacks?

Power is seldom an ally to romance. Women own much of
the nation's wealth, are adored, worshiped, and publicized.

Condensed from "Town & Country", 717 5th Ave., New York City 10022, November, 1969.
©1969 by the Hearst Corp., and reprinted with permission.

Yet, writing in *Women, Society and Sex,* Marynia Farnham notes, "The more men and women are rivals, the less they are lovers. You cannot fuse these two pictures very easily. You cannot have, in any animal society that we know of, a situation in which there is not a position of dominance and a position of non-dominance. You cannot have two absolute equals in one home. Somewhere, somehow, there has to be a woman in the home who is a woman and a man in the home who is a man; and without that the children in the home have no parents. The more the woman intensifies her struggle to rival men, the more she will be hostile."

"Men and women used to fall in love, quarrel, kiss, and make up. Now no one 'falls in love,' " notes social observer Elaine Kendall. "Instead, people experience a mutual attraction that sometimes leads to an emotional involvement, which is hardly the same thing. At best it's self-conscious; at worst joyless." Miss Kendall thinks that "guilty parties in the death of romance are the avant-garde artists and writers: novels so explicit that no imagination is needed; electronic music to grit one's teeth by; plays that show life the 'way it really is' and then some—all are calculated to turn the wine in the air into vinegar." She finds it "hard to believe that this is the way everyone wants life to be. What is needed is less relationship and more romance. And songs that make you want to dance all night."

Women today in our double-time-paced society must be as agile as men to survive. "Who in our major cities," asks a Chicago psychologist, "has the time to be romantic, to savor the niceties; for all the moments that make life bearable?"

The love-historian Morton M. Hunt says, "Romance makes love no longer merely a game and sensuous delight, but a source of reassurance and genuine affection."

Others, too, believe that romance feeds human values. "When you lose a feeling for romance," says Dr. Green, "you may as well be dead. Healthy romance involves a young attitude throughout one's life, a joy in experimenting, a joy in finding out what strong feelings are all about. You experiment with fantasies about ways of getting along with people. Without this kind of experience, you can't develop as a human being. I pity the kids who don't take the time or won't risk dealing with fantasy. I pity anyone who wants only facts."

He adds that romance spawns good feelings, and good feelings make life and love and marriage endurable. "I like to think that we will arrive at another dimension of romance. Possibly more practical. Less neurotic. Look at history:

romance was always enjoyed by the rich and privileged. And, since we are one of the richest nations on earth, I hope we will find time to enjoy life more, to enjoy love more (and I am not referring to sex), to enjoy being human beings who can communicate with a smile, a glance, a touch of the hand. That is the noblest form of romance: quiet communication, in the mere look of an eye across a room. If we lose this, we have lost touch with humanity and are ready for robots to make love for us, for by then we will have become robots, too."

Three Words for Love

English uses one word for three very different things

By Fulton J. Sheen

Rightly it has been said that the Greeks had a word for it. They had three words for love.

The first was *eros*. That is generally what is meant by sex love; it is something biological, glandular, instinctive, emotional. It does not always distinguish between the pleasure and the person.

Often the wine can be drunk and the glass forgotten. *Eros* creates the illusion that there is deep affection for the other person, but what really happens is that the ego is projected into the other person. What is actually loved is the pleasure which the other person gives. The frosting on the cake is eaten but the cake is ignored.

Erotic love sometimes turns to hate. This could never be if the other person was really loved, because love would exist whether the other person reciprocated love or not. When the ego feels that it no longer is receiving the pleasure it expected, there develops a contempt on the grounds that one has been "cheated."

This is a very immature kind of love. That is why its sponsor, Cupid, is generally pictured as a child who has never grown up. When one reads of divorces after a few years of married life, one can be certain that it was an erotic love which was at its basis. As a Russian writer has so well put it, "If unreciprocated love is hard on the heart, sometimes reciprocated love can be worse."

Condensed from "The Power of Love", ⸀1964 by Maco Magazine Corp., 757 3rd Ave., New York City 10017, and reprinted by permission, 96 pp. 60c paper.

The second Greek word for love is *philia.* This is the kind of love which exists both in friendship and in marriage. In erotic love, the other person is replaceable; in *philia,* the other is irreplaceable.

Philia is based on some kind of community of feeling, interest, or service. The intellect rather than the glands dominates the affections. This was the kind of love that Damon had for Pythias, that made Jacob serve seven years to win the heart of Rachel, that a wife like Elizabeth Barrett Browning expresses for her husband: *I love thee with the breath, smiles, tears of all my life!/And, if God choose, I shall but love thee better after death.*

The third word for love was not much used in classical Greek; it was a love so noble and divine that Christianity alone made it popular. That word is *agape.*

The Greeks did not need such a word because Plato held that there could be no real love between God and man, inasmuch as the gods, being perfect, desired nothing; therefore, they had no love for man. Aristotle argued the same way. He said that there was too great a disproportion between man and God for any love to exist.

When God sent his only Son to this world to save it, then was born a love between God and man which the Greeks could not and did not understand.

That kind of love was best expressed by *agape.* In contrast to it, the word *eros* is nowhere found in the New Testament; the word *philia* is found 45 times, but the word *agape* is found 320 times.

Once *agape* began to exist, then if flowed down to illumine even the *eros. Eros* became the sensible expression of the divine love; fraternal and friendly love was also sanctified by the *agape* inasmuch as we were to regard everyone else as better than ourselves. The only true lovers or friends are those whose love is explained by the *agape* of Him who so loved the world He sent his only begotton Son to redeem it.

Chapter IV
The Ages of Man

"Had youth but knowledge; had age but strength." "Grow old along with me, the best is yet to be." English literature is full of psychological reflections on the differences in people at different stages of life. Shakespeare did it best when he recounted his seven ages of man—from the infant mewling and puking in his nurse's arms to the old sans teeth, sans eyes, sans taste, sans everything. A book of this size can only indicate what science has to say on so enormous a subject but this chapter tries in a rough way to follow the course of human reactions from their beginnings to their end on this earth.

The Lady Who Invented Finger Painting

"It is automatic psychotherapy," says Ruth Shaw

By Anne Siegle

Miss Ruth Faison Shaw, a frail but lively woman who is now consultant at the department of psychiatry at the University of North Carolina, invented finger painting. She developed the technique in 1929 while teaching at a school she had founded in Rome.

One of her students, a little Italian prince, cut his finger, went to the bathroom for iodine, and failed to return. Miss Shaw went to get him, and found him streaking the wall with a finger dripping in blood and iodine. Unabashed, he told her he wasn't a bit sorry and didn't care if he was punished. He had always wanted to smear, he said, and it had turned out to be just as much fun as he had thought it would be. The other children, caught up with the idea, wanted to join in the fun.

Well, maybe they should, Miss Shaw thought. And maybe they could if she could figure out an alternative to blood and iodine. As far as she knew, all coloring materials contained lead or arsenic, and had to be thinned with turpentine.

The problem was solved by the man who came to repaint the disfigured bathroom wall. He carried squills of newspaper that contained earth pigments to mix with his basic paint. The pigments were the same as those used by da Vinci and Michelangelo. All were harmless.

A suitable base was found by more luck. A young priest, who taught her pupils Latin, handed Miss Shaw a recipe for a colorless beauty lotion compounded by Caesar's alchemists for Cleopatra. He had come across it in the Vatican library while browsing through some ancient cookbooks. It might just do the trick thought Miss Shaw, and she set about preparing a batch. The result didn't quite duplicate the original. She had to make do with substitutes for "essence of palm tree" and "honey with mountain snow cooked seven

Condensed from the "SK&K Psychiatric Reporter", 1500 Spring Garden St., Philadelphia, Pa. 19101. July and August, 1967. ᶜ1967 by Smith Kline & French Laboratories, and reprinted with permission.

times in ass's milk," but the result was fine: a colorless, edible substance that had the feel of thin mud, only "nicer." Finger painting was born.

It was an instantaneous success. The paintings not only were fun for the children to make but seemed to make some unexpected changes in their behavior. Stammerers began to speak more easily; chronic bed wetters were cured; and the boy with a serious reading difficulty was soon teaching younger children to read.

Miss Shaw's discovery changed her life. As news of the technique spread, educators, painters, psychiatrists, journalists began appearing at the small school to learn more about it. She was invited to lecture at the Sorbonne, and soon found herself giving demonstrations all over Europe. In 1932 she returned to America, taught at the Dalton school in New York, and opened the Shaw Finger Paint studio. She wrote books and articles about finger painting, acted as a consultant to psychiatrists, psychologists, and teachers, and gave demonstrations to schools and hospitals. In 1959, she returned to North Carolina to begin her affiliation with the university.

She told me, "Soon after I began letting the children smear—it was one of them, by the way, who coined the term *finger painting*—I realized it would be presumptuous of me to assume that what I saw in a child's picture was just what *he* meant to say. So I would have the child tell me about the picture. It might not look to me like what he said it was."

The same colors and symbols, she found, not only meant different things to different persons, but also to the same person at different times. Even so, certain colors and symbols did seem to have more or less universal meanings.

"That subject fascinates me," Miss Shaw said, "but please don't take anything I say about it as being necessarily true for any one case. And at best these things are useful only as clues."

Some other clues: blue is the favorite of boys; red, of girls. Yellow is also a favorite color of girls; green is a favorite with many intelligent children, particularly boys.

"When I see a little boy wallowing in red, I look for, and almost always find, a dominating mother. After a while, he may experiment with adding other colors, find out that when he adds green it 'kills' the red, turns it to gray. This symbolic killing usually gives him great satisfaction. For a while, gray may be his favorite color, used over and over again.

"Otto Rank once told me that red, most girls' favorite color, has been used throughout history to represent female forms. Babylonians used it that way, for example. Girls who are very fond of yellow are usually coquettish, very conscious of boys. Did you know Mae West was a finger painter? She painted almost exclusively in yellow."

Miss Shaw went on to say that purple is often the choice of people with serious sexual conflicts. Black used alone seems to indicate fear, insecurity, or guilt. Used with other colors, it often indicates depression. Potential suicides, no matter what colors they use, generally add black.

The repetition of various symbols may also furnish clues. Drawings of mazes seem to indicate deep, often sexual, conflicts; drawings of eyes, guilt feelings and fear of being spied on. Potential suicides often draw boxes endlessly or draw a strong central object, perhaps a tree, menaced by other objects such as pistols, sticks, swords. Sometimes the central figure is Christ on the cross, and the figure will be erased and redrawn again and again, getting smaller each time.

"Have you come across many tendencies that reveal suicidal tendencies?" I asked.

"Yes, and that is always frightening. There was one tragic case I will never forget. I was teaching the technique to a group of young psychiatric residents, and one young man kept drawing a single, centrally placed apple tree with an equal number of apples on each side of it. One day he drew a sharp limb coming from the tree and after several similar pictures, someone hanging from the limb. I was upset, and told his supervisor about it. But the resident seemed well enough by other standards, so nothing was done. When he set up practice, he bought a farm with an apple orchard. Six years later, he was found hanging from one of the trees."

I asked, "If finger painting is a form of psychotherapy, isn't there danger in letting teachers unschooled in psychotherapy use it with children?"

"No, all you have to do is accept what the child is doing. We all have our monsters. If you let the child draw his, let him kill his teacher or father, he doesn't have to tell you about it, and you don't have to give him any advice. Apparently the symbolic act itself is enough to help correct harmful emotional experiences. You don't have to be a psychotherapist. The psychotherapy is automatic."

Yes—But . . . .

*The Christian virtue of hope has practical
application in a hard-boiled world*

By Pearl Buck

Change is the environment of a child, and unless he learns to enjoy change, his own and that of the world about him, he will be filled with fear. Yet his security depends on freedom from fear!

May I suggest a solution, one which in my own lengthening life I have found to be true? It is the "yes-but" technique: that of find the positives to offset the negatives of life.

Truth and decisions can be arrived at only through examination of alternatives. In a country where everyone has the right to express his opinion there is always a yes-but. It is well for a child to realize that what appears in the press bears the bias of editorial opinion and reflects the need for money. For example, if a child is asked to read and report on the news as *Time* magazine gives it, the yes-but might be *Newsweek* or the *Wall Street Journal*.

The same yes-but approach can be used after reading a book, in discussions, in presentations of every subject. The voice that cries out against the evil ways of present-day young people must be measured against the yes-but of figures that report delinquency among a really low percentage of a certain group. Most young people are as fine a lot as our nation has ever seen.

Children catch fears from what they hear their elders talk about or how they see them react. Impassioned arguments about food and water shortages fill the minds of even young children, and they picture a future in which they may not have enough to eat and drink. The yes-but of this situation is easy. A child should know that, according to agricultural scientists, if we really farm our land as well as people do in the small countries of Belgium and Holland, we can feed ten times the present number of people now on earth! This is not

Condensed from the "Instructor", Instructor Park, Dansville, N.Y. 14337. October 1966, as reprinted in the "Education Digest." 416 Longshore Dr., Ann Arbor, Mich. 48107. December, 1966. ⓒ1966 and reprinted with permission of F. A. Owen Publishing Co.

to mention the millions of acres which are not now producing food at all, or the food to be had from chemicals and from the sea.

Since food can always be plentiful if we work for it, we need not worry about overpopulation. As the undeveloped countries improve their schools, and the world's people acquire more education, the earth's population will cease to explode.

As for shortage of water, the yes-but is that we have not begun to tap our sources of water. Desalinization of the sea is now practical. Deserts are not totally dry; even under the Sahara there is an enormous amount of ground water. It will be pumped up and once again the desert will bloom as it did in past ages. Then, too, we know how to purify water so that it can be used over and over. And we are learning ways of increasing rainfall by seeding clouds with chemicals.

Is there a yes-but to war? Certainly! There are many. It is better to stop a war before it begins, and the best way to accomplish this is to study history and find out why people reach the point of fighting. War is like a sickness. If one discovers what causes it, one can find first a cure and finally a prevention. Some day there will be no more war.

Switzerland and Sweden never go to war. They know better. Sweden used to be a very warlike country. The Swedes kept a bigger and bigger army until at last there were not people enough at home to support the soldiers. Then the Swedish people decided that war was stupid. A hundred years ago they decided never to fight another war, and they never have. The day will come when people will learn how to get along, first by understanding each other's points of view, and next by coming to an agreement. Children who learn to try to understand and agree instead of fighting will become sensible grown people who will seek other means than war to solve their problems.

Some children these days worry about getting into college. The yes-but here is that not all people should go the same colleges. There are many kinds of schools, and somewhere there is a school to fit each individual need, or there soon will be if people work at it. But going to school does not complete one's education. School should merely teach people how to learn. The important thing is to keep on learning as long as you live. The one thing that is indispensable for the educated person is to enjoy learning.

There is a yes-but to every fear, even to the fear of death! It is right and natural for children and young persons to be afraid of death. That is nature's way of making them want to stay on earth until their work is done. But when old age draws near, the fear gradually fades away.

Old persons have their own yes-but. What lies beyond this life? It will be exciting to find out when the time comes.

If people keep their minds alive, if they realize there is always a yes-but to help them, if they are willing to work in the direction it points out, then there is a solution to every problem, a relief for every fear.

You and Your Brothers and Sisters

If any

By Ethel Kaplan

Were you an only child? The eldest? The youngest? To find an important key to your personality, take this simple test.

1. When I was a child, I enjoyed going to school. Yes/No.

2. My parents helped me make most of the decisions in my life. Yes/No.

3. My family and friends think I'm too ambitious and work too hard. Yes/No.

4. I worry a lot and am easily depressed. Yes/No.

5. When things happen to go wrong, I prefer to be alone. Yes/No.

6. I tend to resent restrictions and circumvent them when I can. Yes/No.

7. I enjoy being with people who are considered to be unconventional. Yes/No.

8. I enjoy large cocktail parties where I can meet new people. Yes/No.

Eldest and only children tend to answer Yes to the first four statements and No to the last four. For younger children, the pattern is reversed.

A second child is usually unlike the first. In the struggle to assert himself against his rival, each child develops merits corresponding to the other's faults. Untidiness and neatness, sentimentality and matter-of-factness, gentleness and brutality are some of the contrasts. Two sets of Biblical brothers, Cain-Abel and Jacob-Esau, illustrate sibling rivalry and the different personalities it produces.

Condensed from "Science Digest", 1775 Broadway, New York City 10019. February, 1967. ‹1967 by the Hearst Corp., 959 8th Ave., New York City, and reprinted with permission.

"How can two children born of the same parents and raised in the same environment be so different?" a parent may ask. But no two children have the same environment. The second child has parents who are older and more experienced. They may be richer or poorer than when the first child was born, sicker or healthier, more or less preoccupied. One child has an older sibling and the other a younger one, so they grow up in different environments.

After being the center of attention the first-born finds himself dethroned by the new baby. According to psychiatrist Alfred Adler, this traumatic experience turns the first-born into a power-hungry conservative. His desire to be in control shows first in his protective behavior toward the younger one. But this tendency to shield and guide may reflect a desire to keep the younger child subordinate.

Why are first-borns conservative? "The mothering of a first-born child is usually a more tenser process than the mothering of a second," says psychiatrist Irving Harris. Because eldest children are closer to their parents, they are more likely to adopt the parents' attitudes.

Eldest children also tend to be worriers. Moreover, when they feel anxious, they like companionship, whereas a later-born child prefers to face stress alone. But the first-born's greater need for others is not always a handicap. It helps him to work in a group and he frequently becomes a leader.

First children usually have a highly developed moral sense. Suppose that a mother, before leaving home, tells her two sons not to dip into the cookie jar. The younger son, eager for a cookie, is likely to disobey. But the older son, anxious to please his mother and his conscience, will resist temptation.

Because first sons are closer to their mothers, as adults they tend to develop more intense feelings about women, and to romaticize them. Later sons tend to think one woman is not different from another.

First-born speak earlier and better than later-borns, perhaps because in childhood they converse mostly with adults. Greater verbal ability helps the first-born do well in school. But other influences are also involved, says Dr. William Altus. "His curiosity, dependence upon adults, and greater conscience development make him respond better." First-borns continue in school longer than longer than later-borns do; they are over-represented in college populations.

Verbal ability, academic interest and drive to succeed are traits which explain why eldest children often become famous. Although in the general population later-borns outnumber first-borns almost two to one, in more lists of prominent people (such as *Who's Who*) first-borns are in the majority. Eldest children often achieve enough success to impress their parents and associates, but seldom satisfy their own ambitions.

Like eldest children, only children tend to be serious, ambitious, conservative, conventional, moralistic. The only child will probably feel even greater pressure to conform to adult expectations and succeed because he is the center of his parents' lives.

The only child does not escape rivalry or stress. He competes immensely with his father for his mother's attention. (A girl competes with her mother for her father's attention.) The three-member home may become a battleground on which the parents fight each other for the child's love while the child plays one against the other.

Mothers tend to pamper only children, which makes them dependent and timid. Then, too, the one-child family provides no opportunity for the youngster to learn to share the limelight or compete for it.

The only child may find himself at a loss when he goes out into the world (even into kindergarten) and discovers that he is not automatically the center of attention. Parents should send only children to nursery school or place them in other situations where they will be forced to compete and cooperate with other children.

The later-born child is more likely to be an individualist, less concerned about parental or peer-group approval. Because parents are busier and more confident when raising a later-born child, they are more permissive with him and less attentive. The younger child grows up more self-sufficient but also perhaps resentful of having been slighted. Anthropologist Margaret Lantis describes two quite common later-born personality patterns: "He is likely to be either placid, easygoing, cheerful, friendly, or else stubborn, rebellious, independent. What these two patterns have in common is indifference to adult scolding and relative isolation from adults."

Whether it is the first haircut, the first day of kindergarten, the first date or the final exam, facing the unknown is easier for a later-born. He has lived it all vicariously with the older child, and the possibility of failure bothers him less.

"Middle children tend to feel that life is unfair," says Dr. Rudolf Dreikurs. After all, the middle child is not pampered as the baby of the family nor honored as the first-born. But the birth of a new baby is less traumatic for a second child than for a first because a middle child cannot be the only youngster in the family. Also, the middle child is seldom spoiled by the smothering attention that parents may lavish upon an only child or a youngest. Somehow middle children withstand the pressures from both sides and grow up with no more psychological injuries than the others.

The baby of the family escapes the unpleasant experience of dethronement but has many pacemakers to chase. "Because he is so much stimulated and has so many chances for competition, he often runs faster than the other children and overcomes them all," says Adler, and he reminds us of Joseph, David and Saul in the Bible.

Sometimes a youngest child will have difficulty settling upon a single ambition because he wishes to excel in everything. If he scatters his energies, he is unlikely to achieve as much as the first-born. Some youngest children feel inferior because everyone else is older, stronger, and has more experience. Most tragic of all is the pampered youngest child who is content to remain all his life the petted and protected baby of the family.

If a big gap exists between two youngsters, both may develop like only children. Other environmental factors (age, sex, number of siblings, and socio-economic states of parents) also affect personality.

There is no ideal family size, no ideal spacing between children. Every family constellation has his own problems. What is most important is the parents' awareness of how each child interprets his own situation within the family. Remember that the first child is more likely to be "good": obedient at home, conscientious about schoolwork, eager to please. He is also more likely to be bookish, timid, frightened of new situations. It is futile to advise the typical first-born child to relax and stop worrying. He takes life seriously, and if rebuked for this, he will only tend to worry more, because he is extremely sensitive to criticism.

A later-born child is less eager to fulfill adult expectations. Never urge him to "be a good boy like your big brother." The more parents indicate displeasure with his behavior, the more likely he is to rebel against them, or perhaps ignore them.

Although the later-born is less frequently frightened and worried, when he does become anxious, he is more likely to go off by himself than to seek adult support. Parents should not expect a later-born to confide in and consult with them as much as his elder brother did. Nagging a later-born child about being secretive will only encourage him to be more so. Take an interest in whatever he chooses to share, but don't demand to know more than he wants to tell.

You Can Keep Your Youth

The clues are moderation and zest for life

By Barbara Croft

Many a woman who got straight *A's* in school and showed a special flair in art or music has felt after her marriage that she's mentally vegetating. Her "housewife" complex has convinced her that she is probably unable to hold a job or take a responsible position in a volunteer group. The idea that she can be as competent as a business executive would astonish her. Dr. Ward C. Halstead, professor of psychology and medicine at the University of Chicago, has confirmed that many housewives are younger, mentally, than they feel or the calendar tells them.

The only price for youth is that we use our brains to capacity. People who keep alert often don't show signs of aging before their 80's.

Dr. Halstead was struck by two facts: brain power doesn't necessarily deteriorate with age; education, economic background, and experience don't always give people greater brain power. "Stretch your brain by giving it more to do," he urges. "Be a person with a purpose, meeting a challenge."

The key word is *purpose.* The best brain in the world is valueless until it's used. The housewife can be assured that her brain isn't deteriorating only if she really uses it. Says Dr. Halstead, "It doesn't really matter what the goal is, as long as you're enthusiastic about it. Creative cookery is just as creative as mixing chemicals.

"You have only to look around to see where your interests can match human need. The best defense against aging is to start early to develop creativity.

"The facts show that those who remain mentally active will often be much younger than their years."

With more women returning to employment after their child-bearing days, it's comforting to learn that though we may be academically rusty, the quality of our brain may be unimpaired. Education for older persons and "intellectual

Condensed from "Chatelaine", 481 University Ave., Toronto 2, Ont., Canada. August, 1964.
©1964 by Maclean-Hunter Publishing Co., Ltd., and reprinted with permission.

rust-proofing" courses are available for younger women with families.

People have always searched for a way to stay young. Some seem to have a source of vitality unknown to others. Grandma Moses danced a jig on her 100th birthday. Chancellor Konrad Adenauer reluctantly retired at 87. Titian was cheerfully painting when past 90. Improvement in medicine, diet, and sanitation have increased life expectancy, but nobody has yet actually prolonged life.

Scientists are trying to find out what happens as the body cells age and disappear. Clive M. McCay, research scientist at Cornell university, fed rats a diet adequate in all but calories. Lean, always a little hungry, and smaller than their well-fed brothers, these rats stayed healthy. Does this mean we'd be likely to live longer if we always went a little hungry? Probably. Doctors say it's better to undereat than overeat.

Does the body degenerate because something harmful accumulates or because something vital gradually disappears? There is a "planned obsolescence of the human body. You don't hear as well after you're ten. Your eyes start to deteriorate not much later. After you're 25, your muscular system isn't as good as it used to be. You lost some of your sense of taste around 50, some of your sense of smell around 60.

A Gallup Poll report covered 402 persons across the U.S. over 95 years of age, including 152 men and women in the correct male-female ratio. The pattern which emerged showed moderation in everything, zest for life, serenity. Heredity appeared to be a factor.

The "rules" that came out of Gallup study were simple: Don't be fussy about food, and never, never overeat. Don't worry. Work at a job you love. Be sure to get lots of exercise. And sleep — 85% of the people in the study had at least eight hours of sleep each night. The important common denominator really wasn't their record age; it was the zest they had for life.

You'll feel younger and more energetic if you observe the good-diet rules. What you eat is less important than how much. Or how little. A light but nourishing breakfast will keep you younger than the quick-lift quick-letdown tea-and-toast racket. Fresh fruit and vegetables are more youth-retaining than candy and cookies.

Insurance companies in the U.S. and Canada found that, of 6 million men in their 20's, at least 10% were overweight. In the 30-40 age group the figure had gone up to 20%. In the age group group 40-69, the one third whose weight was 10%

over the normal were running an increased risk of death. Overweight puts a heavy strain on the heart, arteries, and kidneys. The report also indicated that the risk to health is reduced as weight is reduced.

Since we have a body that wears out, it's up to us to make it last. The difference between beneficial exercise and exhausting expenditure of energy is good organization of work and rest periods. Develop a creative interest in whatever you have to do, or find something that absorbs you.

Keeping busy doesn't mean cramming every minute with activity. When the late Al Smith found his schedule crowding him he would announce, "I have a previous date with myself," and retire to his office for a short rest.

"The greatest single obstacle in the way of successful aging, writes biochemist Robert de Ropp, "is lack of challenge."

Here are 23 ways to be younger than you are.

1. Collect something or make a scrapbook.
2. Enroll in a night-school course or read a biography of someone you know by name only.
3. Work for the Red Cross or missions.
4. Buy a magazine you've never read before, or see a foreign movie.
5. Make an effort to meet someone you don't know, at church or club.
6. Shop at a different store.
7. Dress a doll in a national costume.
8. Track down full titles of "initials" organizations (NATO, SEATO, SAC, FAO, etc.) and find out what they do.
9. Get curious about mythology or find out how ordinary people lived in the Middle Ages. Consult your library.
10. Track down the origin of 20 words on this page.
11. Pick a book "blind" from your library shelves every month.
12. Pick a country and read everything you can about it.
13. Write the history of your local church, city hall, oldest buildings, or your own family.
14. Volunteer for the next church or club job to come up.
15. Learn to identify dogs, flowers, trees, or become an authority on something.
16. Discover what the UN Commission on the Status of Women is doing.
17. Study flower arranging or make a miniature garden.
18. Go to a city-council meeting.
19. Collect pictures and thumbnail sketches of current world leaders.
20. Dine at a different restaurant once a month.

21. Take a walk turning left, then right, at each alternate corner.
22. Grow plants from orange pips, sweet potatoes, avocado seeds, carrot tops.
23. Try one new household hint from every magazine you see.

Over the Hill at 40?

"Nonsense!" say the experts

Many men over 40 underestimate the toughness of the human body and fail to use the vigor they possess. Some men increase their sleep after 40 until it becomes enervating. The man who gets more than eight hours of sleep is likely to have less energy than one who gets less sleep.

There is no physiological basis for the so-called male change of life.

A man's capacity to handle liquor diminishes after 40, and some men develop a reaction to alcohol that is almost an allergy.

Frustrations and tensions are responsible for as many heart patients as ulcer patients.

These are conclusions of a panel of authorities at the University of California. Four experts who took a look at the general health of middle-aged men pointed out that the middle years are relatively disease free for most men. Middle age should be, according to them, the prime of life, a pleasant plateau from which one can handle his problems and pleasures with full appreciation of his capabilities.

There are no significant changes in the organs of a middle-aged male. Unless he has a history of heart complications, the few cardiovascular changes that occur before 55 will not limit his physical activity. There are no important changes in the function of the thyroid and adrenal glands, and the secretion rate of cortisone and its level in the blood remains stable.

Yet there is a high rate of suicide, divorce, breakdown, and

Condensed from the "University of California Clip Sheet", 131 University Hall, Berkeley, Calif. 74240. ©1966 by the University of California, and reprinted with permission.

neurotic behavior in men between 40 and 55. Do they undergo unknown functional changes? Do they set their standards too high? Can they avoid bad behavior symptoms that appear after 40?

Answers to these questions have come from UCLA authorities on both the foibles and the fortitudes of men in the middle years. As a psychiatrist, Dr. Charles Wahl is familiar with their behavior patterns. As a physician specializing in cardiology, Dr. Harold Bernstein knows how behavior can affect vital organs. As an endocrinologist, Dr. Josiah Brown is an authority on how aging affects the glands. Dr. Laurence. E. Morehouse is a professor of physical education who knows how the body responds to exercise and recreation. These experts are all concerned about the middle-aged man's tendency to overdo. Dr. Bernstein says that sluggish circulation brought on by too much bed rest is a real health hazard in middle age. Overdependence on medication is another extreme. Looking for quick panaceas in the medicine cabinet is increasingly commmon after 40; and indiscriminate self-treatment can do great harm.

According to Dr. Morehouse, even suppplemental vitamins are superfluous for the man who eats a variety of foods every day. Some men of middle years go overboard in selecting certain foods and avoiding others. High-cholesterol in the average daily diet is no threat to the cardiovascular system of the normal middle-aged man. Dr. Morehouse feels that emotional tension is more important than diet in increasing the amount of cholesterol in the blood. "There's no reason why a two-egg breakfast should hurt an active man in good physical condition," he says.

Obesity, however, *is* bad. "Consider," says Dr. Wahl, "how few really obese people you see over 60 years of age." He calls overeating one of the chief hazards of middle age. Assuming that the older man is less active than the younger, he maintains that the caloric intake of men 40-55 should be one third less than that of males between 25 and 40.

Both the psychiatrist and the heart specialist found the effects of alcohol injurious to men who over-indulge during middle age. Dr. Bernstein said that both liquor and strong stimulants are dangerous if used as substitutes for rest and recreation.

Dr. Brown, the endocrinologist, noted that a great number of men achieve a lifelong goal at this age, one which they have worked hard and aggressively to attain. They assume added responsibilities in becoming sales manager, dean, or supervisor. To retain their status, they devote practically all their time and psychic energy to the job.

Dr. Wahl pointed out that some men tend to blame all sorts of symptoms—forgetfulness, self-doubt, worry, depression — on a mythical male menopause. These symptoms are of psychic origin, he insists.

The fossilized executive is a headache to his business colleagues as well as to his family, for he becomes unable to adapt to any change. His rigid viewpoints are the despair of his associates, for he cannot adjust to new ideas or new methods. For him, Dr. Wahl suggests contacts with new people outside the family and usual social circles, or a simple adventure like trying a new restaurant. It is curiosity, he emphasized, that keeps us from becoming prematurely ossified.

Many a middle-aged man feels old when his children leave the household. The void often creates a gap between man and wife. A man may suddenly discover that he cannot even talk with his wife.

All of these reactions to middle age represent character patterns familiar to every psychiatrist, says Dr. Wahl, but none of the responses can be attributed to mere physical change.

Many men over 40 fight their own fitness. One of the greatest dangers is falling into sedentary ways, either because of job confinement or sheer laziness. All of the panel members agreed on the importance of physical recreation, pointing out that before 40, a man exercises to better his performance, but that after 40, he exercises to better his chances for survival.

What is the proper amount and type of exercise for a middle-aged man? Dr. Morehouse says that the male approaching 40 should do two things. First, if he is not reasonably adept at bowling, golf, tennis, or swimming, he should take instruction in some form of physical recreation. Second, he should take an inventory of his physical activity in the course of his regular dialy schedule. He should look at his occupation, such chores as gardening and maintaining the home, his sports activity, and what he is doing in the way of calisthenics, to see if he is getting enough activity.

Start walking more, but don't settle for a window-shopping stroll. Take a brisk posture walk holding the belt line level and raising the breastbone. Then start devoting part of your weekend to a pleasant physical activity like golfing, bowling, dancing, or swimming. Ten minutes of regular exercise every other day produce noticeable results.

The sagging, dragging middle-ager will begin to exhibit a total change in his attitude. He will enjoy his meals more and show more interest in his home. Even his physical appearance will improve.

Move around, but do not rush around. Keep an open mind and a closed refrigerator. The man who pursues many activities, balancing work with play, will stay fit long after middle age.

I'm Glad I'm 60

Do you think youth is the happiest age?
Think again

By Thyrza Funk

I never thought the day would come when I would go past 60 and say, "I'm glad I'm here!" Do I want to be child again? Not me.

Childhood. The happiness of childhood is a fat myth. The pains of a child can be as bad as rheumatism. I remember waiting for my first date with the dentist. I was the youngest of seven. The others all had teeth drilled. For a whole week, I listened to their stories and writhed in pain.

A children's party is supposed to be the height of happiness. My six-year-old friend Elsie had a birthday party. She was the daughter of the town banker. In New York City Elsie would have been the first of the 400. The day of the party, after a middle-of-the-week bath, I was dressed in Sunday clothes and pinned to the corner of a clean white handkerchief. I carried another hanky all gussied up with crocheted edging and wrapped in tissue paper. That was the present for Elsie. With my ground crew milling tensely around, I was blasted off the launching pad for my solo trip into society.

I flew around the block. I could see some people at the door, so I went on past the front walk. I walked a few million miles back and forth, trying to make my speeches. Agonies of childbirth are nothing compared to the suffering of the next half hour. The sun came in the form of Elsie's father. Tall, dignified, with a generous black mustache, he had always seemed unapproachable. But today he took my hand in his, and before I knew it I was in.

Condensed from the "St. Anthony Messenger", 1915 Republic St., Cincinnati, Ohio, 45210. April, 1966. ©1966 by the Franciscan Fathers of St. John the Baptist Province, and reprinted with permission.

Now that I am 60, I know that doors of gold swing both ways. When I have to face up to a roomful of strangers who are smarter, richer, older, or younger than I, my heart still pounds, but now it is with the excitement of adventure and not from fear. At 60, I can enjoy differences.

Teen-age. Persons in the second decade of life are also victims of the old saw that only the young are happy. "They're only young once. Let them have a good time. Soon they'll be unhappy over jobs, taxes, war, and setting a good example for their children." Not many parents are as wise as the cartoon father of the teen-ager about to leave for a date. He says, "Sure, I was young once. That's *why* I say you have to be home at 11 o'clock."

Talk to young people in groups, and you are sure that their problems are unimportant. But talk to them confidentially, and you will learn that they have their share of unhappiness.

When teen-agers are asked what they think is the happiest part of life, their answer is always, "The 20's. Then you're free to choose all the fun things yourself. Then you have made all the pesky decisions about military service, and jobs, and getting married."

A teen-age girl is like no other. Nobody loves her except her mother. Between her giggles and her pouts, sometimes even her mother has doubts.

"What do you think of your chances of being happy when you're 60?" I asked several teen-agers. The response to that question was exactly what mine would have been at that age, "Ugh!" The consensus was that 60 was strictly Dullsville.

20's. Youth looks forward to his 20's as his chance to adjust one planet to its correct orbit. I never want to repeat the experience of realizing that I did not know everything. I'm glad I'm 60!

30's. "Which decade of *your* life was the best?" I asked a friend. There was no hesitation to her answer. "In my 30's. When the boys were small. I was needed. That was the best."

I reminded her of the time her eldest son was asked by his kindergarten teacher if he lived far from school. "Oh, no," he said. "It doesn't take anytime to get home. Every day mother says, "Goodness! Are you home *already!*"

40's. After I plucked from my dark hair the first 100 hairs that shone like headlights in the night (the first 100 white hairs are the hardest), I decided I would have to fight the 40's some other way. So I asked my doctor what advice he could give me to help me through the Desperate Years. "Go home and act natural," he snapped. And I did.

Today I can have any color hair I choose without the usual

step of removing the color before dyeing. But I'm too busy to dye. I'm glad I'm 60!

50's. And what about the 50's? I know one woman who can't enjoy her 50's because they lead straight into the 60's. She begins each day by reading the vital statistics in the morning paper. She worries about eternity, but she suffers from emptiness when the rain cancels the Women's club garden party. She wastes hours feeling sorry for herself, which is like a run in your hose; it always gets worse!

60's. And I'm glad. There never has been a time when I have enjoyed such freedom. Teen-agers look forward to the 20's so they can be free. A convict in the Joliet State penitentiary escaped to freedom by climbing the ladder to the catwalk around the water tower. The warden refused to endanger anyone's life by sending a guard up after him. Maybe I'm at the Top of the Tower with no place to go but up.

But I am free to read what and when I want to. Never again will I plod through great blocks of black print without any gossipy "he said's," just because it was assigned.

Recently I spent one whole day dusting our books, after years of hurriedly vacuuming the bookcases five minutes before the guests arrived. I never dared to let one book fall open or I would get caught reading instead of cooking.

Another choice that makes my age the best is that of volunteer work that is really volunteer work. There is nothing that can make a person feel so rich as to do some worth-while work regularly without pay in dollars. Every decade brought its special demands along that line. There were PTA, Campfire, Sunday school, community beautification, and all such. I was official Blockhead during the war. I was liaison agent for collections of grease, newspapers, tin cans, and scrap rubber. I hated all the volunteer jobs that required doorbell ringing and selling tickets, except the Mothers' March of Dimes. The spirit I met at every door was the same as in Thailand. There the householder who puts rice into the begging bowl of a Buddhist monk also thanks him for the opportuntiy to serve the cause.

Recently, I read about Nancy Malinosky, top student in a class of 397 graduating seniors at Baldwin Wallace college. A polio victim, she had spent 15 of 21 years confined to a wheel chair. But after practicing secretly for six months, she arose when her name was called, and walked alone to receive her diploma from the president. I'm glad I lived to see polio conquered.

The derring-do of the 60's differs from that of the 20's. When you are older you know you don't always have a choice of weapons for improving the world. Sometimes you have to use a frying pan, map, or doorbell you hate to ring.

Lately, I've been saying a flat No to requests to do volunteer work. Here is a secret fact of life I hope no woman ever reads until she's 60: the first No was the hardest.

Not so long ago, I read of a newsman for BBC who retired to the Greek island of Corfu. There he is helping both the English and the natives with their English. Well into his 60's, he says, "I'm happier than I've ever been in my life."

I enjoy the company of creative people because they make my feel so young. I'm 60 going on 70. That has the same sound of music as 16 going on 17.

Senility is Also a State of Mind

Not all the forgetfulness of the aged is caused by physical disease

By Douglas S. Looney

Forget everything you ever thought you knew about senility, that terrible trick of the mind that makes us foolish when we grow old. Nature, it seems, may have precious little to do with our aging brains going into eclipse. There is growing evidence that senility may be avoidable, and even reversible.

The answer lies not so much in miracle drugs, although a breakthrough there may someday help; not so much in treatment, although several methods appear to be helping. More than anything, it lies in establishing your own strong psychological defenses against it.

"Senility is an invention of modern Western society," says the State Communities Aid Assn. of New York city and Buffalo. "It is one of the most damaging self-filling prophecies ever devised."

Senility is one or more of a lot of shortcomings as we grow older: impairment of orientation, memory, intellectual func-

Condensed from "The National Observer", 11501 Columbia Pike, Silver Spring, Md. 20910. March 31, 1973. ⟨1973 by Dow Jones & Co., Inc., and reprinted with permission.

tion (including comprehension and calculation), and judgment. Its extent is influenced by one's personality, emotional stability, environment, and expectations.

Senility damages the brain and often causes bizarre actions, dismaying family and friends. Dictionaries equate senility with old age, but experts say there is no inexorable connection. Dr. Mort Ward of the Philadelphia Geriatric Center suggests, "It is not so much whether you are senile as whether others think you are."

One of the big keys to senility is anxiety. One in six people over 65 is senile: a lot more fear they are. "I lose my eyeglasses five times a day," says Dr. James Folsom of the Veterans Administration in Washington, D.C., "and nobody says I'm senile. But if somebody old does this, everyone gets hysterical."

But just as you cannot tell a child there is no monster under the bed, so you cannot brush off a person's anxiety about senility. With some it is a profound fear. Dr. Ewalt Busse of the Council on Aging and Human Development at Duke University says, "People are more fearful of being incapacitated than dead." A Michigan State University researcher adds, "Senility becomes a psychopathological defense against death." The solution he suggests is what he calls "terror reduction."

At the Philadelphia Geriatric Center, Bernard Liebowitz says, "It is the frightening thing of not having control." And another staff member shakes his head: "The trouble is you live with senility, you don't die."

"Don't anybody hold my hand," insists Mrs. Sarah Seidenberg, a resident. "I can walk fine." Asked where she was born, she responds, "In bed," and chuckles. She throws up her hands at the suggestion of senility, saying, "God forbid." She works two hours a day. She often goes on excursions to Atlantic City, N.J., for fun and to New York for shopping "because Philadelphia is too slow." She is 103 years old.

Keeping your mind in shape is of first importance in avoiding senility, experts say. The brain must be used to ward off flabbiness caused by lack of mental gymnastics.

Col. Harland Sanders, the 83-year-old Kentucky Fried Chicken originator, was reached in a Los Angeles motel in the midst of a 300,000-mile, five-week trip around the world. "You'll rust out quicker than you'll wear out," he says. "I'll just go on about my business doing the best I can until the Grim Reaper calls me." And senility, Colonel? "I'm not going to get senile, so what do I have to worry about?"

Traditionally, the main cause of senility has been thought

to be arteriosclerosis, hardening of the arteries. This largely hereditary ailment affects nearly everyone to some degree, clogging the blood vessels with calcium and cholesterol. But autopsies fail to show any constant relation between arterio-sclerosis and senility. Some people have excessive artery hardening (allowing less oxygen and blood to reach the brain and thus supposedly impairing function) but have functioned normally throughout life. Others get senile without significant arteriosclerosis.

If senility does destroy gray matter (and doctors are in-clined to think it does), even this is considered of relatively minor import in many cases, simply because most of us fail to use our brains fully anyway. Far more important is which cells are destroyed. Says Dr. Ward: "I think your best bet is to hope you lose only unimportant ones."

Brain disease is another factor in senility. Some think that the disease may come about because we all have a sort of latent virus that sometimes is set off, sometimes not. Other possible causes of senility include exposure to radiation, early nutritional deficiencies, isolation, bereavement, and alcoholism.

Mrs. Muriel Oberleder, assistant professor of psychiatry at Albert Einstein College of Medicine in New York City, says, "Frankly, I believe that most people bring senility upon themselves." The VA's Dr. Folsom agrees: "I think some people have been born senile. They have never had an original thought. They don't grab life. They let life grab them."

But researchers still are as uncertain about senility's cause as they are about its cure. Nearly all consider senility far from hopeless. Here are some of their suggestions. Keep in mind that the human brain probably starts deteriorating between 20 and 30.

Be active. "It's far better," says Folsom, "to slip on ice and break a hip than to slip on a rug and break a hip. Too often we make sure people are seated in a comfortable chair rather than being up exercising."

Eat properly. The young too often eat on the run. The old too often settle for a meal out of a can.

Be interested. An old Alabama farmer moved to town but he still returns to his farm daily to check the cows and chickens. "They need me, and I need them," he explains. Mrs. Ernest J. Wakefield, 82, of Kensington, Md., gets up at 5:30 A.M. daily and reads current literature for two or three hours. "I sure would get mad if somebody called me senile," she says.

Be smart. Arthur Waldman, consultant at the Philadelphia Geriatric Center, says senility appears to come more often to the lower end of the intellectual ladder than the top.

Control stress. This by-product of modern living seems to do our brains no good.

Vitamins may help. Ascorbic acid (vitamin C) is popular; B-12 shots are given regularly. Placebos might do as well, but if you think something helps, that is part of the battle.

Get adequate sleep. But older people should avoid constant dozing, which in turn prevents sleeping at night, which gives them time to worry about lots of things — like senility.

Give yourself pep talks. Folsom suggests a daily dose of: "I'm not going to give up my interests by pieces. I will pick up new ideas and not live in the past." Mrs. Margie T. Wild of Portland, Ore., a cousin of Folsom, says she discovered that she was getting senile. How did she avoid it? "I refused to let it happen to me."

Learn new skills. If you you have led an intellectual life, take up bricklaying. If you are a bricklayer, try reading.

Think about second and third careers. Colonel Sanders started what he calls "this chicken thing" when he was 66.

Don't get fat.

Do things for others. The geriatric center's Dr. Ward says 25% of people over 65 live alone. That leaves too much time for self-pity. Look outward.

Don't fret about memory lapses. "By the time you are in your 60's," says Dr. Busse of Duke, "you know a lot of people, so of course you forget some of their names." Mixing up names of children is natural at age 70, even as it is at age 40, when we may be experiencing our first minor memory losses. Network television commentator Chris Schenkel forgot his own name while reporting the Mexico City Olympics in 1968. Nobody thought him senile.

Don't think you are becoming stupid. You're not. Research shows that you will keep your IQ as the years go by.

"Don't give up things with the excuse, "I'm getting old and forgetful." If you play tennis today, play tomorrow. If you go to church this Sunday, go next Sunday (even if it's cold). If you went to concerts last spring, go this spring. Giving up anything is a long step toward senility.

Inspire yourself. Look at Mrs. Elmer Broders, 77, of Kansas City, who ice skates daily. Or look at history's greats who have avoided senility: Supreme Court Justices, Schweitzer, Moses, Segovia, Casals, Toscanini.

Curb your anxieties. "The climax of middle-age fears is senility." says Mrs. Oberleder.

Many of us, young and old, can take these strides ourselves to ward off senility. But how do we cope with friends and relatives who seem to be getting senile? Some of us respond badly. Why? "Many people just can't deal with anything that's not pretty," says Dr. Liebowitz, "and senility isn't pretty."

Ward says the trick is "simply to give old people a little bit of interest in still being alive." In her No-nonsense book, *How to Help Older People,* Julietta K. Arthur sums up an old person's needs: "Somewhere to live, something to do, someone to care."

Avoid endorsing senile behavior. Folsom explains, "We reward them for being forgetful. We say, 'Oh, mother has lost her glasses. Let's all help look.' Then mother realizes that's the only way she can get attention."

Give older people aids. When Mrs. Wakefield reads, she uses a ruler with a magnifying glass. That makes good sense, especially if the alternative is not to read at all. Listen to older people, share their ideas, try to be sympathetic to their concerns. Two researchers at Louisiana State University wrote recently, "It's important not to take away all of life's pleasures purely in the interest of prolonging life." Write things down for them.

Alcohol for the senile? Says one prominient authority. "A little sherry sure beats Geritol." Avoid a smothering kind of love. Just because an older person forgets to record a check on the stub does not mean he is unable from now on to write checks. Because he forgets to tie his shoes, it does not mean that he must always wear slippers.

One way to cope with senile behavior (doctors often make a diagnosis of senility when they cannot figure out what else could be wrong) is through a common-sense concept called "reality orientation" which was developed by Dr. Folsom. His formula requires repeated emphasis on *now*: "What day is today?"

"It's Monday morning. That means it's time to go to therapy." "It's noon, so it's time for lunch." Says Dr. Folsom, "Our biggest problem is convincing family members that senility is not hopeless."

And it's not. Examples abound of people diagnosed as senile who then recover. A cotton broker in Mississippi became increasingly irritable, threw his wife out of their home, and locked the door. After intensive reality orientation under Dr. Folsom, he returned to a normal life. His wife later wrote, "Thank you for giving me may husband back."

Following surgery a person often will awake with "instant senility." This can be erased quite soon, insists Folsom, by patience, perserverance, and by not letting the patient "get away" with senile behavior.

Dr. Carl Eisdorfer, a psychiatrist at the University of Washington, explains, "To the layman, names, dates, and places may be small matters, but the alternative is nothing. It's life in front of a television set where the vertical hold is always shot."

Some specific treatments may help. Most exciting are hyperbaric chambers, where oxygen at above-atmospheric pressure permeates the brain much better than at ordinary pressure. Eleanor Jacobs of the VA hospital in Buffalo has had considerable success, but she claims no miracles. She says that some results have been good with arteriosclerosis cases, but results are poor where there is brain disease.

Miss Jacobs says hyperbaric work is going on at a half-dozen centers. "I think the best hope in hyperbarics," she says, "is in preventive treatment. I don't think this is the final answer for senility." One of the drawbacks is that the treatment (at Buffalo, two 90-minute sessions a day for 15 days) doesn't seem to have much lasting effect.

Pharamaceutical companies are trying to develop and effective antisenility pill. Dr. Ward cautions that older people can tolerate only about one-third to one-half the dosage that younger people can, and he notes, "It's very easy to produce a row of zombies."

One authority says, "Off the record, I'd think pills are probably worthless. For the record, I would say there is evidence on both sides, but it needs a lot more research."

Dr. Nathan Kline, director of research at the Rockland (N.Y.) State Hospital, is testing a Romanian-produced drug, a derivative of procaine. "So far we haven't proved it doesn't work," he says. "All we have now are extravagant claims coming in from abroad.

There has been work on thinning blood to make it pass through clogged arteries, but hemorrhaging is a problem. Expanding arteries has a chance, although Ken Pommerenck of the New York State Communities Aid group wonders about the wisdom of "expanding brittle pipes." Marjorie Fish Lowenthal of the Langley Porter Institute in San Francisco says, "We're searching around as we did with polio."

Dr. Busse of Duke thinks that we will have medical cures for senility within a decade. But a skeptic there says, "Do him a favor and don't quote him on that." Mrs. Oberleder agrees with him.

The biggest part of the answer seems to be in active and vibrant living, refusing to give up on your brain at 65.

How Long You Will Live

*If you answer the questions you
will have a good idea*

By Harold J. Taub

How long you will live cannot be predicted. Yet by seeing where you fit within certain statistics you can make an educated guess about your life span. That is exactly what happens when you apply for life insurance. The insurance company can make a fairly safe bet on how long you are going to live. Then, by shading the odds in its own favor, the company can make money on your premium.

The following questionnaire uses the same statistics an insurance company would use to determine the premium rate. It is based on studies published by the National Center for Health Statistics of the U.S. Public Health Service and by the Bureau of the Census, from studies made by insurance companies, and from medical sources.

Answer all the questions that relate to you. You may find some of them exasperating. For example, although statistically doctors are known to die sooner than men in many other professions, a doctor also knows that those members of his profession who take care of their health have a very good chance of living long lives, as many do. So a doctor who watches his own health might think it nonsensical to have to deduct from his score because of his profession.

It is not nonsense, however. Every doctor is exposed to greater risks of infection; he is also exposed to X rays and other dangers peculiar to his profession. Although no single category can be considered entirely accurate as applied to any particular individual, the totality of the categories provides a statistical profile that has meaning.

It is the final score that counts. It will give you a good idea of how many years you probably have left on the basis of who and what you are and how you are now living. It may also move you to change habits that are making inroads on your health and the length of your life.

Condensed from "Pageant", 205 E. 42nd St., New York City 10017. January, 1966. ∘1966 by Macfadden-Bartell Corp., and reprinted with permission.

1. *Present age.*

a. If you are now 45 years of age or younger, you start off with a life expectancy of 78. Enter the number 78 in the box at the right. [ ]

b. If you are over 45 but under 60, you were born too soon to benefit from modern advances in sanitation, child nutrition, and preventive medicine. This is reflected by your starting out with a score of 73. Write 73 in the box.[ ]

c. If you are past 60, U.S. vital statistics show that you have already passed so many of the hazards to life that your life expectancy has gone up. If your age is between 60 and 65, enter a 78 in the box at the right. If you are between 65 and 70, you start out with a score of 80, and if you are past 70, there is no point in trying to score yourself. You are doing fine. You aren't going to change any habits, anyway. [ ]

2. *Sex.*

a. If you are female add 2 to your starting figure.[ ]

b. If you are male, subtract 2 [ ]

3. *Race.* Although there is absolutely no hereditary difference between white and Negro children, statistics show that Negroes do die younger, probably because of the more difficult environment in which they live.

a. If your racial background is Negro, subtract 6. The figure for whites remains unchanged. [ ]

4. *Geographical location.* Although no one has yet succeeded in explaining why it should be so, there is no doubt that the length of life varies considerably from one region to another. This may be related to way of life, climate, altitude, or mineral content of the soil. Whatever the reasons, where you live has a definite bearing on how long you will live.

a. If you live in a state in the Rocky Mountain time zone or in Alaska, Hawaii, or New Mexico add 3 to your score.[ ]

b. For all other sections of the country, subtract one [ ]

5. *Occupation.* The two occupational extremes — highly privileged jobs in which you have no boss and those requiring hard physical labor — hold out the greatest promise of long life. The one exception is the medical profession, where the special risks to which every doctor is exposed more than nullify the advantages of being self-employed in high-status work.

a. If you are a farmer or outdoor laborer of any type, add 2 to your previous total. [ ]

b. If you are a top executive for a large company or own your own business, add 2 to your score. [ ]

c. If you are a housewife in a well-to-do home, add 2. [ ]

d. If you are a junior executive in a large or small busin-
ness, subtract 2.   [   ]

e. Male or female, if you work steadily at any indoor occupation other than housekeeping and do not occupy a top
position, subtract 1.   [   ]

f. If you are a doctor, subtract 3 from your previous total
unless your work brings you into frequent contact with X-ray
equipment. In that case, subtract 9.   [   ]

6. *Marital status.* Married persons, regardless of whether or
not they are happy, tend to live longer than single ones. The
reasons probably are greater regularity of habits, more sleep,
and better diet. Even the unhappily married may be envied in
this respect by the single people they frequently envy.

a. If you are past 30 and are divorced or have never been
married, subtract 4 from your previous score.   [   ]

b. Widows and widowers subtract 2.[   ]

c. Even if you are now married but have been divorced
more than once, subtract 4.   [   ]

d. If you are below the age of 30 and/or are now married
with a reasonable expectation that your marriage will endure,
your score is unchanged.   [   ]

7. *Heredity.* Those who come of long-lived stock will also
tend to live longer than the average, all other things being
equal.

a. If you had one grandparent on either side who lived past
the age of 80 or is still alive and in good health, add 2 to your
total.   [   ]

b. If you have 2 or more such grandparents, add 5.[   ]

c. If either of your parents or any of your grandparents died
before the age of 60 of heart disease, stroke, arterial disease,
or cancer, subtract 4 from your total.   [   ]

d. If either of your parents is or was diabetic, subtract 2.
                                                     [   ]

8. *Diet.* It is not very important which foods you avoid and
which you prefer if your general diet is well-balanced and
nutritious and you avoid overeating. There are, however, a
few elements of the diet that recent medical studies have
shown have a definite bearing on length of life.

a. If your drinking water is hard, making it difficult to get
suds from soap and perhaps leaving a metallic taste in your
mouth, add 1 to your total.   [   ]

b. If your drinking water is naturally soft or you use a water
softener, subtract 1.   [   ]

c. If you are a man and a heavy eater of high-calorie foods,
such as cakes, candy, sweet desserts, and heavily sugared coffee, and lots of butter, bread, and potatoes, you are a can-

didate for diseased arteries, heart attack, and early death. Subtract 6 from your previous total. This does not apply to women, who can eat such foods with an unchanged score
[   ]

d. If you tend to eat lightly except for one very heavy meal each day subtract 4.   [   ]

e. If you eat many times during the day but never eat a full meal, add 2.   [   ]

9. *Drinking.* The use of alcohol in any substantial quantity is now known to be a strong contributory factor in the development of liver disease, which in turn permits the development of many other health problems. Alcohol is not a direct killer, but it helps those forces that will shorten your life.

a. If you customarily do not drink at all or drink no more than one martini or one or two glasses of beer a day, add 1 to your total.   [   ]

b. If you are the so-called moderate drinker, having two, three, or four drinks a day, subtract 2.   [   ]

c. If you are a heavy drinker or an alcoholic, subtract 5.
[   ]

10. *Smoking.* Doctors now say that the smoking danger is not confined to lung cancer but is also a contributing cause of the diseases of the heart and coronary arteries that are the top killers in the U.S.

a. If you smoke more than 20 cigarettes a day, subtract. 6.
[   ]

b. If you are a heavy smoker of cigars or a pipe, subtract 2.
[   ]

c. If you abstain from tobacco or smoke fewer than 20 cigarettes a day your total is unchanged.   [   ]

11. *Sleep.*

a. If you make certain of getting at least 7 hours' sleep every night, add 2 to your score.   [   ]

b. If in addition to a full night's sleep, you nap for at least half an hour each day, add 2 more.   [   ]

c. If your sleep is irregular and frequently insufficient, sub-tract 3.   [   ]

d. If you habitually use sleeping pills, subtract 5.[   ]

12. *Exercise.* Recent medical investigations, while not yet conclusive, tend to show that exercise is an important element in maintaining health as well as your figure. Many doctors think that a regular daily program of the proper exer-cise is the best preventive of heart attacks.

a. Add 2 if you follow such an exercise program.[   ]

13. *The air you breathe.* Chronic bronchitis, emphysema.

and other chronic diseases of the lungs are prematurely killing increasing numbers of people yearly. They result primarily from the growing pollution of the air. Thus far, there seems to be no solution to the air-pollution problem, which increases in direct proportion to the density of population.

a. Those who live in cities of a million or more people must subtract 4 from their previous totals.   [   ]

b. Those who live in smaller cities subtract 2.   [   ]

c. If you live in a small town, an outlying suburb, or in the country, add 1.   [   ]

14. *Accidents.* Auto-accident deaths have reached epidemic proportions. Nearly as many people die of driving cars as die of cancer. Though the cancer rate might be diminished at any time, the car-death rate is climbing steadily. No estimation of how long you will live would be complete without an assessment of your driving habits.

a. If you habitually drive at a speed of 60 or more on the open road, subtract 5.   [   ]

b. If you sometimes sneak through a red light, pass another car in a prohibited area, neglect to signal for a turn well before turning, or commit other so-called minor violations, subtract 3.   [   ]

c. If you drive a car and have less than normal (20/20) vision, subtract 3.   [   ]

d. If you cultivate such driving habits as maintaining a substantial distance from the car in front of you and obeying all speed and traffic regulations, even though they may seem foolish and unnecessary, you are the only type of driver with a really good chance of never having an accident. Your total, then, would be unchanged, FINAL SCORE   [   ]

You final score indicates how long you can hope to live, taking into account the statistically established favorable and unfavorable ways that you as an individual differ from the average person. It does not and could not consider such factors as your possibly being afflicted with a fatal disease. It presupposes that you are in an average state of health now. That is why it was possible to begin with a life expectancy of 78 years, the latest estimate of the Metropolitan Life Insurance Co.

There are elements of your health profile that you cannot change, but there are also many others that can be altered to your benefit. You now have an excellent idea of what chance you have of realizing your normal life expectancy. You have learned how you can improve your chances. The rest is up to you.

What's in a Name?

Mental health, among other things

By Arthur Henley

Most children are able to live with their names. But, according to a new psychological study, unusual names can sometimes lead to severe personality disturbances.

Sylvester's was an extreme case. His parents named him that because they wanted him to be unique, but Sylvester was not. His name, in his social class, made him an object of ridicule for his playmates. To prove his manliness, he attempted foolhardy stunts. This won him the attention he craved, as well as a nickname, Silly. Being neither the egghead his parents wanted nor the blockhead his classmates derided, Sylvester had emotional conflicts that increased during his teens. In his freshman year at college he attempted suicide. The reason he gave: "I hate my name."

Dr. Robert C. Nicolay, a psychology professor at Loyola University of Chicago, and Dr. Arthur A. Hartman, director of psychology for the Psychiatric institute of the Cook County Circuit court, took a large sampling of unusual names from court psychiatric clinic files and compared them with an equal number of more popular names — James, Elizabeth, David, John, Joseph, Mary — drawn from the same source. They found more than four times as many psychotic individuals in the group with unusual names.

Dr. Hartman says that in a psychological test in which the question "Who are you?" is asked, in almost every case the answer is "I am George," or "Jane," or whatever the child's name might be. A child strongly identifies himself, not by sex or nationality but by his first name, and his first name is often the key to his conduct. If he cannot live up to what his name suggests to him, he is likely to become very maladjusted.

Clarence was such a youngster. Constantly harassed and humiliated by other boys, who sneered at his "sissy name," he struck back with fists. In time, he turned his animosity against

Condensed from the "Ladies Home Journal", 641 Lexington Ave., New York City 10022. June, 1970. ‹1970 by Downe Publishing Inc., and reprinted with permission.

all society. At 16, after many arrests for delinquent behavior, he was sent to a state reformatory.

In some social circles, the name Clarence may be appropriate, as are Sargent (Shriver), Edsel (Ford), Nelson (Rockefeller), Hubert (Humphrey), Dwight (Eisenhower). In fact a high proportion of unusual names appears in *Who's Who.* This could mean that the possessors were comfortable with their names because they were accepted by their set. Or it could mean, as Dr. Hartman suggests, that they "possessed strongly integrated personalities, welcomed the challenge imposed by their unusual names, and strove harder to make good."

When such a person achieves prominence, his unusual name becomes an asset. But it is a mistake for a parent to give a child a highly unusual name as an aid to success. A recent study of Harvard university undergraduates showed that young people with peculiar names were likely to fail and become neurotic. Names such as Reginald, Horace, Percy, and Egbert place a child on the defensive. And the responsibility lies with the parents, who, according to evidence turned up by Dr. Nicolay and Hartman, "inflict their own problems, their own hostilities, and the subsequent influence of an unfavorable home environment on their kids."

Most parents would not name a boy Cain, yet some do. And there is a grotesque humor in Mr. and Mrs. Baer naming their son Teddy, or Mr. And Mrs. Rabbit naming their daughter Bunny, or Mr. and Mrs. Hamm naming their daughter Virginia.

Some parents go further. Many women who wanted a daughter but gave birth to a son simply take a feminine name and modify it to suit a boy. Marian becomes Marion, Frances becomes Francis. This is sometimes the parents' unconscious way of rejecting the child's sex. Their attitude can rub off on the child; when it does, that child can fail to develop a healthy sexual identification.

In one case, the parents had their hearts set on a boy, for whom they had chosen the name Michael. When a girl was born, they decided to name her Michaela. Michaela soon was shortened to plain Mike by everyone the little girl came to know. Her parents also revealed their preference for a male child by their rough-and-tumble treatment of their daughter and the way they subtly encouraged her to dress like a tomboy. This served to reinforce Michaela's sexual confusion, and she grew into a troubled adolescent who could not form attachments to either sex.

"There is every reason to believe, says Dr. Nicolay, "that

when a child is given a name that creates confusion as to sex (Carroll, Bobby, Sydney), or connotes snobbery (Cecil, Dilys, Stoiddard), or is an object of ridicule (Newt, Lulu, Cuthbert), the child's personality may suffer great emotional damage."

No one takes his name more seriously than the child himself, as evidenced by a survey conducted recently at Ohio university by Dr. James L. Bruning, in association with Barbara A. Buchanan, a graduate student in psychology at Pennsylvania State university. Approximately 1,350 freshmen and sophomores, male and female, were asked to state their preferences in names. The best-liked names were Michael, James, and Wendy; the most disliked were Alfreda, Percival, and Isidore. The male students considered Sue, Elizabeth, and Linda the most feminine names, and Sydney, Ronnie, and Jerry the least feminine. The female students considered Dave, Kirk, and Michael the most masculine.

Name styles change with the times. In a general way, it is safe to say that Fanny is out, Barbra is in; Guy is out, Mark is in. Nevertheless, the most popular and most widely accepted names still remain John and Robert for boys, Mary and Elizabeth for girls.

"A name that is poorly regarded by the child who carries it," says Dr. Hartman, "can become as great a stumbling block as a physical handicap, and no child should be made to go through life with a handicap when it can so easily be eliminated." He urges parents whose child dislikes his or her name to allow the child to change the name, or at least to adopt a nickname or to use a middle name.

In *Romeo and Juliet*, Shakespeare asked, "What's in a name?"—and answered himself: "That which we call a rose by any other name would smell as sweet." But now there appears to be more to a name than Shakespeare suspected. It is clear that living up to a name can be far easier and more pleasant when it is the kind of name a child wants to live up to.

Chapter V

How Do I Cope?

"The world is so full of a number of things, I'm sure we should all be as happy as kings," Stevenson wrote. But of course, kings are not necessarily happy and the number of things in the world includes many that work against, rather than for, happiness. Man is in a kind of perpetual battle against both his physical and mental environments. A certain amount of strategy and tactics for the battle has been built up by scientific studies and some of that is presented in this chapter concerning the workings and control of the human mind.

Where Ideas Come From

Science is homing in on the mysterious human process

By Dr. Sam Glucksberg

Where do new ideas come from? In our research at Princeton, we have found that creative behavior is inherent in man's nature, even in a young child learning to talk. When he says "mama" he is merely imitating, but when he says, "Daddy goed away," instead of, "Daddy went away," he has put together "go" and the past tense "-ed" to create a word he has not heard before. He has produced a useful, novel act by combining a new behavior with old habits.

Gutenberg, inventor of the printing press, knew about wood engraving, coin stamping, wax seals, and the wine press. Given these elements, the printing press might almost invent itself. But how are they to be put together? How does a man happen to think of them all simultaneously, and then conceive a use for the combination?

It happened to Gutenberg one autumn afternoon, when he took part in the wine harvest. His ray of light was the new association between the wine press and the seal, which together form the essential idea of the printing press.

Must we leave things to chance, hoping that people like Gutenberg just happen to be in the right places at the right times? At Princeton, our aim is to discover the mechanisms of the creative process so as to foster creative behavior.

We study fairly simple forms of it, using problems which involve using a familiar object in a novel way. For example, the ordinary use for hammer is driving nails. This function may become so fixed in our mind that other possibilities, use as a pendulum weight, electrical conductor, weapon, or bell clapper, may be blocked out.

We are all familiar with the curious situation in which we leave a problem we cannot solve and find that the answer pops into our mind several hours, days, or even weeks later, often when we are not consciously aware of the problem at all. The solution has been there in our minds, but for some

Condensed from "Think", Armonk, N.Y. 10504. March-April, 1968. ⸰1968 by International Business Machines Corp., and reprinted with permission.

reason has been inhibited by a competing idea.

Strong motivation inhibits problem solving. Evidence from both animal and human-learning experiments has shown that increasing motivation strengthens strong habits more than weak habits. We reasoned, then, that increasing motivation in our problems, where the incorrect habit of thought is the strongest, would actually decrease the chances of success in solving the problems.

We gave a candle and a box of tacks to our students and told them to find a new use for them. The solution is to take the tracks out of the box and then use it as a candle holder, a new concept of combining the ideas of tack box and candle holder. Half of the students worked for chance of winning $25, while the other half worked for nothing. The group working for a high reward came up with only half as many solutions as the other, and their average solution times were twice as long. High motivation simply reinforced the tendency to persist down blind alleys with the strong but incorrect initial ideas. High rewards for performance, or anxiety over the possibilities of failure, inhibit creativity.

After people are given, say, four easy problems where common objects must be used in novel ways, they go on to solve more difficult problems more readily. How they do this is not perfectly clear. We must ask what specifically these persons have learned.

We asked all the persons of one group who had been given practice problems to write a hint that would be useful to someone else who might get those problems. Once all the hints had been collected we gave them to a second group. This second group, like the group that had provided the hints, was given the electrical circuit problem. (A simple electric circuit must be completed. Not enough wire is supplied, but a screwdriver, to tighten and loosen the screw terminals, is provided. The problem is solved by using the blade of the screwdriver to conduct electricity.) The puzzling aspect of this study was that the hint-receiving group was not helped by hints at all.

We began to explore some relations between thinking and language. The way we use an object may well be influenced by the name we use for it. What would happen if we gave the screwdriver a new name.

Calling it wire, of course, solves the problem in advance. So we used a nonsense word to remove the cluster of habitual ideas associated with the word screwdriver. We called it *job*. The problem solvers now had a word that was free from interfering associations. When the screwdriver had a new, meaningless name some students used it instead of wire even before they ran out of wire.

In another experiment, we used a number of different tools, and called each either wrench or pliers. Since the tool had to be used as if it were wire, would the rhyming of pliers and wires help people to think of the functional similarity between the two? It did, but we still do not know whether persons judged to be creative in the world outside the laboratory think the way our problem solvers did.

The next phase of study must include systematic comparison of creative and noncreative persons in standarized laboratory tests. But even at this stage we can offer some general conclusions about the nature of the creative process.

1. The separate elements needed for creative combination must be available. In the circuit problem, the potential solver must know that wire is missing, that metal conducts electricity, and that the screwdriver is made, in part, of metal. Before a person can think of an answer in an association test, the elements of the answer must be in his mind.

2. It is the combination of the necesary elements that produces original ideas. Any procedure which makes relevant combinations easier will encourage creative behavior. Such procedures include releasing inhibitions and freeing thought by new ways of talking about things.

3. Creativity is not confined to a few gifted people. As we have been able to show, people can be influenced to behave in creative ways, and can be trained to increase their creativity.

4. Perhaps most important, we feel certain that the process by which the mind produces new ideas can be studied systematically. There is no reason why we cannot develop effective techniques to teach creative thinking. The day we can do this is not far off.

Pills to Make You Smarter

*At long last, Cylert offers an
easy answer to hard problems.*

By Lester David

You have a rough problem, but your brain is fagged and
answers don't come. You reach for some pills, gulp one. Your
scrambled wits reassemble themselves and soon you are as
sharp as a tack again.

You are a student with a dismal future in math and science.
You just don't dig numbers, equations, and formulas, and
there are failing marks on your record. A pill or two, taken as
directed, will help you soak up more math and science than
you ever thought possible.

The medicine that may do all this and much more is a
brownish yellow, aspirin-size tablet called Cylert. This is the
learning and memory drug medical science has been seeking.

The future, if further research confirms early findings,
should be dazzling. Everyone will be using the drug to step
up brain voltage. Elderly persons suffering from senility will
find their memories improved. There is even some hope that
retarded children may be helped.

The drug is so promising that three separate investigations
on human subjects are under way in major medical centers.
Dr. D. Ewen Cameron, a distinguished psychiatrist at Albany
Medical center, has been conducting tests on elderly persons
at the Veterans Administation hospital in Albany for many
months. Two other studies are in progress, one in the East,
the other in the Midwest.

Reports thus far show that Cylert does indeed improve
human memory, and apparently has no bad side effects.

Cylert apparently increases the production of a key
chemical found in the brain, RNA or ribonucleic acid, which
is thought to be vital in memory and learning. Scientists call
RNA the memory molecule.

When Dr. Cameron injected the RNA substance itself into
some 50 aged patients at McGill university in Montreal,

Condensed from "Mechanix Illustrated", 67 W. 44th St., New York City 10036. July, 1966. ‹1966
by Fawcett Publications, Inc., and reprinted with permission.

175

Canada, he found memory improvement in many instances. The patients were suffering from senile psychoses, with memory disturbance a prominent symptom. (The RNA did nothing for other symptoms.)

"The effects," Dr. Cameron reported, "lasted three or four months. Until now, nothing has ever improved memory. Now we can do something we were never able to do before."

The development of Cylert resulted from a series of fascinating explorations conducted all over the world on one of science's most baffling questions: how man thinks and learns. Three young scientists, Drs. Glasky and Lionel Simon, both biochemists, and Nicholas P. Plotnikoff, a neuropharmacologist, tried a memory experiment with rats in Chicago. The test cage was small wooden chamber with a grid flooring and an escape platform outside the box. The floor was electrified so that rats treading upon it could be given a mild shock.

On the first day of school the rats were allowed to remain inside the chamber for 15 seconds, after which a buzzer sounded for the next ten seconds. In the next five seconds current was applied and the buzzer sounded simultaneously. The idea was to find out how fast the rats could learn to escape.

On the second day of school half the test rats got Cylert in their food 30 minutes before being put through the buzzer-shocker test; the others got nothing. Testing proceeded with the doctors watching.

The ones that got Cylert learned to avoid the shock within five to seven seconds. The untreated rats took much longer. Final results: rats given the chemical learned four to five times faster than untreated rats.

Additional testing disclosed that Cylert-treated rats retained what they had learned for weeks but the others did not.

Cylert contains a brain stimulant, magnesium pemoline, which boosts the production of RNA in the cells. It has been used in Europe for the past several years as a mild central-nervous-system stimulant. It is not related chemically to pep pills or amphetamines.

Doctors are not sure how RNA manages to improve brain performance, but one theory is that RNA molecules carry thoughts in coded form, much as DNA molecules carry genetic information. DNA (deoxyribonucleic acid) has been called the code of life because it governs inheritance and all our functions. RNA has been called by many scientists the code of memory and learning. When a particular thought occurs to you, it is coded upon an RNA molecule, or upon a protein molecule made by RNA, and stored in one of the billions of nerve cells of your brain. It remains there, ready to come to mind whenever you want to call it up.

Scientific evidence that RNA definitely is involved in memory has come from many parts of the U.S. and Europe. Neurobiologist Holger Hyden of the University of Goteborg, Sweden, discovered that learning can increase the RNA in the brains of rats considerably. Dr. Hyden analyzed the RNA content of untrained rat brains, then taught a large number of rats to perform intricate laboratory stunts. After months of training the brain cells of the educated rate were again analyzed. Hyden discovered a 35% increase in RNA!

At UCLA Dr. Allan Jacobson set a food cup inside a rat cage. When clicking sound was heard it meant that there was food in the cup. No sound, no food. A group of lab rats soon learned to go to the cup when they heard the sound.

Step 2 was to inject RNA from the brains of the educated rats into seven untrained rodents, who were put into the cage and the cups set out. Even though none had prior instruction, they responded to the clicks.

At the University of Michigan Dr. James McConnell, a psychologist, taught flatworms to respond to electrical shocks. Then the worms were ground up and fed to other worms, who inherited their eduction! The RNA in the educated flatworms was passed on to the untrained ones, and with it the trained response to the shock.

A team of investigators at the Mental Health Research institute of the University of Michigan divided goldfish into two test teams. Into the brains of one group the researchers injected two antibiotic drugs. The others got no drugs. Then both teams were trained to avoid electric shock traps set out in their tanks.

The fish that did not receive the drugs remembered for months where the traps were, but the treated ones forgot within three days! The memory-destroying drugs they got are Puromycin and Acetoxycycloheximide, both of which impair the manufacture of RNA in cells.

How soon will you be able to get smart pills from your drug store? Cylert is now classified as an experimental drug. According to the food-and-drug laws, the manufacturer must present adequate evidence of safety and effectiveness to government authorities before permission to market it is granted.

The Needless Tragedy of Suicide

Community planning could end the disease

By Jack Star

In Boston, an old-age pensioner dialed HA 6-6600 and said that he had just bought a revolver and intended to kill himself. In Los Angeles, a middle-aged housewife called DU 1-5111 and said she would rather die of poison than of cancer. These and other telephone numbers provide a help for potential suicides. They let them cut through social agency red tape and get the help they need quickly.

In one year, more than 20,000 suicides were recorded in the U.S. About another 20,000 went unrecorded because they were disguised as accidents or because of a reluctance to call suicide by its right name. Several million Americans have survived attempts at suicide. It has become the third leading cause of death among teen-agers 15 to 19.

In Chicago's Cook County hospital, attempted-suicides are brought in by the hundreds a year. A young nurse in the emergency room says, "We often see the same patients again and again. Their wrists have old scars."

Doctors know that a suicidal gesture may very well precede the real thing, that the woman who takes a few pills too many is giving a cry for help. Often cries go unheard. At Cook County hospital, 90% of the suicidal patients are discharged without further treatment after their stomachs are pumped out or their wrists sewn up. "We send 10% of them, the worst risks, to a state hospital so they won't be able to harm themselves," says Dr. Vladimir Urse. "What can we do with the others? There are no out-patient clinics I can refer them to. It takes months to get an appointment, and how many patients on welfare can afford $2 or $10 a visit?"

Three-quarters of all those who kill themselves go to a physician within a few months before their deaths, yet often their symptoms remain undetected. Dr. Stanley F. Yolles, director of the National Institute of Mental Health, says, "In over half the suicide deaths, there is a history of previous, spontaneous, suicidal communication, either direct: 'I'm going to shoot myself'; or indirect, 'How do you leave your body to the medical school?' " He says that physicians should learn to recognize the signals.

Dr. Philip Solomon, of Harvard Medical school, says that psychiatrists alone cannot do the job, because there will never be enough of them nor enough physicians, nurses, and clergymen.

It is better to let lay people tackle the problem, under supervision, rather than do nothing. In Boston, Dr. Solomon serves as vice-president of Rescue, Inc., a nondenominational suicide-prevention group organized by a Catholic priest, Father Kenneth B. Murphy, after police had twice summoned him to talk would-be suicides out of leaping to their deaths.

In seven years, Rescue, Inc., whose telephone number is in the front of the phone book under the police and fire numbers, handled 11,000 calls. Not all were from persons thinking of suicide; many dealt with problems of sickness, poverty and loneliness.

Trained volunteers (including a druggist, two Trappist monks, an Episcopal priest, and a paint chemist) refer callers to an appropriate social-service agency, psychiatric clinic, or doctor. If the caller is facing a serious crisis, a volunteer may go to his home.

Los Angeles' Suicide Prevention Center receives 5,000 calls a year. The callers are questioned adroitly to gauge their stress. They are rated on a lethality scale that takes into account whether they have a specific suicide scheme in mind (where, when, how), and whether they can count on friends and relatives. Older persons rate high on the scale; so do homosexuals, alcoholics, and persons living alone. A divorce, death, or separation also means increased danger.

Says Dr. Robert E. Litman, chief psychiatrist, "One young woman called at midnight, refused to give her name, and said only that she had taken many pills. During the conversation, she revealed that she could hear the ocean, and was then in a church. Then she collapsed. With the clues, the police were able to find her and take her to a hospital in time to save her life."

Nearly two-thirds of the callers need little more than reassurance, or perhaps the help of a phone call to the right person. In some cases, the right person may be a friend or relative, in others, a therapist who has seen them in the past.

A third of the callers appear to be approaching a suicidal crisis, and it is with these that the center is proving its worth.

A training manual points out that the patients have contradictory feelings, "wanting to die and wanting to live at the same time. A person may take a lethal dose of barbiturates and then call someone for help before he loses consciousness. Most people have a stronger wish to live than to die. It is this fact which makes suicide prevention possible."

At the center, such patients are greeted with hope the moment they enter the door. An interviewer confronted a 40-year-old man who was having trouble with his wife, his job and his health. "Look," he said, "you have some problems, but they're not so bad. We have seen worse. You need some advice." While the patient is kept busy taking a psychological test, the interviewer calls in his wife. Sometimes a psychiatrist will prescribe a drug that dispels depression.

Doctors are finding an increasing number of mysterious deaths among those who use barbiturates and also drink.

"Many persons are living on the thin edge of death because of their daily intake of drugs, and I include alcohol," says Dr. Tabachnick, a psychiatrist at the center.

Investigators found that barbiturate addicts "purchased and stored sleeping pills by the hundreds. They took large amounts of barbiturates day and night and were unable to get through even a day without drugs. Such persons frequently placed themselves in a rather deep stage of anesthesia almost every night." For them, even catching a mild infection or twisting their necks into an awkward position might mean death.

The National Institute of Mental Health is preparing to coordinate all research on suicide. Dr. Bunney and Dr. Fawcett are attempting to detect hard-to-spot depressions in potentially suicidal patients by testing their urine.

Dr. Mish Zaks, associate professor of psychiatry at Northwestern university, is trying to uncover potential suicides through a do-it-yourself written exam that can be given to any group. He thinks that his test, with answers that can be checked in only 15 minutes, will detect suicidal tendencies in persons who may not even be aware of them.

Is suicide a disease? Are people who kill themselves mentally ill? Dr. Grinker, of Chicago's Michael Reese hospital, says, "Everyone, at some time or other, has the wish to kill himself or to die for some personal reason. He enjoys the fantasy of such an ending and of the grief of those left behind. But what differentiates the wish from the act? We have no satisfactory answer."

Some psychiatrists think that most suicidal persons suffer from manic-depressive disease, depressed phase. Instead of showing the typical alternating periods of jubilation and dark despair, the patient sinks into silent withdrawal. His appetite may diminish, he loses weight, he awakens at 4 a.m. and can't get back to sleep. He loses interest in work and play. He may complain of headaches, abdominal distress, and have other vague, hypochondriacal symptoms. He usually keeps secret his feeling of deep sadness, worthlessness, and unhappiness.

Depression is undoubtedly a major factor in suicide, but some students say that mental illness is not always responsible for it. Jack P. Gibbs, professor of sociology at Washington State university, points to strange riddles in suicide statistics.

1. The suicide rate (number of deaths annually per 100,000) increases regularly with age, from 0.3 among children 5-14 years old to 26.0 for persons 85 and over. Presumably, the problems of aging (poor health, financial problems, death of friends) are responsible. But, asks Dr. Gibbs, why is it that the rate rises only for white males, not for white women or Negroes?

2. The male suicide rate is three times that of females — but not all through life. Among persons of less than 20 years of age the male rate may exceed the female rate in a given year by less than one per 100,000, but at 75 and over, the differences maybe as much as 50 per 100,000.

3. The Negro suicide rate is 3.9; the white rate is 11.4. But in Seattle the Negro rate rose to 10.2 (For some reason, as the Negro murder rate declines, the suicide rate increases.)

Dr. Schneidman of the L.A. Suicide Prevention center doubts the Freudian theory that suicide is murder turned inward. "We now know," he says, "that people will kill themselves for many reasons, not only hate and revenge, but also shame, guilt, fear, hopelessness, loyalty, pain, and even boredom."

Except for such primitive (and presumably happy) peoples as the Caroline Islanders of the South Pacific and the Kafirs of the Hindu Kush, suicide is an international disease. But it varies inexplicably from country to country. Japan has a high rate: 26. Catholic Ireland has a very low rate: 2.5. But Catholic Austria has one of the highest rates: 25. Sweden and Denmark are near the top with suicides, but their neighbor, Norway, is near the bottom, and no one can explain why. The Swedish and Danish rates are about double the U.S. rate of 10.5.

West Berlin leads Europe's cities with 37, but East Berlin (unreported) is probably just as high. In the U.S., where suicide is the tenth leading cause of death, the highest rates are in the Western mountain regions and the Pacific Coast. San Francisco leads all cities. Los Angeles, Seattle, and Portland also rank high. Thirty years ago, cities had a 60% higher rate than rural areas, but today there is little difference.

Married men between 35 and 44 have a rate of 16.7; single men, 29.8; widowers, 81.7; and divorced men 112.6! Suicide hits all social and economic levels evenly, but certain occupations are more vulnerable.

In Los Angeles county, every month, at least one physican kills himself. ("I suppose it's because they feel they can't ask for help," says a psychiatrist.) Policemen are a high-risk group, and so are peacetime soldiers. "The surest way of reducing the suicide rate is to start a war," says Dr. Stengel.

Every possible method is tried. The more violent methods indicate the seriousness of the inner disturbance and forecast the likelihood that another attempt will be made. Women try suicide three times more often than men, but three times as many men die. The men use more violent means, like shooting or hanging, women usually take sleeping pills.

Of the 20,819 suicides in a recent year, firearms accounted for 9,595; hanging, 3,057; analgesics and soporifics, 2,666; motor exhaust gases and carbon monoxide, 2,211; jumping, 791; other liquids and solids, 733; drowning, 576; cutting, 417. Barbiturates were responsible for nearly 2,000 of the analgesic deaths.

Alcohol plays a big part in suicide. Dr. Berger, of Wallace laboratories, reports that alcohol was found in the blood of 617 Maryland suicide victims. He says, "Alcohol often intensifies and heightens the prevailing mood. In a depressed patient, it may deepen the depression. In other patients, it may increase their aggressiveness, which, when turned against oneself, will lead to suicide."

Five hundred children and adolescents die every year by their own hands; 100 of them are in the 10-14 group. Dr. Lourie of George Washington university reports, "A three-year-old tried to kill herself by throwing herself in front of cars in order to join her beloved five-year-old sister who had died a month before. A four-year-old boy attempted to jump out the window a few months after his 20-year-old brother had committed suicide."

Dr. Louris says that 10 of 40 suicidal children he studied were seeking punishment for guilt. Others sought escape from an intolerable situation. He found their suicidal tendency stemmed from the earliest years of childhood "when they learned to hurt others by leaving them."

Suicidal children are often those who do not take part in school activities outside the classroom as members of athletic teams, orchestras, dramatic clubs. In every case the child had no close friends.

Dr. Joseph D. Teicher of the University of Southern California found that all but 12% of adolescent suicide attempts occurred at home, often with parents in the next room. But the parents might just as well have been miles away. "The adolescent suicide is cut off from persons with whom he can discuss his problems," said the researchers. In 72% of cases studied, the young persons "had one or both natural parents absent from the home (divorced, separated, or deceased), and 20% of them had a parent who attempted suicide. In the 15 to 19-year-old group, deaths by suicide are exceeded only by deaths from accidents and cancer. Suicide is the second leading cause of death among college students.

Our attitude toward suicide is becoming less punitive as we learn more about mental illness. In England, it was unlawful until 1961 for anyone to try to kill himself. From 1946 to 1955, the English put to trial 5,800 persons and found 5,500 of them guilty of attempting suicide. Three hundred were sent to prison. In the U.S., nine states still have laws against attempting suicide; other states prosecute suicidal persons for disorderly conduct.

"This is typical of our attitude toward suicide," says Dr. Tabin, a psychiatrist in Champaign, Ill. "We can't face up to the sickness, so we call it crime and send the criminals to prison. It is time we faced up to the truth."

Dr. Schneidman of the Los Angles center is heartened by new developments. He says, "Soon every community will have some kind of suicide-prevention center, just as it has a fire department.

The Pain In Rain

How weather affects health

By James C. G. Conniff

Every person is a living barometer. Cooling air, in advance of a low-pressure front, with the humidity rising is a typical pre-storm situation. If affects people. As the barometer falls, up go crime, suicides, accidents, absenteeism, engineering errors, and bank miscalculations.

The World Meteorogical organization has just published a book, *A Survey of Human Biometeorology*, which confirms what grandfather has been saying all along: arthritis, rheumatism, and corns alert you to changes in the weather.

The biometeorologists found that body tissues, freed from the weight of the atmosphere, swell because moisture content expands. This can increase limb diameter as much as an inch and, in the arthritic, clamp the flesh painfully against joints.

The WMO survey rounds up thousands of findings about the complex links between man and what the insiders call sferics, short for atmospherics.

Eighteen biometeorologists pinpointed the influence that weather has on everything from disease, to the way we think (sharpest at about 40°, barometer up), work (most efficiently around 65°, low humidity), talk (more clearly and slowly on a rising barometer), hear (best at 50°, less well as humidity increases), and react (response is impaired by changes in the atmosphere's electrical field).

One study traced the paths of storms across 50 of Europe's largest cities for years and tabulated in their wakes accident-rate increases as high as 40%. The evidence of a connection between highway carnage and sferics is so overpowering that the biometeorologists say flatly there can be no question about it.

The survey also shows why that brilliant inspiration you had looks embarrassingly routine 24 hours later. Moodiness, bleak outlook, foggy thinking are all tied up mysteriously

Condensed from "Columbia", Columbia Plaza, New Haven, Conn. 06507. May, 1966. ‹1967 by the Knights of Columbus and reprinted with permission.

with brain function. That depends more on weather than scientists once thought. When you feel depressed on a rainy day, it is not just your imagination. It is because the falling barometer affects your brain.

Like the joints of the arthritic, the brain becomes cramped by internal pressure from its own moisture-distended tissue. Since the skull does not give, confinement of the brain is more intense. It crushes its own blood vessels until they are unable to carry enough oxygen to nourish the brain tissue that is compressing them. With a reduced brain-oxygen supply, you are bound to feel low and think poorly.

Although surgeons have long consulted the weather, especially when scheduling operations for high-risk patients (hot, humid spells put an added burden on circulatory systems), it is only recently that we are finding out just how subtly weather affects health.

For example, the survey reports that there is a general rise in blood pressure after a stretch of marked atmospheric cooling. Since sharp, long drops in temperature occur most frequently during autumn and winter, persons plagued by hypertension should avoid undue exertion then. Heart attacks strike most often during weather extremes of both humid cold and heat. Dry heat, once a person adapts to it, actually reduces the work of the heart.

A sudden drop in temperature, coupled with a falling barometer, plays hob with the asthmatic patient. Best condition for the asthmatic: a sustained high-pressure front like those which prevail in dry, warm Arizona and New Mexico.

Glaucoma is another sudden reactor to very hot or very cold days. Detached retinas rise in frequency during late spring or early summer but are relatively rare in winter. In bright sunny weather conjunctivitis increases. The same weather conditions provoke epileptic seizures, especially when the seizure-prone person is driving along a glaring road bordered by fence posts, poles or trees set close together or when there are sudden rapid changes in light intensity as on entering and leaving tunnels.

You build up to it, of course, but the tense ulcer type is more likely to suffer an acute perforation during drastic changes in air masses. These are most frequent, as are perforated ulcers, in May and November.

Weather effects even your teeth. Biometeorologists note that the colder the climate the more carbohydrate and sugar-laden the menu. Dental caries are inevitable under such conditions.

Warmer climates exact their price, too. It is no myth that

life goes on at a slower pace in the tropics. It has to: less glandular output, hence less energy.

Studies of the tropics reveal that because the body has heat-disposal problems wherever external temperatures are high, a tropical people have short bodies. One important plus for the tropics: lowered insulin needs let diabetic patients do better there. They often can give up medication completely.

The over-all weather-to-population studies demonstrate that seasonal temperatures influence even the sex ratio in birth rates. Somehow, more boys are conceived in hot weather run a higher risk of being less bright than they could be if the mother, like most people in summertime, eats less food, especially protein, during the vital third month when the baby's brain structures are being formed.

What climate is considered best for health? Ideally, the quiet air masses which for centuries the health resorts of western Europe have capitalized on to lure those in need of physical and mental repair. The lee of high mountains, where low-pressure areas seldom move in, is also ideal. So is any coast where there are bright days "with the white sails flying and the flung spray and the blown spume and the sea gulls crying."

Banishing the Blues

*Depression is a serious disease
that calls for medical help*

By Lawrence Galton

A 35-year-old engineer suddenly loses his appetite. He cannot sleep, reports severe headaches and chest pains. A medical check show nothing physically wrong. But the doctor, refusing to leave it at that, questions him closely. He discovers there have been several such attacks. Always they have come during periods of pressure on the job. Always they have been accompanied by feelings of discouragement.

The doctor doesn't prescribe a medicine chest full of drugs, one for each symptom. He prescribes one **drug** to fight mental

Condensed from "Parade", 733 3rd Ave., New York City 10017. Jan. 2, 1966. ©1966 by Parade Publications, Inc., and reprinted with permission.

depression, and before long all symptoms disappear.

A young housewife suffers from overwhelming fatigue and constant abdominal distress. She has tried vitamins, tonics, and other remedies without result. When finally she consults a doctor, he notices a kind of dullness and mental withdrawal. When he finds no physical explanation for her troubles, he gently asks if anything has happened to make her feel depressed. She had lost her mother eight months before, had grieved for some time, but thought she had recovered. The housewife, too, is treated for depression and quickly relieved.

Mental depression is being recognized as a critical medical problem. It is "the most challenging one that confronts the modern physician," says Dr. Frank J. Ayd, Jr., of Baltimore, a psychiatrist. "More human suffering has resulted from depression than from any other single disease," declares Dr. Nathan S. Kline, a Lasker-award winner for mental-health research. "The great masquerader," Dr. Seymour Diamond of the Chicago Medical school calls it. Says Dr. Paul H. Ornstein of the University of Cincinnati, "It has many faces and often hides behind physical complaints without betraying its presence by an obviously sad or despairing mood." The California state medical society calls depression "one of the most common conditions encountered in medical practice."

Is depression in disguised form right now affecting someone in your family, or a friend or a neighbor? Here is what doctors have been discovering about its symptoms and disguises, and what you can about it.

All of us have our ups and downs, days when we feel on top of the world, others when we feel low. But depression is another matter. It is a chronic change of mood, an extended lowering of the spirits. It can be triggered by a loss of a loved one, of money, or a job. Such a depression is called *exogenous*, meaning it comes from outside.

But there is another common type of depression. Suddenly a person decides he is a failure in life. Self-confidence and a self-esteem vanish. Everyday problems seem too much to cope with. This is *endogenous* depression, coming from within, perhaps as the result of some body-chemical upset.

Doctors think depressions often are both endogenous and exogenous. They argue there has to be an endogenous (internal) factor, otherwise a death in the family or other loss would lead only to temporary normal sadness.

When a depression does set in, there is a general lowering of vitality. In one study Johns Hopkins investigators found that depressed persons can be harder hit when common illnesses strike. They gave psychological tests to a group of employees at Fort Detrick, Md. The following winter, when flu broke out and many of the employees were affected, those who had been found mildly depressed took three weeks or longer to recover. Others were over their flu in three to 14 days.

Some medical men think that depression may open the door for other illnesses. Dr. Edward J. Kollar of the University of California has noticed that many persons become sick for the first time, or begin to suffer from some chronic disorder, or decide to undergo surgery when they are depressed.

"During my five-year experience as chief of a large general hospital," he says, "I became aware of the large number of patients who had masked depressions. Anyone ill is entitled to react to his illness with depression. But people were depressed *before* they developed the illness."

Even when depression is the result of illness, doctors have discovered that treating the depression may help to treat the illness. Antidepressant drugs, for instance, seem to help in rheumatoid arthritis and chronic ulcerative colitis cases in which depression is present. Dr. M. D. Sanger of Brooklyn, N.Y., has used the drugs on asthma and eczema patients who have failed to benefit from usual treatment and who were found to be depressed. Of 113 persons tested, 89 showed improvement.

At the Neuropsychiatric institute of the University of California, Los Angeles, physicians tried antidepressant drug treatment on patients with Parkinson's disease. The patients had not been able to dress, cook, or keep themselves clean, and were all depressed. After three weeks, almost 90% could care for themselves. Some could even do simple jobs.

Depression can also cause a wide variety of symptoms that resemble those of physical ailments. In a four-year study, doctors at Massachusetts General hospital, Boston, found fatigue the single most frequent symptom of patients diagnosed as depressed. Sometimes the patients felt so exhausted they could not get through their daily work. Yet at the same time they reported they could not sleep well. They would doze off, then wake up early in the morning and toss for hours. Any sudden tendency to wake up very early can be a sign of depression.

Headaches are another common symptom. In studying 423 patients with depression, Dr. Diamond found that 84% complained of headache. Depressive headaches, he says, are not limited to one area, tend to be worse in the morning than in the evening, and often resist all ordinary remedies. But once recognized for what they are, they can be relieved with antidepressant drug. Dr. Diamond also found that 75% of depressed patients lost weight, from five to 20 pounds. Other symptoms included breathing difficulty, dizziness, weakness, urinary disturbance, palpitations, nausea.

Dr. Jack R. Ewalt, Harvard psychiatrist, warned a group of family doctors that "depression symptoms are frequently referred to the gastro-intestinal tract," and urged a check for depression when patients complained of abdominal pains that could not be explained by organic difficulties.

Many elderly persons considered senile are really only depressed. "The depressions of the geriatric patient often remain undiagnosed," says Dr. Sidney Cohen, chief of Psychiatry service, Wadsworth Veterans Administration hospital, Los Angeles. "There is the feeling that he is too senile to be depressed. Depressions can contribute to or even cause senile confusion."

Until 1938 there was almost nothing doctors could do about depression. Then came electroshock therapy, and the use of drugs.

No one drug is a cure-all. The drug that helps one patient may have little effect on another. Some physicians prefer to use drugs only when psychotherapy does not work. They report that psychotherapy alone often accomplishes wonders. It can be brief and given by a family doctor, sometimes in only a few sessions in which the patient is told the reason for his physical compaints, is encouraged to talk out worries, and is given the needed reassurance.

Another new development is Indoklon, an inhalant drug. A few sniffs can be as effective as electroshock for severe depression.

Now, a whole new electroshock technique has shown promise. Ordinarily, brief bursts of current are applied to both sides of the brain. In the new method, they are applied to just one side. Dr. Winston L. Martin of the University of Texas, Houston, has found that it is fully as effective, and it minimizes the temporary confusion and memory disturbance that sometimes follow conventional treatment.

But the big problem with depression is not treatment but recognition. Depressed persons often shrug off their blue feelings as results, not cause, of their aches and pains. When they do seek medical help, they often fail to mention their dejection. Some vehemently deny feeling depressed out of a mistaken belief that there is something shameful about it.

There is not. It is one of the most common of all disorders and it hits people in all walks of life. And if patients tell their doctors about it they can save a lot of needless treatment, expense, and misery.

Accident Prone?

*The persons most likely to get
into serious trouble can be*

By John Fetterman

Dr. Hans Hahn, of Transylvania college, Lexington, Ky., has spent most of his life looking for people who like to have accidents, and in this field the jovial 65-year-old professor has few peers. He estimates that about 25% of all people, including himself, are accident prone, in industry, home, or auto.

At the Kentucky Utilities Co., he singled out a worker as highly accident prone. Soon after, the man was killed in a power-line accident. Skeptical Kentucky state police brought him ten motorists, two of whom had long records of minor accidents. He correctly identified the two accident-prone drivers. Dr. Hahn's work has stirred interest among insurance companies, railroads, aircraft manufacturers, and trade unions, each with special reasons for wanting to identify people who like to have accidents.

His tests are deceptively simple. In one he takes his subjects to a small stage and points to the orchestra pit, strewn with broken glass. "It would be most unpleasant to fall upon the sharp glass," he warns. Then the subjects are taken back about 16 feet and blindfolded. Each one must then walk toward the edge. One may grope fearfully with the first step. The next, however, may walk boldly to the edge and only be prevented from plunging over by guards.

The supercautious man, explains Dr. Hahn, is the neurotic driver who gropes through traffic and causes others to have accidents. The carefree extrovert is the driver who follows too closely, races trains to crossings, and "has absolutely no margin of safety for himself or others."

The normal, safe driver will usually take three or four sure

Condensed from the "National Observer", 11501 Columbia Pike, Silver Spring, Md. 20910. April 19, 1965. ᶜ1965 by Dow Jones & Co., Inc., and reprinted with permission.

steps, then refuse to advance closer to the waiting disaster.

"I believe that the margin of safety is a deeply rooted trait that shows accident proneness in the form of carelessness," says the professor. All his tests are devised to pinpoint a subject's margin of safety, which may be affected by fatigue, strain, and boredom. Thus some of the tests involve laboratory reproductions of highway stresses.

In one test, subjects are told to press a button whenever a light flashes. Even the accident-prone subject responds well at first. Then a bell signal is substituted for the light, and the two are mixed with no discernible pattern. Finally, the danger signals are speeded up. Many persons tend to panic, try to outguess the signals or quit in despair.

Again, the subjects are put before a board on which 100 numbers are scattered at random. Each is told to point out specific numbers. Only about one in 10,000 finds all numbers in the five minutes allowed.

The safe driver will find between 25 and 50 of them, because he is searching out and seeing only the important things such as the other car approaching from a side road. The accident-prone driver will look at a dozen numbers before he finds the one he wants. This driver will focus so strongly on one quest that he misses all other signs. He may see the car come out of the side road, but will therefore miss the other car approaching head-on.

A subject may merely add long columns of figures for an hour. Some grow irritable. These are the ones who grow tired of analyzing and reacting to constant danger signals in traffic: blinking lights, hand signals, whistles, changing lights, and horns. Others do well for most of the hour-long test, then their accuracy and attention explode, and they prove themselves to be the most dangerous of all. At the crucial moment they quit reacting to all danger signals.

The fatigue factor is important. Tests that go fast do not mean much. In Europe they know that a test must be long and tedious to discover anything. Germany's railroads now use the professors' tests, as does the 1.2 million-member German coal-mine union.

His ultimate goal is to develop therapy for the accident prone. But it won't be easy, "Accident proneness is something you are born with," says Dr. Hahn, "and it may be you can never get rid of it."

Gamblers . . . Who can't Quit

The cure is the same as for alcoholics:
total abstention

By Barbara O'Connell with Melvin Herman
and Flora Rheta Schreiber

Sam made $125 a week as the traffic manager for a manufacturing concern, and he owed $100 of it. Every week he would borrow from one creditor to pay another. At finance companies, he renewed loans time after time so he would not have to pay them off.

One day he totaled up his debts: $3,600. Not a big sum, but an impossible one for him. Depressed, he put down the pencil he had used to add up the figures and reached for the telephone. "Hello? This is Sam. I want to make a bet." When he hung up the telephone, he was almost happy. This time, he might win.

Sam is a compulsive gambler. For 25 years (he is now in his 40's) he has bet on horses, athletic contests, cards, pool, or anything else. For Sam, the gambling season is always. Now he is in debt, his wife is sick, and his children need clothes for school. But for the moment, Sam is content. He paces up and down the room and looks at the telephone. He might win. He will win!

In the U.S. are 6 million compulsive gamblers who throw away some $20 billion a year. Gamblers Anonymous, an organization that helps gamblers kick the habit, is opening new chapters every year. Gambling fever can attack anyone. Some gambers are rich, others are poor. Sam makes a small salary and wagers small amounts. High-salaried executives roll up debts in the hundreds of thousands of dollars. But all compulsive gamblers must lose. They never quit while they are ahead.

What makes them act like that? Most of the 20 psychiatrists who have published studies think compulsive gambling comes from unresolved problems in the person's life. They

Condensed from "Science Digest", 959 8th Ave., New York City 10019. April, 1968. ʿ 1968 by the Hearst Corp., and reprinted with permission.

think that many of the problems are carried over from child-hood in the form of conflicts with members of the family. Psychiatrists say that the gambler has a deep-seated feeling of guilt. He wants to punish himself. If he wins for a while, it is not enough. So he wagers more. If he loses, he is depressed. Although he seems to the cheerful enough on the surface, he lives on the brink of a depression intensified by a loss of self-esteem.

"Compulsive gamblers gamble in an attempt to ward off an impending depression," says Dr. Ralph R. Greensen, of Beverly Hills. As a result, plush gambling places are usually full of depressed people. Such gambling centers often figure in suicides. Threatened by debts, family troubles, and jail, desperate gamblers often take their own lives.

Members of GA who man a 24-hour-a-day phone service report a number of suicide threats. "I've got one foot out the window," a caller told a member recently. "Hold on," the member advised calmly. "Come to the meeting this afternoon and I'll go to your creditors with you. You won't have to go to jail."

The gambler equates fate with God and the omnipotent father of his early childhood. Luck is a lady who is both mother and saint. Fate is all-powerful, but Luck has a loving, protective side. The compulsive gambler is out to woo Luck, conquer Fate, and defeat his opponent, logic and even the "establishment." All this is riding on one throw; he is not playing just for money.

All compulsive gamblers show the same faulty thinking, the family man the loner, the woman as well as the man, the prosperous as well as the down-and-out. "I once thought I was smarter than anyone else," says Henry P., a reformed gambler who almost ruined his business before he gave up gambling.

Henry's history is typical. Betting on horses became his first love at 15, but he was always eager to gamble at gin rummy, poker, or dice. "I don't remember a day I was out of debt," he says. When he got out of the army in 1945 with a lit-tle nest egg, he gambled it away. Soon a high weekly salary was going the same way. He began stealing from his brother and from his employer. In 1950, he went into the dress business. Being intelligent and energetic, he built up a $3.5 million business, but gambled it away. By 1960, he was bankrupt.

"But the thing that gambling most affects is the family," he says. "My wife didn't have a chance. I wished her dead. Once I threw her bodily out of the car because she tried to stop me from gambling. She developed a bleeding ulcer. But I didn't consider myself bad, I didn't want to feel 'no good.' "

Like Henry, a typical gambler begins casually. He visits the race track with a friend. Perhaps he wins a large stake on his first trip and comes away with a euphoric feeling. Luck will be eternally his. Besides, it is exciting. Once hooked, he cannot keep from spending the family savings, cadging loans from friends, and getting into debt with loan companies. He may even go to jail. Gamblers Anonymous now has three chapters in jails, the membership composed of convicts who have landed there through gambling. It has 85 chapters in the U.S., 15 chapters in Europe, and several more in Canada. It was started in California by a reformed gambler. Like Alcoholics Anonymous, it works by demonstration of fellowship. In GA, the compulsive gambler learns that he does not stand alone.

One evening in Manhattan, 20 men, an average number for a GA meeting, sat around a table. There were no women. GA has women members, but they are a tiny minority of the membership. A chairman introduced one of the men, John, by his first name. No last names are used. John, a husky man in his 30's, stood up. "I'm John and I'm a compulsive gambler. I've been in Gamblers Anonymous for five years and I haven't placed a bet in that time. Before that . . ."

The story he told is typical: the early introduction to gambling, the quick development of the passion, the bouncing checks, the lost business, the faltering marriage. Most typical, perhaps, was John's obsession with gambling. "It was the last thing I thought about before going to sleep and first thing I thought about when I woke up," he says. "I spent 90% of my time thinking about it."

The chairman introduces each man in turn and each relates his tale. They speak in firm, clear voices with a lawyerlike grasp of timing and gesture. "We couldn't talk to groups before," one explains later. "We were all loners. But we've been telling the same story in GA for years, so we're pretty good." The stories vary only in the details.

In another room in the building, a group called Gam-Anon, composed of relatives of gamblers, was meeting at the same time. It draws mostly wives, both those who have husbands in GA and those whose husbands are still gambling. On this particular evening, a young woman and attractive redhead asked for advice about her husband, who refuses to admit he is a compulsive gambler. The women offered suggestions based on experience.

"Put all money in your own checking account."

"Don't cover his checks, let them bounce. Just keep the money you need for household expenses."

"Remember, he can't help it, he's sick."

The Gamblers Anonymous program is based on total abstention. Like alcoholics, gamblers who indulge their weakness cannot stop. They must give up gambling completely. The prescribed way is to take one day at a time. Members are advised to tell themselves, "I didn't gamble today, I won't gamble tomorrow." Some do it the hard way. After his first meeting, Henry told himself, "I'll never gamble again." It worked. He cancelled a bet he had on the Kentucky Derby and never made another wager.

After a few meetings a new member and his wife got together with a panel of experienced members for advice on their financial situation. "They tell you how to pay up," explains Sam, who joined GA after his debts reached $3,600. "After two years in GA, I only owe $700. They want you to pay off slowly, otherwise you might get overconfident." Sam is now an ex-gambler.

ARE YOU A COMPULSIVE GAMBLER?

Most compulsive gamblers will answer Yes to at least seven of these questions, which are taken from Gamblers Anonymous publications.

1. Do you lose time from work because of gambling?
2. Is gambling making your homelife unhappy?
3. Is gambling affecting your reputation?
4. Have you ever felt remorse after gambling?
5. Do you ever gamble to get money with which to pay debts?
6. Does gambling cause a decrease in your ambition or efficiency?
7. After losing, do you feel you must return as soon as possible and win back your losses?
8. After you win do you have a strong urge to return and win more?
9. Do you often gamble until your last dollar is done?
10. Do you ever borrow to finance your gambling?
11. Have you ever sold any real or personal property to finance gambling?
12. Are you reluctant to use "gambling money" for ordinary expenditures?
13. Does gambling make you careless of the welfare of your family?
14. Do you ever gamble longer than you had planned?
15. Do you ever gamble to escape worry or trouble?
16. Have you ever committed, or considered committing,

an illegal act to finance gambling?

17. Does gambling cause you to have difficulty in sleeping?

18. Do arguments, disappointments, or frustrations create within you an urge to gamble?

19. Do you have an urge to celebrate any good fortune by a few hours of gambling?

20. Have you ever considered self-destruction as a result of your gambling?

What Science Has Discovered About Hope

Lack of it can have lethal physical consequences

By Martin E. P. Seligman

Helplessness, the loss of control over one's life, can bring on sudden, unexplained death. Rats, roaches, dogs, prisoners, and rejected old folks have all been victims.

Major F. Harold Kushner, a physician who spent nearly six years in a Viet Cong prison camp, told me particularly chilling tales. He saw men killed by their own state of mind. They simply lost the will to live, and died of helplessness.

Ronald was typical. He had been a rugged, intelligent Marine from a crack unit. When Dr. Kushner came to camp in 1968 he was impressed with Ronald's physical and mental strength. Although he had been a prisoner for two years, weighed only 140 pounds, and every day had to carry large loads of tree roots on his back, he never griped. "Grit your teeth and tighten your belt," he used to repeat.

The reason for Ronald's resilience became clear to the physician. Ronald was convinced the Viet Cong were going to release him soon. They would periodically release a few men who had cooperated with them, and Ronald had. The camp commander indicated that he was next in line, that he would be released in about six months.

But six months later, some very high VC officials arrived to give the prisoners a political course. The prisoners were given to understand that the outstanding pupil would be released. Ronald became the leader of the group, and the VC led him to expect release within a month. But a month came and went, and one day it finally dawned on Ronald that the whole thing had been a hoax. He was not going to be released after all.

He became depressed, stopped working, refused food, and lay on his bed in a fetal position sucking his thumb. Dr. Kushner and the other POW's tried to bring him around. They hugged him, and babied him, but early one December morning, Ronald died in Kushner's arms.

This is only one of a number of such deaths witnessed by Major Kushner. In each case psychological disturbances led to death. Hope of release had sustained Ronald. When he gave up hope, when he believed that nothing he could do would get him out of the camp, he died.

In my work on helplessness over the last decade, I have had the same experience with laboratory animals. When rats, chickens, monkeys, and even cockroaches learn that their actions are futile, that they have no control over their lives, they become susceptible to death.

Conversely, learning that they can control their environment prolongs their lives. I do not know what physiological mechanism is at work, but much evidence indicates that being placed in a helpless situation and reacting passively increases the risk of death, for both human beings and animals.

Curt Richter of John Hopkins medical school was one of the first researchers to connect helplessness with sudden death. Seventeen years ago he was studying differences in response to stress among wild animals and domestic Norway rats. He found that most wild rats would usually swim for about 60 hours in a large tank of warm water before they drowned. But a few rats died within minutes.

Richter retraced his procedures until he discovered the reason. The rats had died quickly were those he had gripped until they stopped struggling. When he placed them in the water, they would often dive suddenly to the bottom and drown. At first he thought they had been scared to death. Like Ronald, when they confronted a hopeless situation, they simply gave up. Their sudden death was submissive death, from helplessness.

Richter was able to prevent submissive death by teaching the rats that their situation was not hopeless. He held the rats briefly and then freed them, immersed them in water for a few seconds and then took them out again. In this way the rats learned to hope. They became aggressive, tried to escape, and showed no signs of sudden death.

For several years my colleagues and I have studied the effects of inescapable events on rats, dogs, and people. In one experiment, we give rats physically harmless but inescapable electric shocks. Then the rats receive shocks while in a box from which they can easily escape. But they do not attempt to flee. Instead they run around, and then settle down, passively accepting the noxious punishment. Their earlier experience has taught them that shock is inescapable, that they are helpless. But when we allow them to escape shock repeatedly before we give them inescapable shock, they keep trying to escape even in a hopeless situation. Their previous experience has taught them that they can avoid the shock.

L. S. Ewing observed submissive death in creatures as lowly as the cockroach. Cockroaches have clear dominance hierarchies, and when subordinate cockroaches are repeatedly attacked by dominant roaches, they die. Characteristically, there is no sign of external damage; the physiological mechanism of death remains unknown. But their defeat may have produced helplessness, with death as the consequence.

When we cage a wild animal in a zoo, we deprive it of its natural environment and, more important, of control over its own actions. This may explain why so many newly acquired wild animals die, often en route to the zoo.

Hal Markowitz of the Oregon Zoological Research Center in Portland has markedly improved the health of the zoo's apes simply by giving them control over their food rather than doling it out to them.

Death from helplessness among animals is distressing enough, but submissive death among human beings is much worse. Yet I believe that human beings die following feelings of helplessness. The death of a loved one upon whom they have depended, a sudden loss of power, prestige, or purpose, the loss of physical abilities in old age, all may lead to early death. George Engel documented 170 cases of sudden death during psychological stress.

A 22-year-old girl with malignant paraganglioma was still able to take drives with her mother. On one such outing the mother was killed in a car accident. The girl was not injured, but within a few hours she lapsed into a coma and died.

This girl had been totally dependent upon her mother. It seems plausible that feelings of helplessness after her mother's unexpected death could have caused the girl's own sudden death.

A 45-year-old man found himself in an unbearable situation and decided to move to another town. But just as he was ready, difficulties developed that made the move impossible. In an anguished quandary, he nonetheless boarded the train. Halfway to his destination, he got out to pace the platform at a station stop. When the conductor called "all aboard," he felt he could neither go on nor return home. He dropped dead on the spot. His dilemma had made him helpless. With nowhere to return, nowhere to go, he gave up and died.

Mysterious voodoo deaths provide evidence that helplessness contributes to sudden death. More than 30 years ago physiologist Walter Cannon described several incidents.

A Brazilian Indian condemned and sentenced by a so-called medicine man is helpless against his own emotional response and dies within hours. In Africa a young man unknowingly eats a taboo wild hen. On discovery of his "crime" he trembles, is overcome by fear, and dies in 24 hours. In New Zealand a Moari woman eats fruit that she later learns has come from a tabooed place. By noon next day she is dead. In Australia a witch doctor points a bone at a man. The man rapidly sinks in spirits and prepares to die. He is saved only at the last moment when the witch doctor is forced to remove the charm. All these people believed they were doomed to die, that there was nothing they could do to change their fate.

For two decades Engel, Arthur Schmale, and William Greene have been investigating the consequences of psychological loss on physical disease. In one study they interviewed 51 healthy women who had regular Pap tests. Each woman showed some "suspicious" cells, but none was cancerous. During the interviews, the researchers learned that 18 of the women had recently suffered some kind of psychological loss that made them feel hopeless. The investigators predicted that these 18 women would be likely to develop cancer. Eleven of them did. Only eight of the remaining 33 women developed the disease.

Further evidence comes from a British study of 4,500 widowers. During the first six months after their spouses' deaths, 213 of these men died. That rate was 40% higher than the expected mortality rate for their age group.

I believe that depression, the common cold of psychopathology, is really the belief in one's own helplessness. In psychological post mortems of 26 sudden, unexpected deaths among Eastman Kodak employees, depression was the dominant state of mind. When these depressed persons became anxious or angry, they had heart attacks.

David Glass of the University of Texas reported that

coronary-prone people are highly susceptible to becoming helpless when subjected to stress in the laboratory. Other research has shown that depression prolongs recovery from virus infections.

Helplessness makes people more susceptible to pathogens in the environment, so when one of our parents dies, or when our own spouse dies, we must be particularly careful. I suggest bi-monthly physical checkups during the first year following such a loss, or any major life change.

The staffs of hospitals, mental institutions, old-age homes, prisons, and other institutions pay too little attention to the effects of helplessness. The usual doctor-patient, caretaker-aged jailer-inmate relationship allows the inhabitants no sense of control. In hospitals, the doctors knows all; patients are expected to sit back calmly and rely on the staff to make them well.

This extreme dependency may be helpful to some patients, but others will not recover unless they can assume greater control over their lives. In a physically or mentally sick person, loss of control may be enough to tip the balance toward death.

A woman who had remained mute for nearly ten years was shifted to the first floor in her hospital while her unit was being redecorated. The third floor, where she had been living, was known among the patients as the chronic hopeless floor. In contrast, the first floor was commonly occupied by patients who were free to come and go. Patients there could anticipate discharge fairly soon.

All patients who were temporarily moved from the third floor were given medical examinations just before the move, and the patient in question was judged to be in excellent medical health, though still mute and withdrawn. Shortly after moving to the first floor, she surprised the staff by becoming socially responsive. Within a two-week period she ceased to be mute and was actually becoming gregarious. But then the redecoration of the third floor was completed, and all previous residents were returned. Within a week after return to the "hopeless" unit, this patient, who, like Snow White, had been aroused from a living torpor, collapsed and died. Autopsy revealed no pathology of note, and it was suggested at the time that the patient had died of despair.

One of the groups most vulnerable to death by helplessness is the aged. In America growing old means losing control. Forced to retire at 65, sent to an old-age home, ignored by relatives, the old person is systematically stripped of control over his life. We kill many of our older people by denying

them choices, purpose in life, control over their lives. Many
of these deaths are premature and unnecessary.
N. A. Ferrari made a study of perceived freedom of choice
in 55 women over 65 years old, average age 82, who applied
for admission to an old-age home in the Midwest. Miss
Ferrari asked them how much choice they had in moving to
the home, how many other possibilities were open to them,
and how much pressure relatives applied to them. Of the 17
women who said they had no alternative, eight died after four
weeks and 16 were dead by ten weeks. Apparently only one
persons out of the 38 who had an alternative died soon after
admission. These deaths were called "unexpected" by the
staff.
Such deaths should no longer be unexpected. We should
expect that when we remove the last vestiges of control over
the environment of an already physically weakened human
being, we may kill him.
We need to make some life-prolonging experiments. Take
two groups of patients in a home for the aged. Give one group
control over their daily lives: a choice about omelets or
scrambled eggs, going to the movies on Wednesday or Thurs-
day, blue or red curtains, between sleeping on the first or
second floor. The other group would be treated the way our
aged are usually treated: no choices. I predict that the group
with choice will live longer and be happier.
Many of us have known people who died shortly after they
were forced to retire at 65. The same logic that forbids
discriminating against blacks and women should apply to
firing a person simply because he is 65. Not only is it
discriminatory, in that individual merit is not taken into account, it may also be lethal. Deprive a person of work and
you remove his best source of control over his life.
Children also show death from helplessness. Ren'e Spitz
first reported on "anaclitic depression," or "hospitalism."
Two conditions produced it: if infants were raised in foundling homes with minimal stimulation, they became torpid
and unresponsive. Alternatively, when infants between six
and 18 months were separated from their prisonmate mothers
who were placed in solitary confinement, depression also
developed. Of the 91 children that showed hospitalism in the
foundling home, 34 died within two years. Death was caused
by respiratory infections, measles, and intestinal disorders.
It is unlikely that the physical conditions of the home were
bad enough to produce a 40% death rate. But what does lack
of stimulation mean to an infant at precisely the age when he
is developing control? Helplessness.

A wide range of physical conditions—heart failure, cancer, viral infection, malnutrition, and asthma—are found in cases of sudden, submissive death. Since the terminal conditions are so varied, it seems unlikely that any one physical event can be the cause.

Our inability to identify a single physical cause should not blind us to the reality of the situation. Even before we fully understand the physical basis of helplessness, we can combat it psychologically by building control into the lives of persons who are thrown into vulnerable situations.

We also can see the importance of controlling our own lives. Perhaps Dylan Thomas expressed it best:

"Do not go gentle into that good night. Old age should burn and rave at close of day; Rage, Rage against the dying of the light . . ."

Do You Know How to Change People's Minds

Psychologists suggest simple methods of persuasion that can be used in everyday life

By John E. Gibson

1. If you want someone to do you a big favor, get him to do you a small one first. True or false?

2. One of the best ways to get someone to change his mind about something is not to talk to him about it at all. True of false?

3. The best way to get people to do what you want is to soften them up with a humorous approach—use jokes or witticisms to put them in a receptive mood. True or false?

4. The best way to convince someone of your good points is to let somebody else mention them. True or false?

5. The most difficult person to influence is the individual with low self-esteem. True or false?

ANSWERS

1. True. Stanford University studies have demonstrated that complying with a small request makes a person much

Condensed from "Family Weekly", 641 Lexington Ave., New York, N.Y. 10022. Nov. 10, 1974. ᶜ1976 by Family Weekly, Inc., and reprinted with permission.

more prone to comply with a larger one later. This principle, as one leading investigation observed, is extremely useful in persuasion.

2. True. If a person has made up his mind about something, to talk him out of it—no matter how persuasive you are—is likely to arouse resentment and provoke argument. Psychological studies show that the best way to operate is to marshal your most persuasive facts but instead of directing them at the person you want to convince, arrange for him to overhear them. Example: Excuse yourself while you "make a phone call," during which you wax as eloquent as you can with your most convincing arguments, favoring the point you wish to put across and permitting the other party to "overhear" your conversation. Research has shown that "persuasions counter to the attitude held by a person were more effective when 'overhead' than when the same persuasion was made directly to the subject."

3. False—at least where young people are concerned—according to a series of studies at Ohio State university, where humor was found to be an unreliable ingredient when used in connection with persuasion. Results of tests showed that "in general, humor did not increase, and sometimes decreased, the persuasive effect of the message."

4. True. University studies have shown that another person will be far more impressed with your good points if they are presented by a third party rather than by yourself. However, if the person you wish to impress is likely to hear negative things about you, it's far better if he hears about them directly from you.

5. False. Studies shows that he is the easiest to influence. As Profs. John R. Wenburg and William W. Wilmot observe in their definitive treatise, *The Personal Communication Process,* "the low-esteem person . . . is far easier to persuade because he has little confidence in his own personal opinions."

Visceral Learning

It may be a new human faculty

By John E. Pfeiffer

Recent studies indicate that man may be able to adjust his own blood pressure, regulate his heart rate, kidney function, blood flow, stomach contractions and brain-wave rhythms by "visceral learning."

Work is still at an experimental stage, but clinical trials at leading medical centers have already yielded important results. It may not be long before "visceral learning" replaces drugs and surgery in treating heart disease, epilepsy, and other ailments. Healthy persons may benefit as well as patients. One day, for example, desk-bound business executives may be able to keep in top physical condition by mentally controlling their own blood pressure and heart rate instead of jogging.

Pioneer experiments were conducted by Neal Miller, a 60-year-old psychologist at Rockefeller university in New York. For nearly two decades he has been waging, and is now winning, a battle against an old and firmly held notion about learning.

The traditional belief is that we can acquire skills (driving, golfing) because skeletal muscles which move our limbs, shoulders, and eyes are under voluntary control of the brain, but that we cannot control or train our internal organs. Heartbeats, for instance, are governed by the involuntary nervous system, automatically and independently of the will.

Famous feats such as those achieved by yogis, who have long regulated heart rates and other visceral processes, were thought to be produced indirectly, by the relaxing of skeletal muscles, which in turn produced the internal changes. Direct control was considered physiologically impossible.

Disproving this dogma turned out to be a formidable task. Miller was helped by a volunteer who stepped forward in the summer of 1962, Jay Trowill, a graduate student. His project

Condensed from "Think", Armonk, N.Y. 10504. September-October, 1969. ᶜ1969 by International Business Machines Corp., and reprinted with permission.

was to devise a way of teaching animals to control their heart rates.

He spent about a year and a half simply trying to find the right experimental animal, which turned out to be the rat. He ruled out indirect effects of the skeletal muscles on the heart by injections of the ancient South American arrow poison, curare, a drug that paralyzes skeletal muscles without affecting the muscles of the heart. Curare paralyzes breathing muscles, thus demanding some form of artificial lung.

Trowill supplied one for his rats, but promptly ran head-on into further problems. Rats, like people, learn best by being rewarded for doing the right thing, but how do you reward a paralyzed animal? The answer involved brain surgery. Trowill implanted electrodes in certain nerve clusters near the base of the rat's brain. Studies conducted during the past 15 years show that these particular clusters operate as "pleasure sites." When they are stimulated, the animal has sensations of intense satisfaction.

Finally, Trowill needed a kind of robot monitor, equipment which would pick up regular electrical pulses produced by contracting heart muscles, recognize brief period of faster-than-average and slower-than-average heart rates, and automatically trigger the device that transmits pleasure signals to the brain. One day, while thumbing through an equipment catalogue, Trowill found a device that would do all this.

Trowill's immobilized, wired-for-pleasure, and electronically monitored rats were soon performing according to expectations. Every time their heart rates increased spontaneously, the robot apparatus gave the rats their reward: intense feelings of pleasure. Of course, the animals did not know what they were doing. But they like the stimulations, and the only way they could get them was by increasing their heart rates.

That is exactly what they did, although *how* they did it remains to be explained. After about an hour of training, 15 out of 19 rats tested increased their heart rates by an average of 5%, or some 20 beats per minute. (The average rat heart rate is about 400 beats per minute.) Furthermore, 15 out of 17 rats rewarded for decreasing their heart rates did so.

The heart-rate changes were small but definite and statistically significant, and indicated the possibility of visceral learning.

Miller and Leo DiCara, his chief assistant, improved on Trowill's results by continually "raising the ante." That is, as soon as a rat increased or decreased its heart rate by a certain amount, say 20 beats per minute, no further rewards were provided until it attained further changes at still higher levels of 25 or more beats per minute. In this way, they gradually reached a point where they could produce changes of about 20% in either direction, so that a rat with a starting heart beat of 400 beats per minute could be trained to attain slow rates of about 320 and fast rates of 480.

Similar results were obtained for other visceral responses. The rats learned to control the contractions of their intestines, increasing or decreasing them by up to 40%; double or half the rate at which their kidneys produced urine; raise or lower their blood pressure; and regulate the amount of blood flowing in their stomach walls. They also learned to produce fast or slow brainwaves, depending on how they were rewarded.

These and other experiments reveal that visceral learning is not only possible, but that in many ways it resembles the process we go through in acquiring any basic skill. A novice learning to play golf or drive a car does not coordinate all at once. At first he makes awkward and unnecessary motions. In swinging the club or shifting gears he has difficulty building individual actions into single smooth sequence. True economy of effort, what we call good form, comes with increasing practice.

There is also a kind of "good form" in visceral learning. Some rats being trained to control intestinal contractions, for example, may also alter heart rates by small amounts. But the effect is least marked in the best learners, and usually diminishes with continued training. When practice has been completed, one and only one function, the rewarded function, is learned. An animal trained to lower its blood pressure will show no significant changes in heart rate. Rats have learned to dilate blood vessels in their right ears but not in their left ears, and vice versa, indicating a degree of selective control which surprised even Miller.

Miller's hunch has long been that "people are at least as smart as rats." In research at the Cornell Medical center, a typical study involved a man suffering from abnormally fast heart rates, 95 to 100 beats per minute, compared with a normal average of 70. The patient sat in an easy chair, with wires running from his chest and leg to a monitoring device that recorded his heart rate. Doctors told him that they were trying to train him to slow down his heart, and that whenever a slight slowing occurred spontaneously he would hear a beeping tone. He needed no further information and no special reward; the desire to achieve a healthier heart rhythm was incentive enough. Unlike the rats, the man knew what he was supposed to do. But aside from relaxing, which has no appreciable effect in such cases, he had no idea of *how* to go about it. He simply *tried* to make the beeps as frequent and long-lasting as possible, and somehow that worked.

The patient made some improvement during the very first session, which lasted an hour. After three weeks and 30 sessions, the end of his experimental training period, his heart rate had dropped to a low-normal figure of about 65 beats per minute.

In other studies at the Harvard Medical school, David Shapiro, Bernard Tursky, and associates have spent more than six years investigating the control of visceral functions. Currently, some of the most important tests involve blood-pressure changes among healthy as well as ailing persons.

Psychiatrists have long taught that what happens to us during childhood may influence our behavior for the rest of our lives, and much of that behavior involves functions. A boy afraid of going to school may exhibit a wide range of symptoms, from stomach-aches, headaches, and palpitations to faintness and pallor. Whether these symptoms develop into a set lifelong pattern depends on the reactions of his parents.

If they happen to be particularly upset by their son's stomach pains, they will "reward" them. They will decide that he ought to stay home, and he will "use" stomach-aches not only during his school days but throughout life whenever he finds himself under stress. Obscure muscular pains, low backache and stiff neck, constipation, fainting spells, and other difficult-to-treat ailments may often be traced to such early conditions and conditioning.

Miller thinks that it may be possible to produce this kind of behavior among young rats, starting at weaning age (about 20 days). If he succeeds, psychiatrists will have fresh clues to the causes and treatment of neuroses and psychosomatic disorders. Even more significant, the new insights may bring about major changes in family relationships, child rearing, and education.

Drugs and Your Brain

*Researchers are hard at work
trying to find out what happens*

By Murray E. Jarvik

The now famous drug LSD was discovered by Albert Hof-
mann accidently in Basel, Switzerland, in 1943. It is a
semisynthetic compound of plant origin, a derivative of ergot
(a fungus which infects rye). It acts like marijuana and
mescaline but is much stronger and produces more bizarre
mental states. Recently Maimon Cohen has reported the finding, frightening in view of its nonmedical use, that LSD can
damage chromosomes which control heredity. Despite
thousands of scientific papers dealing with LSD, we have little idea of what it does to the brain, and we don't know how it
does it.

Hallucinogenic drugs like LSD have always appealed to
unconventional figures in literature and the arts. Thomas de
Quincey and Samuel Coleridge, at the beginning of the 19th
century, recommended opium, and Paolo Mantegazza in
1859 wrote a highly colored account of the beatific effects of
coca. Freud approved of cocaine, and advised his fiancee to
take it. Charles Baudelaire was called the "De Quincey of
Hashish," and with Arthur Ribaud and Paul Verlaine, ac-
claimed the drug. More recently, Aldous Huxley declared
that the "doors of perception" could be opened by mescaline
and LSD.

Many jazz, swing, bop, and other musicians claim that
marijuana and other stimulant drugs enhance their playing or
composing. There are also artists, poets, scientists, and inventors who say that LSD, marijuana, or amphetamine in-
spired them, but controlled experiments to test these claims
are lacking. Drugs do not ordinarily instill beauty, wisdom,
or virtue to the taker.

Drugs do change our perception of the world, and when
our world becomes unbearable, as in terminal cancer, drug

Condensed from "Psychology Today", 1330 Camino Del Mar, Del Mar, Calif. 92014. May, 1967.
©1967 by CRM Associates, and reprinted with permission.

use is justified. The question is whether it is justified for the relief of unhappiness, dissatisfaction, or boredom. Timothy Leary founded a religious body, the League for Spiritual Discovery (LSD), which advocates the use of psychedelic drugs. In reaction, city, state, and federal legislative and enforcement bodies have tried to control the distribution and use of behavior-affecting drugs. But the government is trying to make rules about substances which are still poorly understood.

During the first half of the 20th century drugs were occasionally used to affect human behavior.

Morphine, cocaine, and barbiturates were tried in the treatment of mental illness, but proved ineffective. In 1908 the Englishman W. H. R. Rivers reported on the influence of drugs on motor and mental efficiency. In 1924 Clark Hull studied the effect of pipe smoking and coffee drinking on mental efficiency.

Research was spurred in the 1930's and 1940's by military interest in the application of drugs. Both Allied and German soldiers were given amphetamines to combat sleeplessness and fatigue. The drugs were found to diminish fatigue, but whether they could raise performance above normal levels was an open question which is still not fully answered.

During the mid-1950's research on new drugs became big business. The Psychopharmacology Service Center, established within the National Institute of Mental Health, contributed millions of dollars for study of the psychological effects of drugs.

Psychologists are now in general agreement that certain psychological functions depend upon specific chemical substances just as taste and smell receptors respond to specific drugs. Sodium dehydrochlorate and saccharin, injected into the arm, respectively produce a bitter or sweet taste on reaching the tongue. Digitalis and LSD, taken by mouth, produce visual effects.

The brain is full of chemicals which are waiting to be investigated by psychologists. Nucleic acids and particularly ribonucleic acid (RNA) have been assigned a special role in learning by some. Puromycin and cyclohexamide interfere with both memory and learning. But the experiments are difficult to perform and behavior cannot be seen in a test tube full of chemicals from the brain than the theme of a mosaic can be determined from an analysis of its tones. But ultimately it ought to be possible to look at the chemical structure of a new drug and predict whether it will be useful as an antipsychotic, an antifatigue agent, an appetite stimulant, and so forth. One can evisage the day when drugs may be used not only to reduce pain, suffering, agitation, and anxiety, but also to enhance the normal state of man, to increase pleasure, facilitate learning and memory, reduce jealousy and aggressiveness. We can hope that such pharmacological developments will come with, but not as a substitute for, a more ideal society.

You and Your *n* Ach

How much success you enjoy depends largely on how much you really want it

By David C. McClelland

A few persons are challenged by opportunity and willing to work hard to achieve something. The majority really do not care that much.

For 20 years, psychologists have tried to understand this curious difference. Is the need to achieve (or the absence of it) an accident? Is it hereditary or environment? Is it a single human motive or a combination of motives: the desire to accumulate wealth, power, fame? Is there a way that we could give this will to achieve to people, or even to whole societies, who now lack it?

A study was made of 450 workers who had been thrown out of work by a plant shutdown in Erie, Pa. Most of them stayed home for a while and then checked with the U.S. employment service to see if their old jobs or similar ones were available. But a small minority started job hunting. Why? Psychologists have demonstrated that these men possessed a specific type of motivation. Let us call this personality characteristic "motive A" and review some of the other characteristics of the men who have more of it than other men.

Suppose they are confronted by a job in which they themselves can decide how difficult a task they will undertake. In the psychological laboratory, the men were asked to throw rings over a peg from any distance they chose. Most men

Condensed from "Think", 1775 Broadway, New York City 10019. November-December, 1966. ⓒ1966 by International Business Machines, and reprinted with permission. As reprinted in the "Science Digest."

threw more or less randomly, standing close, now far away, but those with motive A seemed to calculate carefully from what they were most likely to get a sense of mastery. They stood nearly always at moderate distances, not so close as to make the task ridiculously easy, nor so far away as to make it impossible. They set moderately difficult, but potentially achievable goals. But they did this only if they could influence the outcome by performing the work themselves.

They prefer not to gamble. If they are given a choice between rolling dice with just one in three chances of winning or working on a problem with a one-in-three chance of solving in the time allotted, they choose to work on the problem.

Obviously they are concerned with personal achievement rather than with the rewards of success. This leads to another characteristic the motive A men show: a strong preference for work situations in which they get immediate information on how well they are doing, as one does, say, in playing golf, or in being a salesman, but as one does not in teaching or in personnel counseling.

Men behave like this because they keep thinking about doing things better. Psychologists can measure the strength of motive A by taking samples of a man's spontaneous thoughts, such as making up a story about a picture he has been shown and counting how many times he mentions doing things better. This yields what is referred to technically as an individual's n Ach score (for "need for Achievement"). Persons who think constantly about doing better are more likely to do better, but why some persons and not others come to think this way is another question. The evidence suggests that their parents had set moderately high achievement goals and were warm, encouraging, and nonauthoritarian in helping their children reach them.

Much public and business policy is based on the notion that people will work harder "if they have to." That idea is not totally wrong, but it is only a half-truth. A simple experiment proves the point. Subjects were told that they could choose as a working partner either a close friend or a stranger who was known to be an expert on the problem to be solved. Those with higher n Ach chose the experts over their friends, whereas those with more n Aff ("need to Affiliate with others") chose friends over experts. Their desire to be with someone they like was a stronger motive than their desire to excel at the task.

The need for power is often confused with the need for achievement because both may lead to outstanding activities.

There is a distinct difference. Persons with a strong need for power want to command attention, get recognition, and control others. They are not much concerned with improving their own daily work.

Not all great achievers score high in *n* Ach. Many generals, politicians, and research scientists must be able to go for long periods without the immedaite reward the person with high *n* Ach requires. Business executives tend to score high in *n* Ach.

You cannot accept what people tell you about their motives. Thus a general may say he is interested in achievement (because he has obviously achieved), or a businessman that he is interested only in making money (because he has made money), or one of the unemployed in Erie that he desperately wants a job (because he knows he needs one). A careful check of what each one thinks about and how he spends his time may show that each is concerned about quite different things.

Men with higher *n* Ach get more raises and are promoted more rapidly because they keep seeking ways to do a better job. Companies with many such men grow faster. There appears to be a correlation between the *n* Ach content in popular literature (such as popular songs or stories in children's textbooks) and subsequent rates of national economic growth. A nation which is thinking about doing better all the time actually does do better. Careful studies have shown this to be true in ancient Greece, in Spain in the Middle Ages, in England from 1400-1800, as well as among contemporary nations.

Contrast these two stories for example. Which one contains more *n* Ach? Which one reflects a state of mind which leads to striving?

Story A (4th-grade reader): "Don't ever owe a man. The world is an illusion. Wife, children, horses, and cows are all just ties of fate. They are ephemeral. Each, after fulfilling his part in life, disappears. So we should not clamor after riches which are not permanent. As long as we live, it is wise not to have any attachment. We have to spend our lives without trouble, for is it not true that there is an end to grievances? So it is better to live knowing the real state of affairs. Don't get entangled in the meshes of family life."

Story B (4th-grade reader): "How I do like to learn! I was sent to an accelerated technical high school. I was so happy I cried. Learning is not very easy. In the beginning I couldn't understand what the teacher taught us. I always got a bad mark on my papers. The boy sitting next to me was very enthusiastic and also an outstanding student. When he found I couldn't do the problems he offered to show me how he had done them. I could not copy his work. I must learn through my own reasoning. I gave his paper back and explained that I had to do it myself. Sometimes I worked on a problem until midnight. If I couldn't finish, I started early in the morning. The bad marks were getting less common. I conquered my difficultues. My marks rose. I graduated and went on to college."

Most readers would agree that the second story shows more concern with improvement than the first, which comes from a contemporary reader used in the public schools of India. Story B has a Horatio Alger quality typical of our own McGuffey readers of long ago. It appears today in the textbooks of communist China.

The *n* Ach level is obviously important for statesmen to watch and in many instances to try to do something about, particularly if a nation's economy is lagging.

If psychologists can detect *n* Ach levels in individuals or nations, before their effects are widespread, can't the knowledge be put to use to foster economic developments? Detection or diagnosis is not enough. What good is it to tell Britain (or India for that matter) that it needs a greater spirit of enterprise? Most informed observers of the local scene know very well that such a need exists. What is needed is some method of developing *n* Ach in individuals or nations.

Since 1960, psychologists in my research group at Harvard have been experimenting with means to accomplish this goal, chiefly among business executives whose work requires a high *n* Ach.

Our courses had four main goals. 1. They taught the participants how to think, talk, and act like a person with high *n* Ach. The men learned how to make up stories that would code high in *n* Ach. 2. They stimulated students to set higher but carefully planned and realistic work goals for themselves over the next two years. We checked back with them every six months to see how well they were doing. 3. The courses also gave the participants knowledge about themselves. In playing the ring-toss game, they could observe that they behaved differently from others, perhaps in refusing to adjust a goal downward after failure. This would then become a matter for group discussion, and the man would have to explain what he meant in setting an unrealistic goal. Discussion could then lead on to what a man's ultimate goals in life were, how much he cared about actually improving performance. 4. The new courses also created a group *esprit de corps*. This membership in a new group helps a man achieve his goals because he knows he has the sympathy and support of the others and because he knows they will be watching.

The courses have been given to executives in a large American firm, and in several Mexican firms; to underachieving high-school boys; and to businessmen in India from Bombay and from a small city, Kakinada in the state of Andhra Pradesh. In every instance save one (the Mexican) we demonstrated statistically, two years later, that the men who took the course had done better (made more money, got promoted faster, expanded their business faster) than comparable men who did not take the course.

This is Living!

Harness all five senses, forget LSD,
and you can feel the heart-throb of creation

By Wylly Folk St. John

Most of us are only half alive. Some try to get a lift by taking dangerous drugs. But LSD is not the answer. Some try to buy excitement, but money is not the answer, either.

There is a way to make life richer, fuller, and more rewarding, without taking any drug or spending a cent. The secret is awareness. Just learn how to turn yourself on.

How long has it been since you felt the throb of your own blood through your veins? Since you tasted your tears? Watched a flower open? Let your skin feel the soft chill of rain?

A child is aware without thinking. Everything is fresh and marvelous to the budding senses. But unless you make a conscious effort to hold it, as you grow older, it will leave you. You have to exercise awareness every day, every hour. Almost every minute. You have to make yourself consciously, constantly, aware of yourself, as well as of everything about you.

Even washing dishes is interesting if you notice the varying textures of water: rough as it rushes out of the faucet, silken with liquid soap, bubbly or smooth against your fingers. What color is water? Really look at it and see. It can make a variety of sounds, too. Listen.

Condensed from the Atlanta "Journal and Constitution Magazine", Box 4689, Atlanta, Ga. 30302. April 28, 1968. ©1968 by Atlanta Newspapers, Inc., and reprinted with permission.

My first lesson in perceiving something beneath the surface came from an artist friend, when I was about 12. I was having trouble getting the right flesh tones into my water-color painting. The artist told me that human skin is not pink and white, that is has shadows of green, purple, and yellow. I looked and, sure enough, it had. Then he pointed out that the shadow of a tree is not gray; it, too, is purple or green. I had thought all shadows were gray. Before, I had just been glancing at the world. That day I learned how to see.

It is not easy to learn how to turn yourself on, but it can be done. Thirty Atlanta men and women learned how in an adult-education class at Emory university, conducted by Dr. and Mrs. Clements, a team of clinical psychologists. The class was called "Self-awareness and Personal Growth." It taught them to become more aware and less suppressed, to feel the here and now, and to experience the present moment. The Drs. Clements are exponents of the Gestalt school of psychotherapy: "The whole is more than the sum of the parts." One should be aware of each individual sense impression, each art or experience, and also of the pattern of the whole, the unity of the whole self.

In one of the early classes, the students were told to close their eyes; then the psychologists paired them off so that each could become aware of how it felt to hold an unknown person's hand, and of his own inner feeling at having his hand held. When they were told to open their eyes, there was a warm communal feeling, hard to describe but very real, as they shared their reactions.

Everybody felt that something emotional had happened.

Another assignment for the class was to imagine in every detail doing something backwards. One of several nuns got out of her rut by imagining herself a city bus driver going over his route backwards. They were told to substitute *I* for it. Instead of, "It is not very nice weather today," say, "I'm not enjoying the weather today." Become aware of your own feeling rather than an abstraction. The rain you do not like may be nice weather to the farmer.

And never say *why* and *because.* "If you hunt reasons," Dr. Clements says, "you leave what you were experiencing. Stay with the question rather than hunting for answers. Instead of rationalizing, just feel. Sensing, feeling, experiencing are aims in themselves. Recognize both positive and negative feelings.

"People are often unaware that voice tones, facial expressions, posture, indicate their feelings. When they become aware of this, they can better understand other's reactions.

"And it is good to be vulnerable to emotion. We grow through pain, too. It is better to be aware of pain than not to be aware at all. You can feel joy only to the extent that you are open to pain. To feel grief is better than not to feel. And it would be healthy for people to learn to express more honest feeling."

An experiment during the last class of the six weeks had the students placed in a circle, holding hands. Then they were told to back away until they lost contact with each other's finger tips, and to be aware of what they felt at the loss of contact. Some felt sad, some lonely, but one woman was delighted. "I feel like an individual," she said.

Another said the awareness she gained in the class would help in her every day depressing routine. She had been rebellious because she *had* to to to the grocery, or to the laundry, or *had* to cook dinner. When she became aware that she actually had a choice, that maybe she didn't have to do those things, if willing to accept the consequences, she felt different about doing them.

You can practice do-it-yourself awareness, without the help of group therapy. First, become conscious of your senses. Tell yourself you are going to perceive every tiny detail more clearly. Resolve to hear the most minute sounds, differentiate between odors and fragrances, orient your taste buds to strange substances as well as appreciating familiar ones. Decide to feel with your tongue and your finger tips. Put your lips against a rose petal.